T0301836

Graduate Migration and Regional Development

NEW HORIZONS IN REGIONAL SCIENCE

Series Editor: Philip McCann, *Professor of Urban and Regional Economics, University of Sheffield Management School, UK*

Regional science analyses important issues surrounding the growth and development of urban and regional systems and is emerging as a major social science discipline. This series provides an invaluable forum for the publication of high quality scholarly work on urban and regional studies, industrial location economics, transport systems, economic geography and networks.

New Horizons in Regional Science aims to publish the best work by economists, geographers, urban and regional planners and other researchers from throughout the world. It is intended to serve a wide readership including academics, students and policymakers.

Titles in the series include:

Graduate Migration and Regional Development

An International Perspective

Edited by

Jonathan Corcoran

Professor of Human Geography, School of Earth and Environmental Sciences, The University of Queensland and Director, Queensland Centre for Population Research, Brisbane, Australia

Alessandra Faggian

Professor of Applied Economics, Director of Social Sciences and Vice Provost for Research, Gran Sasso Science Institute, L'Aquila, Italy, President of the North American Regional Science Council (NARSC) and co-editor of Papers in Regional Science

NEW HORIZONS IN REGIONAL SCIENCE

Cheltenham, UK • Northampton, MA, USA

Published by
Edward Elgar Publishing Limited
The Lypiatts
15 Lansdown Road
Cheltenham
Glos GL50 2JA
UK

Edward Elgar Publishing, Inc.
William Pratt House
9 Dewey Court
Northampton
Massachusetts 01060
USA

A catalogue record for this book
is available from the British Library

Library of Congress Control Number: 2016962546

This book is available electronically in the **Elgar**online
Economics subject collection
DOI 10.4337/9781784712167

MIX
Paper from
responsible sources
FSC
www.fsc.org   FSC® C013056

ISBN 978 1 78471 215 0 (cased)
ISBN 978 1 78471 216 7 (eBook)

Typeset by Servis Filmsetting Ltd, Stockport, Cheshire
Printed and bound in Great Britain by TJ International Ltd, Padstow

To my parents, John and Pearl, for their enduring love and
encouragement
Jonathan Corcoran

To the reason why the world is beautiful . . . I love you Alex
Alessandra Faggian

Contents

Contributors

Roberta Comunian is Lecturer in Cultural and Creative Industries at the Department of Culture, Media and Creative Industries at King's College London, UK. Roberta's research interests lie in the fields of cultural policy, urban studies and knowledge transfer. Her publications cover a range of topics including business investment in the arts, creative graduates and creative careers, creative and cultural industries and their relation to cities and regional economies. She has co-authored more than twenty internationally peer-reviewed journal articles in leading journals such as *European Planning Studies, Geoforum, Urban Studies, International Journal of Cultural and Creative Industries, Cultural Trends, Regional Studies, Papers in Regional Science, Annals of Regional Science* and *Environment and Planning C: Government and Policy*. She has just completed an edited book and a special issue of the *International Journal of Cultural Policy* with the title 'Higher Education and the Creative Economy'.

Jonathan Corcoran is Professor of Human Geography in the School of Earth and Environmental Sciences at The University of Queensland and Director of the Queensland Centre for Population Research, Brisbane, Australia. His research interests lie in the fields of population geography, spatial science and regional science. His publications cover a broad suite of topics including human mobility and migration, human capital, crime and urban fires, each of which has a focus on quantitative methods. He is the co-editor of *Papers in Regional Science* and the *Journal of Spatial Science* and has been guest editor of special issues in the *Journal of Transport Geography, Annals of Regional Science* and the *Fire Safety Journal*.

Cécile Détang-Dessendre is senior researcher in economics at CESAER, a research unit linked between INRA (the French National Institute for Agricultural Research) and AgroSup Dijon, at the Université Bourgogne Franche-Comté, Dijon, France, and deputy-head of the division of Social Sciences at INRA. Her research interests lie in the fields of demography, regional science and labour economics. Her publications cover topics including human mobility, migration, human capital and local labour markets with a focus on urban–rural differentiations. Her studies involve quantitative methods. She is co-author of about 40 publications. Her articles have appeared in journals such as *Journal of Regional Science, Regional Science and Urban Economics, Urban Studies, Land Economics* and *Environment and Planning A*.

Alessandra Faggian is Professor of Applied Economics, Director of Social Sciences and Vice Provost for Research at Gran Sasso Science Institute, L'Aquila, Italy, and is President of the North American Regional Science Council (NARSC) and co-editor of the journal *Papers in Regional Science*. Dr Faggian's research interests lie in the fields of regional and urban economics, demography, labour economics and economics of education. Her publications cover a wide range of topics including migration, human capital, labour markets, creativity and local innovation and growth. She has co-authored over 80 academic publications. Her articles have appeared in journals such as *Oxford Economics Papers, Cambridge Journal of Economics, Feminist Economics, Regional Studies, Papers in Regional Science, Journal of Regional Science* and *The Journal of Economic Geography*. Alessandra is the 2007 recipient of the Moss Madden Memorial Medal by the Regional Science Association International: Irish and British section (RSAIBIS) for the best paper published in the year 2006 and the 2015 recipient of the Geoffrey Hewings Award by The North American Regional Council for outstanding research contribution by a young scholar in the field of regional science.

Rachel S. Franklin is Associate Professor (Research) of Population Studies and Associate Director of the Spatial Structures in the Social Sciences (S4) initiative at Brown University, Providence, RI, USA. Rachel's research is centered on the interaction between geography and demography, from spatial analysis methods for population change to migration to the evolution of population composition. Her current research focuses on the impacts of college student migration on human capital distribution in the United States and on the measurement, impacts, and demographic sources of population loss in the United States and Europe. Other ongoing work investigates the shifting geographical patterns of racial/ethnic diversity across US counties and states. Rachel has also published on migration trends and data in the United States, as well as regional fertility change in Italy. Her research has appeared in *Geographical Analysis, the Journal of Regional Science, the Professional Geographer* and *Spatial Economic Analysis*.

Mika Haapanen is Senior Researcher in the School of Business and Economics at the University of Jyväskylä, Finland. Dr Haapanen's research interests lie in the fields of regional economics, labour economics and the economics of education. His publications often utilise microeconometric methods to study questions related to inter-regional migration, returns to education, post-secondary education and business subsidies. His articles have appeared in journals such as *Regional Studies, Journal of Regional Science, Journal of Population Economics, Environment and Planning C: Government and Policy* and *Applied Economics*. He is currently an associate editor of *Regional Studies, Regional Science*.

Simona Iammarino is Professor of Economic Geography in the Department of Geography and Environment at the London School of Economics and Political Science, UK. She has been Head of Department since January 2014. Simona's main research interests lie in the following areas: multinational corporations, location and innovation strategies, and local impacts; geography of innovation and technological change; regional systems of innovation; and regional and local economic development and policy. Simona has published extensively in major refereed journals, and she is the author of two books that have been widely cited in the academic literature: *Multinational Corporations and European Regional Systems of Innovation* (2003), with John Cantwell, and *Multinationals and Economic Geography: Location, Technology and Innovation* (2013), with Philip McCann. She was one of the co-editors of the journal *Regional Studies* (2008–2013). Simona has long-term experience in externally funded international research projects, and in consultancy projects for various government agencies and international organisations such as the European Commission, the OECD and the UN Economic Commission for Latin America and the Caribbean, among others.

Sarah Jewell is a Lecturer in Economics at the University of Reading, UK. Her research interests lie in the field of labour economics, human capital, time use and the graduate labour market. Her publications cover a range of topics including term-time employment, creative graduates and creative careers, graduate migration, life satisfaction, unpaid work and executive pay and performance. She has published in journals such as *Oxford Economic Papers, Cambridge Journal of Economics, Regional Studies, Feminist Economics, Environment and Planning C: Government and Policy, International Review of Finance* and *Cultural Trends*.

Hannu Karhunen received his PhD in Economics in 2015. His main research interests include the economics of education, the economic effects of student migration and questions related to policy evaluations. His research has been published in the journal *Small Business Economics*. Currently Karhunen is working as a postdoctoral researcher at the University of Jyväskylä and at Statistics Finland.

Norman Maldonado is Associate Professor in the Department of Economics at the Universidad Sergio Arboleda, Bogota, Colombia. His research is focused on the fields of development economics, spatial economics and health economics. Norman's work on spatial economics has been on spatial heterogeneity of innovative behaviour, structural change, industrial localization, agglomeration economies, regional development and migration of human capital, using microeconometrics, spatial general equilibrium and agent-based models. He has worked as a consultant for local governments on spatial policy, land use and spatial equity.

Elisabetta Marinelli is a Scientific Officer at the Institute for Prospective Technological Studies of the European Commission, Sevilla, Spain. An economist by training, she holds a PhD from the London School of Economics (Department of Geography and Environment), UK. She has published articles in journals such as *Regional Studies*, *Technovation*, *Environment and Planning* and the *Journal of Business Research*. Over the years she has researched a variety of topics, including graduates' and scientists' migration, the investment strategies of MNEs, technology foresight and regional development. She is currently working on the implementation of EU regional research and innovation policies, applying participatory research methodology.

K. Bruce Newbold is Professor of Geography at McMaster University, Hamilton, ON, Canada, where he is also the Director of the School of Geography and Earth Sciences. He has held guest positions at the University of Glasgow, UK and the University of California San Diego, USA. Trained as a population geographer, his research interests include migration, immigration, health, and human capital. Bruce has authored or co-authored over 100 academic articles, in journals such as *Social Science and Medicine*, *The Professional Geographer*, *Environment and Planning A*, *Papers in Regional Science* and *The Canadian Geographer*. He has also authored the population textbook *Population Geography: Tools and Issues*, whose 3rd edition is due to be published in 2017. He has received awards for his work and service from the Population Specialty Group of the Association of American Geographers and the North American Regional Science Council.

Virginie Piguet is a statistician at CESAER, a research unit linked between INRA (the French National Institute for Agricultural Research) and AgroSup Dijon at the Université Bourgogne Franche-Comté, Dijon, France. Her publications cover topics including demography, regional migration, spatial differentiation on an urban–periurban–rural gradient, regional economic activity, public spending, local taxation, fiscal cooperation, and agricultural land prices. Her studies involve quantitative methods such as spatial models, simultaneous equation models or panel data models. She is co-author of about 30 publications. Her articles have appeared in journals such as *Population Space and Place, Regional Science and Urban Economics, Regional Studies, International Regional Science Review, Land Use Policy, Economie et Statistique* and *Revue d'Economie Politique.*

Raul Ramos is Associate Professor in Applied Economics at the University of Barcelona, researcher at AQR (Grup d'Anàlisi Quantitativa Regional), Barcelona, Spain and research fellow of IZA (Institute of Labor Economics), Berlin, Germany. Raul's research interests lie in the fields of regional and urban economics, labour economics and the economics of education. His publications include the analysis of different topics including migration, wage inequality and the role of institutions. He has co-authored over 50 academic publications. His articles have appeared in journals such as *Papers in Regional Science, International Regional Science Review, Regional Studies* and *Tijdschrift Voor Economische en Sociale Geografie.* Raul is a member of the editorial team of the *European Journal of Development Research* and has been guest editor of special issues of *Spatial Economic Analysis* and the *International Journal of Manpower.*

Francisco Rowe is a lecturer in Economic Geography at The University of Liverpool, UK. His research focuses on three core areas of human and economic geography: human capital mobility, spatial labour markets and statistical economic modelling. He has co-authored 26 academic publications. His articles have appeared in journals such as *Applied Geography* and *Environment and Planning C.* Francisco has been guest editor of the journal *The Annals of Regional Science* and works closely with the UN Latin American Demographic Centre (CELADE).

Vicente Royuela is Associate Professor at the University of Barcelona, Spain, and an economist and expert in regional science, urban economics and socio-economic development, with an intense emphasis on statistical and econometrics techniques. He is a member of the AQR Research Group and a member of the EOC Committee of the European Regional Science Association, and was the Coordinator of the 51st ERSA Conference 2011. He is the managing editor of *REGION*, the flagship journal of ERSA, field editor of the *Encyclopedia of Quality of Life*, and member of the editorial board of several international scientific journals. He has been involved in European and national (Spanish and Italian) research projects. Furthermore, he has developed consultancy activity for the OECD, the European Commission and the European Parliament. He is the author of dozens of research works, articles and books. His research has been published in journals such as *Papers in Regional Science*, *Urban Studies*, *Spatial Economic Analysis* and *Regional Studies*. He has acted as guest speaker in international conferences and as the invited lecturer of quantitative methods for regional science and urban economics at several universities.

Angelina Zhi Rou Tang is a doctoral candidate within the Institute for Social Science Research, The University of Queensland (UQ), Australia. She is also a Fellow at the ARC Centre of Excellence for Children and Families over the Life Course. Her main research interests lie in the fields of human geography, labour economics and the economics of education. Her honours thesis on the spatial mobility of overseas graduates in Australia has been translated into two refereed publications and featured twice in the national newspaper, *The Australian*. She subsequently won two scholarships, the International Postgraduate Research Scholarship and the UQ Centennial Scholarship, to undertake her current doctoral project which examines the employment outcomes of overseas graduates in Australia.

Viktor A. Venhorst is Assistant Professor in the Faculty of Spatial Sciences at the University of Groningen, the Netherlands. Viktor is also a Research Fellow in the Research Centre for Education and the Labour Market at the University of Maastricht, the Netherlands. His PhD thesis (2007–2011) presents the first study for the Netherlands on the spatial mobility of young recent higher-education graduates. During his post-doc (2011–2014), he extended this research using Statistics Netherlands registry data, applying a longitudinal approach, focusing on issues such as the effects of student entrepreneurship and the longitudinal analysis of regional labour-market dynamics. Other research interests include cross-border commuting, well-being and urban–rural linkages. Together with Dr Gary Bosworth, Viktor is the Winner of the Regional Studies Association Award for Best International Conference Paper Early Career Category 2015, for the paper 'Economic linkages between urban and rural regions: what's in it for the rural?'. He was also winner of the Best Referee Award 2013 for the journal *Regional Studies*, and winner of the 2013 Gratama Science Award based on his societally relevant research and outreach activities. Viktor holds a PhD in Spatial Sciences (Cum Laude) and has a background in economics and demography.

1. Graduate migration and regional development: an international perspective

Jonathan Corcoran and Alessandra Faggian

1.1 BACKGROUND: GRADUATE MIGRATION AND REGIONAL DEVELOPMENT

The number of tertiary-educated immigrants in OECD countries over the decade prior to 2011 increased by 70 per cent to reach 27 million people (OECD, 2013). The number of students seeking education abroad continues to increase, but there is also increasing competition from regional destinations that offer more affordable education prospects which may be more culturally relevant (UNESCO Institute for Statistics, 2016). Student and graduate migration form an integral part of the cross-border mobility of the intellectual elite (Lowell et al., 2004). In 2013, over 4.1 million people were studying abroad, meaning that 2 in 100 students globally were enrolled at a tertiary institution outside of their home country (UNESCO Institute for Statistics, 2016). This suggests that despite the trajectory of immigration rates slowing in recent years, university students and recent graduates have a consistently high degree of spatial mobility (Carree and Kronenberg, 2014).

While the United States, United Kingdom, Australia and France remain the most sought after destinations for students seeking high-quality education, student-based immigration is spreading to new countries and to regional hubs trying to expand their intellectual capital by attracting international students (UNESCO Institute for Statistics, 2016). Attracting international students is critical because many of these highly educated individuals remain in their host countries at the conclusion of their studies, increasing the human capital of the country and providing economic and intellectual gains. Within each host country, regions that have higher rates of education, such as the larger cities, may gain additional benefits. Understanding the locational choices of graduates is essential both at an international and regional level to shape local economic development and help the regions bearing the consequences of a loss of knowledge, technology transfer, investments and trade.

As our economies shift towards a knowledge-based focus, human capital is becoming increasingly relevant (Dotti et al., 2013), and areas with low levels of human capital experience limited growth (Haapanen and Tervo, 2012). According to Rowe et al. (2013, p.179), a 'recognition of the importance of overseas graduates has led many industrialised nations to develop new immigration policies, targeted specifically at this segment of the foreign population'. Thus many countries are strategically focused on attracting highly educated migrants.

1.1.1 The Importance of Human Capital

Human capital is essential for growth and development (Corcoran et al., 2010; Faggian and McCann, 2009). Indeed, a region's human capital is one of the strongest predictors of sustained economic vitality (Abel and Deitz, 2012), as it is linked to increases in economic and population growth, wages, income and innovation (Florida et al., 2008). Empirical evidence suggests that local development is fostered by the presence of a skilled labour pool, which generates knowledge spill-overs and human capital externalities in turn increasing productivity and high-technology activities (Consoli et al., 2013). Ahlin et al. (2014) find that the spatial distribution of human capital is vital in explaining the long-term dynamics of the geography of jobs, incomes and well-being. Highly educated and highly skilled people are a sought-after resource as they are an irreplaceable element for economic success. Shapiro (2006) reports that from 1940 to 1990, a 10 per cent increase in rates of university education led to a 0.8 per cent increase in employment growth in the United States. Thus, graduate migrants are an 'increasingly numerous and strategically important' fraction of the population (King and Ruiz-Gelices, 2003, p.229). They embody newly acquired knowledge and skills, and they are usually more mobile in their choice of where to enter the labour market after graduation (Ahlin et al., 2014). For this reason, regions with a university nearby have a consistent flow of tertiary-educated human capital, providing economic advantages over other regions (Haapanen and Tervo, 2012). Irrespective of the contextual differences in the countries analysed, human capital emerges as a key ingredient for economic growth and development.

1.1.2 Human Capital and Migration

On completion of a college or university degree, a graduate will move to a new region or country if there is a greater requirement for their acquired skills in the new area (Winters, 2012). Evidence shows that in Britain, about 60 per cent of graduates migrate to a new region after graduation (Faggian et al., 2007), while studies in the United States show that 33 per cent of doctoral students migrate after graduation (Stephan et al., 2004). Graduates will base a decision to migrate on a number of factors such as wage and employment opportunities, the local cost of living, amenities and quality of life, as well as their household and family circumstances (Franklin, 2003; Winters, 2012). Young college graduates are often attracted to large metropolitan areas with high wages and a strong labour market, and cultural and recreational amenities may play a further part in college graduate migration decisions. Individual employment outcomes and benefits of education are therefore inherently tied to location decisions (Oosterbeek and Webbink, 2011).

When looking at migration benefits, it is important to remember that migrants are also self-selected (Détang-Dessendre et al., 2004; Kazakis and Faggian, 2016) and hence not representative of the general population. For instance, students with higher grades and qualifications from more prestigious universities, having more employment options upon graduation, tend to be more mobile (Baryla Jr and Dotterweich, 2001; Faggian et al., 2007). There are also clear differences in migration propensity due to other personal characteristics such as marital status, ethnicity, previous migration, and family connections (Faggian et al., 2006; 2007; Mulder and Clark, 2002). Life cycle also plays a role. The propensity to move, for instance, is at its highest within the first couple of years after graduation (Haapanen and Tervo, 2009). Rérat (2014) refers to a triple biography in understanding decisions to migrate. This includes the social familial trajectory (such as sex, household factors, socio-economic background, partners' characteristics); the migration trajectory (such as region of origin, parents' region of birth, location of university); and the professional trajectory (such as field of study, kind of degree, grants, job status, year of graduation). The individual may, in the course of their studies, develop networks inside or outside of their university that enhance their employment prospects in the area. Alternatively, recent graduates may have built strong friendships and grown accustomed to local amenities that make it difficult to move away after graduation. Indeed, these preferences for the place where they attended college may even incline some recent graduates to accept lower-paying jobs to stay in the area that they have grown to appreciate (Winters, 2012).

Along with the circumstances and preferences of the individual, there is also a need to consider regional characteristics that may influence an individual's decision. The probability of individual migration depends on employment rates and the availability of jobs, relative wage levels and cost

of living, levels of income and employment growth rates, amenity variations and crime (Faggian et al., 2006; Venhorst et al., 2011). The availability of high-level jobs in the area is an important factor, as are the available
amenities (Venhorst et al., 2011). The value of expected income is also key,
as are potential career progressions and opportunities to increase skills
(Di Cintio and Grassi, 2013). Conversely, adverse regional and national
economic circumstances may stimulate spatial mobility, as migrants may
need to search further afield for work (Venhorst et al., 2011). With this in
mind, the less developed a country is, the more likely it is that the intellectual 'elites' of such a country choose to move away to further advance
their education and career with a potential for brain drain (Szelényi, 2006).

1.1.3   The Implications of Graduate Migration

An emerging body of literature has investigated the potential positive
and negative economic consequences of highly skilled migration both for
individuals and for the sending and receiving countries (Rowe et al., 2013).
A large and consistent loss of the intellectual elite of a region or country
can have negative consequences for the economic, technological and trade
assets in that area. This loss of the educated population, referred to in the
literature as 'brain drain', depletes the human capital of the area (Lowell
and Findlay, 2001; Szelényi, 2006). The implicit assumption that regions
with local university educational options benefit from the gain in human
capital is only true if these graduates remain in the region (Venhorst et al.,
2010). Therefore, many regions place a high priority on retaining their
graduates in attempts to maintain their human capital, and to encourage
graduates to seek employment in the area to repay some of the cost of their
education that was initially covered by the state or country (Krabel and
Flöther, 2014). Brain drain is of particular concern for local governments
in university towns that act as 'escalator regions' – that is, students enter
the city to receive their education, and then move to another region to
capitalise on the education they received (Abreu et al., 2014). Attracting
and retaining graduates is vitally important to avoid this 'brain drain' and
to maximise human capital in an area. In contrast to 'brain drain', 'brain
gain' has been coined as a term for the educational and economic gains
made by the countries that host highly skilled immigrants for extended
periods, or in many cases, permanently (Szelényi, 2006).

1.2   STRUCTURE

This book provides an international perspective on graduate migration. It centres around three key themes emerging from the literature: mobility and mismatch; push and pull migration factors; and migration and labour-market outcomes. The book is structured into twelve chapters including this introduction. The remaining eleven chapters are organised according to the three themes mentioned above. Chapters 2 to 5 discuss mobility and mismatch, Chapters 6 to 8 focus on push-pull factors and Chapters 9 to 11 detail the labour market and wages for graduates.

1.2.1   Mobility and Mismatch

While new university graduates are geographically highly mobile, there is evidence that some of them – especially in certain fields such as the creative arts – struggle when entering the labour market, resorting to working in non-graduate-level jobs or in a field different from the one for which they are qualified (Abreu et al., 2015; Comunian et al., 2010). This also means that many graduates are not earning to their full remuneration potential. In the literature, mismatches are captured in three forms: qualification, field-of-study, and skill mismatches. Qualification mismatches occur when a graduate holds a higher qualification than is required for their job (Green and McIntosh, 2007). A field-of-study mismatch occurs when a graduate is employed in a field that does not align with their area of tertiary study (McGuinness and Byrne, 2015). A skills mismatch occurs when graduates do not employ the skills that they learnt during the course of their studies in their occupation, including key skills such as literacy, numeracy, problem solving and communication skills (McGowan and Andrews, 2015).

A number of studies on mismatch have concluded that a large share of graduates are over-educated for their jobs and earn less than their well-matched peers. Although Rosen (1972) explains that this over-education may be a temporary consequence of graduates accepting lower-paid occupations which require fewer skills to increase their experience in the field to improve their chances of obtaining a more suitable job in the long-term (see also McGuinness and Byrne, 2015), this does not explain all of the mismatch that occurs. Furthermore, there is evidence of gender and age effects, as well as differences in mismatch across fields of study (Groot and Van Den Brink, 2000). In this book, studies from Australia, Canada, Italy and the Netherlands consider the mobility and mismatch of graduate populations between regions (Chapters 2 to 5).

Chapter 2, by Angelina Tang, Jonathan Corcoran and Francisco Rowe, examines the incidence of education–job mismatch amongst overseas students who remain in Australia after graduation. The authors conclude that post-graduation migration between local labour markets has marginal impacts on lowering the likelihood of experiencing field-of-study and skills mismatches, and that migration also increases the chances of having qualification mismatch as migrants tend to cluster in highly competitive labour markets within the largest capital cities. Chapter 3, by Bruce Newbold, considers the graduate migration behaviours of university graduates in Canada. This study identifies that individuals with higher levels of education, and more employment experience during their studies are more likely to migrate to labour-market opportunities following graduation, while individuals of a visible minority status were more likely to remain. Chapter 4, by Simona Iammarino and Elisabetta Marinelli, analyses the impact of inter-regional mobility on education–job match in the early stage of a graduate's professional career in Italy. Results from this study demonstrate that there are important regional differences in the probability of over-education and a mismatch of the graduate's skills and capabilities. Chapter 5, by Viktor Venhorst, details the effect of the household situation of the graduate's mobility after leaving a higher education institution in the Netherlands. It is concluded that the likelihood of labour-market dynamics varies strongly with the life-phase, with the likelihood of changes declining sharply within a few years of graduation.

1.2.2   Push-Pull factors

As we know from the wealth of scholarship on human migration, many key factors coalesce to influence an individual's decision to migrate. There are several economic and social forces within the home country that serve to 'push' graduates to another region or country with more opportunities. These factors may include poor employment prospects, limited economic opportunities, crime rates, or conflict. However, the decision as to which area they will select is dependent on a variety of 'pull' factors associated with that place. These include more opportunities for employment, higher wages, better facilities, more attractive working conditions, and suitable amenities. In this book, the push-pull factors of graduate migration are discussed in the context of Finland, France and Spain (Chapters 6 to 8).

Chapter 6, by Mika Haapanen and Hannu Karhunen, details the implications of working while studying in Finland. The authors note that migration rates are lower for students who have worked throughout their studies, particularly for those who worked full-time. Chapter 7, by Cécile Détang-Dessendre and Virginie Piguet, seeks to explain migration flows of young educated people in France. These findings demonstrate that graduate migration is predicted by the characteristics of local labour markets, rather than climates and amenities, particularly for individuals with higher levels of education. Chapter 8, by Raul Ramos and Vicente Royuela, analyses the effect of the Great Recession on emigration in Spain. Results show that graduates with higher grades are more prone to migrate, and that previous mobility experiences and foreign language knowledge also impact migration decisions.

1.2.3   Graduate Migration and the Labour Market

Wage discrepancies are noted in research on graduate migration. Specifically, substantial differences are noted in the wages of those who are repeat migrants (those who move to a university, and then move again to employment), return migrants (those who move away to study, and then return to the same region), and those who attend a university in their region of origin. There are also differences between salaries for males and females, with females reporting lower salaries in most conditions. In this book, studies on Mexico, the United States and the United Kingdom (Chapters 9 to 11) investigate the role of migration on salaries at different career points.

Chapter 9, by Norman Maldonado, describes the migration paths of graduates in Mexico. Results demonstrate that the more heterogeneous the migration path, the higher the wage premium. Chapter 10, by Alessandra Faggian, Jonathan Corcoran and Rachel Franklin, examines the salaries of graduates in the United States. Their evidence demonstrates that in the United States, unlike the United Kingdom, repeat migrants obtain the highest wage premium in terms of both mean and median wages. Chapter 11, by Roberta Comunian, Sarah Jewell and Alessandra Faggian, considers the effect of gender on graduate wages in the United Kingdom. Findings show that while late migration has the strongest effect on salaries for women, men earn higher salaries than women in most situations.

REFERENCES

Abel, J.R. and Deitz, R. (2012). Do colleges and universities increase their region's human capital? *Journal of Economic Geography*, 12(3), 667–691, doi: 10.1093/jeg/lbr020.

Abreu, M., Koster, S. and Venhorst, V.A. (2014). Transitions and location choice: analysing the decisions of students and recent graduates. *Spatial Economic Analysis*, 9(4), 349–354, doi: 10.1080/17421772.2014.965552.

Abreu, M., Faggian, A. and McCann, P. (2015). Migration and inter-industry mobility of UK graduates. *Journal of Economic Geography*, 15(2), 353–385, doi: 10.1093/jeg/lbt043.

Ahlin, L., Andersson, M. and Thulin, P. (2014). Market thickness and the early labour market career of university graduates: an urban advantage? *Spatial Economic Analysis*, 9(4), 396–419, doi: 10.1080/17421772.2014.961534.

Baryla Jr, E.A. and Dotterweich, D. (2001). Student migration: do significant factors vary by region? *Education Economics*, 9(3), 269–280.

Carree, M.A. and Kronenberg, K. (2014). Locational choices and the costs of distance: empirical evidence for Dutch graduates. *Spatial Economic Analysis*, 9(4), 420–435.

Cintio, M. di and Grassi, E. (2013). Internal migration and wages of Italian university graduates. *Papers in Regional Science*, 92(1), 119–140.

Comunian, R., Faggian, A. and Li, Q.C. (2010). Unrewarded careers in the creative class: the strange case of bohemian graduates. *Papers in Regional Science*, 89(2), 389–410.

Consoli, D., Vona, F. and Saarivirta, T. (2013). Analysis of the graduate labour market in Finland: spatial agglomeration and skill–job match. *Regional Studies*, 47(10), 1634–1652.

Corcoran, J., Faggian, A. and McCann, P. (2010). Human capital in remote and rural Australia: the role of graduate migration. *Growth and Change*, 41(2), 192–220, doi: 10.1111/j.1468–2257.2010.00525.x.

Détang-Dessendre, C., Drapier, C. and Jayet, H. (2004). The impact of migration on wages: empirical evidence from French youth. *Journal of Regional Science*, 44(4), 661–691.

Dotti, N.F., Fratesi, U., Lenzi, C. and Percoco, M. (2013). Local labour markets and the interregional mobility of Italian university students. *Spatial Economic Analysis*, 8(4), 443–468.

Faggian, A. and McCann, P. (2009). Human capital and regional development. In R. Capello and P. Nijkamp (eds), *Handbook of Regional Growth and Development Theories*, Cheltenham, UK and Northampton, MA: Edward Elgar, pp. 133–151.

Faggian, A., McCann, P. and Sheppard, S. (2006). An analysis of ethnic differences in UK graduate migration behaviour. *The Annals of Regional Science*, 40(2), 461–471.

Faggian, A., McCann, P. and Sheppard, S. (2007). Some evidence that women are more mobile than men: gender differences in UK graduate migration behavior. *Journal of Regional Science*, 47(3), 517–539.

Florida, R., Mellander, C. and Stolarick, K. (2008). Inside the black box of regional development: human capital, the creative class and tolerance. *Journal of Economic Geography*, 8(5), 615–649, doi: 10.1093/jeg/lbn023.

Franklin, R.S. (2003). Migration of the young, single, and college educated, 1995–2000. Special report, US Department of Commerce, Economics and Statistics Administration, US Census Bureau, available at: https://usa.ipums.org/usa/resources/voliii/pubdocs/2000/censr-12.pdf.

Green, F. and McIntosh, S. (2007). Is there a genuine under-utilization of skills amongst the over-qualified? *Applied Economics*, 39(4), 427–439.

Groot, W. and Van Den Brink, H.M. (2000). Overeducation in the labor market: a meta-analysis. *Economics of Education Review*, 19(2), 149–158.

Haapanen, M. and Tervo, H. (2009). Return and onward migration of highly educated: evidence from residence spells of Finnish graduates. Working paper, School of Business and Economics, University of Jyväskylä.

Haapanen, M. and Tervo, H. (2012). Migration of the highly educated: evidence from residence spells of university graduates. *Journal of Regional Science*, 52(4), 587–605.

Kazakis, P. and Faggian, A. (2016). Mobility, education and labor market outcomes for U.S. graduates: is selectivity important? *Annals in Regional Science*, doi: 10.1007/s00168-016-0773-6.

King, R. and Ruiz-Gelices, E. (2003). International student migration and the European 'year abroad': effects on European identity and subsequent migration behaviour. *International Journal of Population Geography*, 9(3), 229–252, doi: 10.1002/ijpg.280.

Krabel, S. and Flöther, C. (2014). Here today, gone tomorrow? Regional labour mobility of German university graduates. *Regional Studies*, 48(10), 1609–1627.

Lowell, B.L. and Findlay, A. (2001). Migration of highly skilled persons from developing countries: impact and policy responses. Synthesis report, International Migration Papers, p. 44.

Lowell, B.L., Findlay, A. and Stewart, E. (2004). Brain strain: optimising highly skilled migration from developing countries. Institute for Public Policy Research Working Paper, 3.

McGowan, M.A. and Andrews, D. (2015). Labour market mismatch and labour productivity. OECD Economics Department Working Papers, doi: 10.1787/18151973.

McGuinness, S. and Byrne, D. (2015). Born abroad and educated here: examining the impacts of education and skill mismatch among immigrant graduates in Europe. *IZA Journal of Migration*, 4(1), 1–30, doi: 10.1186/s40176-015-0039-6.

Mulder, C.H. and Clark, W.A. (2002). Leaving home for college and gaining independence. *Environment and Planning A*, 34(6), 981–999.

OECD (2013). World migration in figures, available at: https://www.oecd.org/els/mig/World-Migration-in-Figures.pdf.

Oosterbeek, H. and Webbink, D. (2011). Does studying abroad induce a brain drain? *Economica*, 78(310), 347–366.

Rérat, P. (2014). The selective migration of young graduates: which of them return to their rural home region and which do not? *Journal of Rural Studies*, 35, 123–132.

Rosen, S. (1972). Learning and experience in the labor market. *Journal of Human Resources*, 7(3), 326–342.

Rowe, F., Corcoran, J. and Faggian, A. (2013). Mobility patterns of overseas human capital in Australia: the role of a 'new' graduate visa scheme and rural development policy. *Australian Geographer*, 44(2), 177–195.

Shapiro, J.M. (2006). Smart cities: quality of life, productivity, and the growth effects of human capital. *The Review of Economics and Statistics*, 88(2), 324–335.

Stephan, P.E., Sumell, A.J., Black, G.C. and Adams, J.D. (2004). Doctoral education and economic development: the flow of new PhDs to industry. *Economic Development Quarterly*, 18(2), 151–167.

Szelényi, K. (2006). Students without borders? Migratory decision-making among international graduate students in the US. *Knowledge, Technology and Policy*, 19(3), 64–86.

UNESCO Institute for Statistics (2016). Global flow of tertiary educated students, available at: http://www.uis.unesco.org/Education/Pages/international-student-flow-viz.aspx.

Venhorst, V., Van Dijk, J. and Van Wissen, L. (2010). Do the best graduates leave the peripheral areas of the Netherlands? *Tijdschrift voor economische en sociale geografie*, 101(5), 521–537.

Venhorst, V., Van Dijk, J. and Van Wissen, L. (2011). An analysis of trends in spatial mobility of Dutch graduates. *Spatial Economic Analysis*, 6(1), 57–82.

Winters, J.V. (2012). Differences in employment outcomes for college town stayers and leavers. *IZA Journal of Migration*, 1(1), 1–17.

2. The role of migration on education–job mismatch: evidence from overseas graduates in Australia

Angelina Zhi Rou Tang,* Jonathan Corcoran and Francisco Rowe

2.1 INTRODUCTION

Driven by a persistent lack of skilled labour, many countries, including Australia, Canada, France, Germany and New Zealand, have progressively adjusted their immigration programmes to target a new pool of human capital: international students who recently graduated from the local higher-education institutions (OECD, 2014a). Of the few countries mentioned above, Australia is the leading nation in the competition for domestically educated overseas graduates (DEOGs) as it has developed a comprehensive migration framework designed to retain this group of talent (Peykov, 2004). A recent addition to this framework has been the introduction of a graduate visa scheme in late 2007. This visa policy permits DEOGs who have completed at least two years of tertiary study in Australia to remain in the country after graduation with full working rights for a period of eighteen months to four years depending on their level of qualification. After the introduction of this scheme, the number of DEOGs remaining in the country rose from approximately 31,000 in 2006–07 to an annual average of 48,000 for the period 2007–10 (Birrell et al., 2011). This marked increase has reinforced Australia's position as the primary overseas study destination of all member countries of the Organisation for Economic Co-operation and Development (OECD) (OECD, 2011).

Despite the potential labour-market benefits of retaining a growing pool of DEOGs, recent work suggests that these graduates are likely to experience education–job mismatch in the Australian labour market (for example, Li and Miller, 2013; Faggian et al., 2015; Tang et al., forthcoming). There is some empirical evidence that they tend to be employed in jobs that require a lower level of education qualification. Understanding the trends of education–job mismatch among DEOGs is highly critical as it can have a number of negative effects on individual career trajectories and national socio-economic development. For the individuals, education–job mismatch leads to lower salary and lower job satisfaction (Rumberger, 1987; Dolton and Vignoles, 2000; Allen and Velden, 2001), as well as long-term negative consequences for career advancement and future work outcomes (Frenette, 2004; Lindley and McIntosh, 2010; Baert et al., 2013). For the host countries, poor economic integration of DEOGs as a result of education–job mismatch is argued to potentially reduce social inclusion among local communities which will in turn affect public acceptance of future immigration (OECD, 2014b). Moreover, education–job mismatch is an outcome that reflects inefficient use of scarce human capital resources (Beckhusen et al., 2013), lowering productivity and constraining economic growth. In Canada, the total productivity loss due to education–job mismatch among highly skilled migrants was estimated to be between C\$5 and C\$11 billion in 1996 and 2006 (Reitz et al., 2014), while it cost the Australian economy about US\$350 million per annum in the 1980s (Stasiulius, 1990).

In view of the detrimental impacts of education–job mismatch, this chapter seeks to rationalise the higher level of mismatch incidence among DEOGs who have remained in Australia since the introduction of the graduate visa scheme. In particular, our study will focus on investigating the role of greater spatial flexibility and mobility in ameliorating the chance of experiencing education–job mismatch. There is a growing body of literature which argues that being geographically mobile – for example, commuting – helps highly educated individuals to secure better employment outcomes, including finding jobs that align with their education qualifications (Battu et al., 1999; Buchel and van Ham, 2003; Hensen et al., 2009). To this end, we examine the relationship between internal migration and employment outcomes through the lens of education–job mismatch to establish the extent to which being a mobile DEOG is a strategy to maximise early labour-market performance in the Australian labour market.

The remainder of this chapter is structured as follows. Section 2.2 reviews the literature on the work outcomes of DEOGs remaining in Australia before introducing existing scholarship on geographic mobility and education–job mismatch. The data and methods are then described in Sections 2.3 and 2.4 respectively before presenting the results and a discussion of the analysis in Section 2.5. The final Section 2.6 offers the key conclusions along with some avenues for future research.

2.2 BACKGROUND

In response to the growing overseas graduate population in Australia, recent research has attempted to gain a better understanding of their performance in the local labour market. While it remains the focus of only a small sub-set of studies, the accumulating evidence provides interesting insights into the post-graduation employment and salary outcomes of international students who remain in Australia. The results reveal that DEOGs consistently experience greater difficulties in transitioning from tertiary education into employment compared to their domestic counterparts. They are less likely to secure a job following graduation (Trevelyan and Tilli, 2010), and those who are employed tend to work in part-time jobs that do not match their education attainment and to earn substantially lower salaries (Li and Miller, 2013; Hawthorne and To, 2014; Faggian et al., 2015; Tang et al., forthcoming). The inferior labour-market outcomes among the DEOGs are argued to result from a combination of factors, including low proficiency level in English (Arkoudis et al., 2009; Hawthorne and To, 2014), poor communication and interpersonal skills (Birrell and Healy, 2008), lack of familiarity with local culture (James and Otsuka, 2009) and their residency status as a temporary immigrant (Li and Miller, 2013). Scholars also suggest that their tendency to concentrate in metropolitan locations with intense job competition may, at least in part, explain the poorer outcomes (Beckhusen et al., 2013; Rowe et al., 2013; Tang et al., 2016).

Recent literature on mismatch incidence among highly skilled labour attempts to investigate the effects of spatial flexibility and mobility on finding employment that better aligns with their education qualification (for example, van Ham, 2001; Büchel and van Ham, 2003; Hensen et al., 2009; Iammarino and Marinelli, 2015). Underpinning this focus is the concept that the demand (that is, jobs) and supply (that is, workers) of labour, skills and knowledge is often spatially disconnected due to the uneven distribution of economic activities and employment opportunities over space in terms of quantity and quality. In order to secure a suitable job, workers are required to close the gaps by being spatially flexible and mobile. To this end, they need to either commute (that is, travel regularly over a certain distance) or migrate (that is, relocate to a new location) to the place where their labour, skills and knowledge is in demand.

Existing work reveals that most workers have limited spatial flexibility and mobility and thus their job search is often restricted to their local labour market (van Ham et al., 2001a; 2001b; Sloane, 2003). Additionally, there is a comprehensive body of work showing that long-distance commuters are less likely to experience education–job mismatch than those who work locally (for example, van Ham, 2001; Büchel and van Ham, 2003; Hensen et al., 2009). In contrast, limited attempts have been made to evaluate the role of migration even though it is argued that migration offers a larger geographical scope of job search and a greater potential in mitigating education–job mismatch. A recent Italian study shows that inter-regional migration significantly lowers the likelihood that recent graduates take up jobs that do not match their education qualification (Iammarino and Marinelli, 2015). The influence of migration, however, varies depending on the direction of movement. In this case, the positive impact was only experienced by those who migrated from the lagging southern region to the highly diversified and dynamic economy in the north (Iammarino, 2005; Iammarino and Marinelli, 2015).

In this chapter, we continue the line of enquiry progressed by Iammarino and Marinelli (2015) to explore the role of migration in ameliorating education–job mismatch among DEOGs who remained in Australia after graduation. Spatial inequalities in economic performance and employment opportunities are also apparent in Australia across the urban hierarchy and the labour-market regions. Metropolitan locales, Sydney and Melbourne in particular, house larger and denser labour markets with a diverse range of occupations, while the smaller labour markets in rural Australia are primarily based around natural resources and public administrative activities (BTRE, 2004). As such, it is argued that migration has the potential to help recent graduates secure jobs that align with their education qualification. To this end, we examine the drivers of education–job mismatch among DEOGs in Australia, paying particular attention to investigating the role of migration in mitigating the misalignment.

2.3 DATA SOURCES

This chapter draws on micro data from the Graduate Destination Survey, which forms part of the Australian Graduate Survey project administered by Graduate Careers Australia. This is an annual survey that collates information on newly qualified tertiary graduates at four months after graduation. It records data on their labour-market outcomes, including paid work status, employment location and occupation, and a range of personal characteristics (for example, age, sex and language background) and course information (for example, field of study, highest level of qualification and work experience during the final year of study).

We used data from five annual surveys running from 2008 to 2012 which captured the tertiary student population graduating in the period 2007–11. This study focused on DEOGs who worked full- or part-time in Australia at four months after graduation and we defined DEOGs as those who self-identified as international fee-paying students (Guthrie, 2008). To study the alignment between education qualification and employment, the analysis concentrated on those who provided valid responses on their field of study, highest level of qualification, occupation and the importance of their cognitive skills to the reported occupation. Following the OECD (Quintini and Broecke, 2014), we excluded two groups of workers: first, self-employed individuals because the cyclical process makes it hard to determine the actual cause-and-effect relationship between self-employment and education–job mismatch (see James and Otsuka, 2009); second, members of the armed forces and legislators because the scope of skills and knowledge required is difficult to define (ILO, 2004). We also limited the analysis to valid responses on the variables of interest included in this chapter.

2.3.1   Definition of Migration

To define migration, we employed the Australian Statistical Geography Standard Statistical Area Level 4 (SA4) as the spatial framework. This structure divides the Australian territory into 88 SA4 spatial units (ABS, 2010). It is purposely built by the Australian Bureau of Statistics to reflect sub-state socio-economic breakdown and to produce labour-force data (ibid.). The spatial units are designed using travel-to-work information to capture self-contained labour-market regions within states and territories where a large percentage of residents living in the SA4 work in the same region (ibid.). They are also structured to account for geographical, social and economic similarities (ibid.). As such, this geographical structure provides a useful framework to capture job-related migration patterns of DEOGs following graduation.

Based on this framework, we distinguished between movers and stayers. Movers are defined as those who relocated to another SA4 for employment after graduation, while stayers are those who remained and worked in the labour-market region where they studied previously. Figure 2.1 presents the sample sizes for movers and stayers and their respective paid work statuses for the five-year period. The majority of DEOGs (indicated by the bracketed percentages in Figure 2.1) migrated to another labour-market region after graduation while slightly more than one-third remained at their university location. Figure 2.1 shows that movers are more likely to work in full-time jobs than stayers who demonstrate a higher tendency to take up part-time employment. This evidence suggests that being spatially flexible and mobile helps improve labour-market performances among DEOGs and thus underpins our analysis to estimate the impact of migration on education–job mismatch.

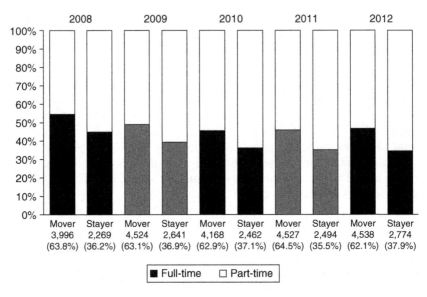

Figure 2.1   Paid work status for mover and stayer, 2008–12

2.3.2   Definition of Education–Job Mismatch

To define education–job mismatch, we followed the OECD's framework for labour-market analysis and captured three forms of mismatch: qualification, field-of-study and skills mismatches (Quintini and Broecke, 2014). First, qualification mismatch is considered to occur when a worker holds a higher or lower level of qualification than that required for their reported occupation. We compared the attained level of qualification to the level prescribed in the Australian and New Zealand Standard Classification of Occupations 2006 (ANZSCO) (ABS, 2013a). Since most respondents (99.6 to 100.0 per cent) held at least a bachelor's degree which was commensurate with the highest level of education in the ANZSCO, this study focused on over-qualification, that is, having a higher level of qualification than the prescribed level. An example of qualification mismatch is a female medical graduate with a bachelor's degree working as a medical laboratory technician (that only requires an associate degree, advanced diploma or diploma) or a taxi driver (that only requires a vocational certificate) (Table 2.1).

Second, field-of-study mismatch arises when workers are employed in a field that does not align with their area of expertise. In our analysis, we compared the reported job to the list of occupations defined by Wolbers (2003) for

Table 2.1   *Examples of education–job mismatch for a female medical graduate with a bachelor's degree*

Example	Qualification mismatch	Field-of-study mismatch	Skills mismatch
1. Works as a resident medical officer which utilises her cognitive skills	*No*	*No*	*No*
	Why? The graduate holds the required level of qualification	*Why?* The graduate remains in her area of expertise	*Why?* The graduate uses her cognitive skills at work
2. Works as a medical laboratory technician which does not utilise her cognitive skills	*Yes*	*No*	*Yes*
	Why? The graduate holds a higher level of qualification	*Why?* The graduate remains in her area of expertise	*Why?* The graduate does not use her cognitive skills at work
3. Works as a taxi driver which utilises her cognitive skills	*Yes*	*Yes*	*No*
	Why? The graduate holds a higher level of qualification	*Why?* The graduate works in a field that does not match her area of expertise	*Why?* The graduate uses her cognitive skills at work

each field. Respondents who did not work in a job that is regarded as a good match for their field of study are considered mismatched. Using the example above, the taxi driver also experiences field-of-study mismatch because the creative arts and services field does not align with the health or medical field; however, this is not the case for the medical laboratory technician since the graduate remains in her area of expertise, that is, the health field.

Third, skills mismatch exists when workers are not using their cognitive skills in their reported occupation. Key cognitive skills include literacy, numeracy, problem-solving and communication skills. We identified skills mismatch based on a respondent's self-assessment on the alignment between their cognitive skills and occupation, that is, respondents are regarded as having a skills mismatch if they self-identified that their cognitive skills were not important to their reported job.

2.4 METHODOLOGY

Following prior research on education–job mismatch (for example, Carroll and Tani, 2011; Beckhusen et al., 2013), we adopted a probit regression framework to analyse the determinants underlying the three forms of education–job mismatch described above. The dependent variable was a binary variable capturing mismatch: 1 if there was a misalignment between an individual's occupation and education qualification; and 0 if there was a match. Separate models were performed to capture the drivers that influenced each form of mismatch.

A range of characteristics were included as independent variables in the regression models to capture individual and spatial variations in the likelihood of experiencing an education–job mismatch. Table 2.2 lists and describes these variables. We included personal characteristics (for example, age, sex and language background), university attributes (for example, field of study, highest level of qualification and work experience during the final year of study) and employment outcomes (for example, paid work status, employment sector and industry of employment), and also controlled for the type of labour-market region where individuals were employed (that is, metropolitan, inner regional or distant areas[1]). Spatial variations in education–job mismatch are expected. As mentioned in Section 2.2, recent research shows that education–job mismatch is more likely to occur in metropolitan areas because competition for jobs is more intense in these regions compared to non-urban locations (Beckhusen et al., 2013).

In order to determine the influence of migration on education–job mismatch, we included a dummy variable as an independent variable in our regression models, taking the value 1 if a DEOG was identified as a mover, and 0 if identified as a stayer. This variable is labelled 'Migrated after graduation'. Formally, the estimated model is as follows:

$$\Pr(m) = \Phi(\alpha p_{s1} + \beta u_{s1} + \gamma e_{s1} + \Delta Mig), \qquad (2.1)$$

where we assume that the probability of experiencing a particular form of mismatch ($\Pr(m)$) is influenced by vectors that capture personal (p_{s1}), university (u_{s1}), employment (e_{s1}) and post-graduation migration characteristics (Mig) as listed in Table 2.2. The aim of this analysis is to determine the influence of these factors by estimating the respective parameters (that is, α, β and γ).

Estimating the effect of migration on education–job mismatch is, however, not straightforward due to potential endogeneity arising from

Table 2.2   Independent variables for the binary probit regression analysis

Variables	Definition
Personal characteristics	
Age	A continuous variable that represents the age of respondent (ranges between 19 and 74)
Age^2	The square of the variable 'Age' that captures the decreasing effect of age
Female	1 if respondent is female; 0 if respondent is male
Non-English-speaking background	1 if respondent has a non-English-speaking background; 0 if respondent has an English-speaking background
Australian permanent resident	1 if respondent holds an Australian permanent residency at reference date; 0 if respondent holds an Australian temporary residency at reference date
Educational characteristics	
Field of study	
Natural and physical sciences	1 if respondent has a natural and physical sciences qualification; 0 otherwise
Information technology	1 if respondent has an information technology qualification; 0 otherwise
Engineering and related technologies	1 if respondent has an engineering and related technologies qualification; 0 otherwise
Architecture and building	1 if respondent has an architecture and building qualification; 0 otherwise
Agriculture, environment and related studies	1 if respondent has an agriculture, environment and related studies qualification; 0 otherwise
Health	1 if respondent has a health qualification; 0 otherwise
Education	1 if respondent has an education qualification; 0 otherwise
Management and commerce	1 if respondent has a management and commerce qualification; 0 otherwise
Society and culture	1 if respondent has a society and culture qualification; 0 otherwise
Creative arts and services	1 if respondent has a creative arts or food, hospitality and personal services qualification; 0 otherwise

(continues overleaf)

Table 2.2   (continued)

Variables	Definition
Postgraduate degree	1 if respondent holds a postgraduate degree; 0 if respondent holds an undergraduate degree
Worked during the final year of study	1 if respondent has worked during the final year of study; 0 otherwise
Employment characteristics	
Full-time employment	1 if respondent has a full-time job; 0 if respondent has a part-time job
Studying while working	1 if respondent undertakes further study while working; 0 otherwise
Employment sector	
Private sector	1 if respondent works in the private sector; 0 otherwise
Public sector	1 if respondent works in the public sector; 0 otherwise
Not-for-profit organisation	1 if respondent works for a not-for-profit organisation; 0 otherwise
Industry	
Natural resources	1 if respondent works in agriculture, forestry and fishing or mining; 0 otherwise
Manufacturing, trade and logistics	1 if respondent works in manufacturing, wholesale and retail trade or transport, postal and warehousing; 0 otherwise
Construction and utilities	1 if respondent works in electricity, gas, water and waste services or construction;0 otherwise
Telecommunications	1 if respondent works in information media and telecommunications; 0 otherwise
Professional services	1 if respondent works in professional, scientific and technical services; 0 otherwise
Financial services	1 if respondent works in financial and insurance services or rental, hiring and real-estate services; 0 otherwise
Administrative services	1 if respondent works in administrative and support services or public administration and safety; 0 otherwise

Table 2.2   (continued)

Variables	Definition
Education	1 if respondent works in education and training; 0 otherwise
Health care	1 if respondent works in health care and social assistance; 0 otherwise
Recreation and other services	1 if respondent works in arts and recreation services, accommodation and food services or other services; 0 otherwise
Employment location	
Major cities	1 if respondent works in a major city; 0 otherwise
Inner regional areas	1 if respondent works in an inner regional area; 0 otherwise
Distant areas	1 if respondent works in an outer regional area, remote or very remote region; 0 otherwise
Migrated after graduation	1 if respondent has migrated after graduation; 0 otherwise

migrants' self-selectivity. Compared to stayers, movers tend to be well-educated (Greenwood and Hunt, 2003), more motivated (Rowe et al., 2014) and have higher aspirations (Rowe et al., 2016) – all characteristics which may be associated with a reduced probability of experiencing an education–job mismatch. This is a self-selectivity problem as individuals have 'self-selected' into becoming 'movers' or 'stayers'. We thus only observe the education–job mismatch outcomes of individuals who self-selected into one of these two groups.

Following work on the effects of migration on individual outcomes (for example, Pekkala and Tervo, 2002; Abreu et al., 2015), we employed a counterfactual treatment effects approach to address this issue. This method permits estimation of the 'average treatment effect' of migration on education–job mismatch, while accounting for non-random migration assignment. To this end, two models were estimated: an outcome model of education–job mismatch (as described above) and a treatment model of migration choice. The treatment model was applied to produce counterfactual outcome data, which were then used to estimate the average difference in the probability of experiencing an education–job mismatch between movers and stayers in the outcome model. These estimates were thus corrected by self-selectivity.[2] The treatment model can be defined as follows:

$$\Pr(Mig) = \Phi(\delta p_{s2} + \varepsilon u_{s2} + \eta e_{s2}), \tag{2.2}$$

where $\Pr(Mig)$ denotes the probability of relocating across labour-market regions after graduation; p_{s2}, u_{s2} and e_{s2} represent personal, university and employment characteristics that are assumed to influence the probability of moving; and, δ, ε and η are the parameters that will be estimated in this model.

The dependent variable was a binary variable, that is, 1 indicating a mover and 0 denoting a stayer, meaning that the migration choice model was estimated using a probit regression framework. In this analysis, we followed previous work on migration studies[3] and controlled for a similar set of personal, university and employment attributes (as listed in Table 2.2), with the exceptions being language background, permanent residency status and employment sector. We also introduced two additional variables to capture the effects of university location and occupation type. There is some evidence that those who studied in regional areas (see, for example, Rowe et al., 2013; Tang et al., 2016) or worked in highly skilled occupations (see, for example, Borjas et al., 1992; Carrington and Detragiache, 1998) are more likely to migrate.

In this study, we used two estimators to estimate equations (2.1) and (2.2): the Inverse Probability Weighting Regression Adjustment (IPWRA) and the Augmented Inverse Probability Weighting (AIPW) estimators (Wooldridge, 2002). Both estimators use inverse-probability weights to estimate the effects of treatment and other covariates on an outcome, with inverse probabilities obtained by fitting the treatment model. The IPWRA estimator uses these weights to produce corrected regression coefficients that are then used to account for non-random treatment assignment modelling the outcome variable. The AIPW estimator uses inverse-probability weights in combination with a bias-correction term to estimate regression coefficients. Both IPWRA and AIPW are known as doubly robust estimators[4] as they require only one model – either the outcome or treatment model – to be correctly defined to produce an accurate estimate of the treatment effects. There is no general solution with respect to the question of which estimator produces a better estimation; however, both IPWRA and AIPW produced consistently similar results when applied to our data. As such, we only reported results based on the IPWRA estimator in the next section.

2.5 RESULTS AND DISCUSSION

Results are divided into two parts. First, we present a descriptive analysis of the employment outcomes of movers and stayers. To this end, we explore the alignment of their jobs to field of study, level of qualification and cognitive skills. Second, we present the results from the regression modelling to assess the role that migration plays in mitigating the three forms of education–job mismatch.

2.5.1 Descriptive Analysis

Figure 2.2 presents the extent of qualification, field-of-study and skills mismatches for both the movers and the stayers between 2008 and 2012. The results suggest that DEOGs who are spatially flexible and mobile are more likely to secure employment that closely aligns with their education qualifications than those who stay put. For example, those who migrated to another labour-market region after graduation appear to have a lower likelihood (30 to 32 per cent) of working in jobs that do not match their areas of expertise (Figure 2.2a). In contrast, a marginally higher percentage of DEOGs (35 to 38 per cent) experience field-of-study mismatch when they remain and work in the labour-market region where they studied previously. Additionally, relocation across labour-market regions following graduation has the potential to reduce the chance of experiencing skills mismatch. Figure 2.2c indicates that less than one-fifth (17 to 21 per cent) of the spatially flexible graduates were regarded as having skills mismatch while up to a quarter of stayers (20 to 25 per cent) self-identified that their cognitive skills were not important to their reported occupation.

There is also some evidence that migration exerts a negative influence on the probability of experiencing qualification mismatch (Figure 2.2b). Nonetheless, the impact does not always hold over the five-year period. It was not until 2010 that post-graduation migration across labour-market regions helped to lower the propensity of having qualification mismatch: 56 to 58 per cent for movers versus 58 to 59 per cent for stayers. Between 2008 and 2009, movers (54 to 58 per cent) appeared to have a higher tendency to work in subordinate positions as compared to those who stayed at their university locations after graduation (52 to 55 per cent). This contradicting pattern is likely a result of the 2008 Global Financial Crisis (hereafter referred to as the 2008 GFC) which has noticeably reduced the number and range of employment available in the Australian labour market (The Smith Family, 2014; ABS, 2015). The economic downturn may have also made the effects of migration on field-of-study and skills mismatches less significant for the years 2008–09, as noticed in Figures 2.2a and 2.2c.

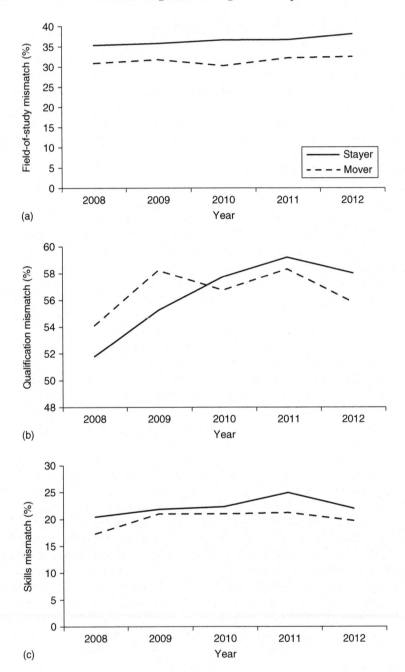

Figure 2.2   Field-of-study, qualification and skills mismatches, 2008–12

2.5.2   Modelling Results

To assess the association and significance of the influence of migration on education–job mismatch, a treatment effects model was estimated for each of the three forms of mismatch. We first present the estimation results from the treatment models which correspond to the process of self-selection in migration before discussing the outputs from the outcome models.

2.5.2.1   Treatment models

Table 2.3 shows the results from the treatment model of migration choice. The regression outputs are in line with existing literature in migration studies. Starting with personal characteristics, the results suggest that female graduates are less migratory than their male counterparts. This is partly because females are often constrained by family and childcare commitments (Mueller, 1982; Bell and Brown, 2006). Additionally, they are under-represented in occupations (for example, manager) and industries (for example, the mining sector) that tend to be more mobile (Bell and Brown, 2006). Nonetheless, we find that older graduates are more likely to move across labour-market regions after graduation, a finding that is in contrast with the common conception that young individuals are more spatially flexible and mobile.

Specialisation in health or education also increases the likelihood of migrating following graduation. In contrast, those who are qualified in natural and physical sciences, engineering and related technologies, architecture and building, or agriculture, environment and related studies are less likely to relocate across labour-market regions, as are those who worked during their final year of studies. This tendency is mainly because the majority of these graduates (56 to 66 per cent) remain employed with the same employer (and highly likely at the same location as well) after graduation. The results also reveal that graduates from regional universities are consistently more mobile than those who studied in a metropolitan location, a finding in-keeping with Rowe et al. (2013) and Tang et al. (2016) that regional areas tend to have lower overseas graduate retention rates. In contrast with previous work suggesting that post-graduate degree holders are less mobile (Abreu et al., 2015), our results indicate that having a post-graduate degree does not affect the odds of moving. The inclusion of occupation and industry of employment in our models may have captured the variation due to education level (Bonin et al., 2008; Nicholas and Shah, 2014).

The results for paid work status are as expected: having a full-time job is found to be associated with a higher chance of migrating after graduation. Nonetheless, it is not clear in this case whether full-time employment is a cause of mobility (for example, O'Sullivan, 2013) or a result (for example,

Table 2.3 Treatment models[a]

	Migration				
	2008	2009	2010	2011	2012
Personal characteristics					
Age	0.061**	0.005	0.063*	0.103***	0.111***
Age^2	−0.001*	0.000	−0.001*	−0.001***	−0.002***
Female	−0.057	−0.091**	−0.093**	−0.031	0.015
Educational characteristics					
Field of study[b] (base: creative arts and services[c])	—	—	—	—	—
Natural and physical sciences	−0.323**	−0.316**	−0.571***	−0.081	−0.175
Information technology	0.009	0.046	−0.028	0.073	0.151
Engineering and related technologies	−0.027	−0.118	−0.255*	−0.149	0.017
Architecture and building	−0.325*	−0.416**	−0.424**	−0.110	−0.342*
Agriculture, environment and related studies	−0.320	0.082	−0.451*	−0.308	−0.205
Health	0.246*	0.286**	0.019	0.108	0.105
Education	0.516***	0.705***	0.308*	0.567***	0.398**
Management and commerce	0.159	0.145	−0.008	0.157	0.135
Society and culture	−0.032	0.098	−0.105	−0.043	0.026
Post-graduate degree	−0.021	0.028	0.027	0.019	0.005
Worked during the final year of study	0.031	−0.064	−0.130***	−0.123***	−0.024
Studied in regional university	1.031***	1.034***	0.854***	0.741***	0.593***
Employment characteristics					
Full-time employment	0.185***	0.122**	0.145***	0.172***	0.249***
Studying while working	−0.0914*	−0.150***	−0.048	−0.010	−0.066

Occupation[b] (base: labourers)					
Managers	0.197	0.186	0.265*	0.289**	0.018
Professionals	0.245**	0.186*	0.278***	0.232**	-0.003
Technicians and trades workers	0.196	0.096	0.187	0.115	0.081
Community and personal service workers	0.047	0.148	0.140	0.038	-0.058
Clerical and administrative workers	0.264**	0.297***	0.253**	0.303***	-0.003
Sales workers	0.129	0.105	0.189*	0.099	-0.137
Machinery operators and drivers	0.079	0.203	-0.080	0.156	0.042
Industry[b] (base: telecommunications)	–	–	–	–	–
Natural resources	-0.122	0.158	0.353	0.073	0.223
Manufacturing, trade and logistics	0.029	0.122	0.197	0.093	0.015
Construction and utilities	0.184	0.128	0.124	0.379*	-0.035
Professional services	-0.223*	0.022	-0.009	-0.132	-0.177
Financial services	-0.154	0.003	-0.028	0.005	-0.144
Administrative services	-0.189	0.076	-0.005	0.004	-0.280*
Education	-0.823***	-0.743***	-0.725***	-0.771***	-0.841***
Health care	0.016	0.081	0.162	0.129	-0.033
Recreation and other services	-0.080	-0.101	-0.083	-0.078	-0.166
Observations	6,265	7,165	6,630	7,021	7,312

Notes:

a. This table reports the results of treatment models relating to field-of-study and qualification mismatches. The treatment models for skills mismatch produced consistently similar results and hence are not reported in this chapter.

b. The categorisation of field of study conforms to the Australian Standard Classification of Education 2001, while occupation and industry of employment follow the Australian and New Zealand Standard Classification of Occupations 2006 and Australian and New Zealand Standard Industrial Classification 2006 respectively.

c. Includes creative arts and food, hospitality and personal services.

Significance: ***1 per cent, **5 per cent, *10 per cent.

Hensen et al., 2009). There is also some evidence that highly skilled workers are more spatially flexible than those who are less skilled (see, for example, Borjas et al., 1992; Carrington and Detragiache, 1998; Chiquiar and Hanson, 2005). Our analysis reveals that managers, professionals, clerical and administrative workers, and sales workers are more mobile than labourers. Turning to industry of employment, working in construction and utilities increases the odds of relocating, while appointment in professional services, administrative services or education lowers the likelihood. The reduced mobility is also observed among those who continued their studies after graduation, partly because they tend to remain at the same higher education institution.

2.5.2.2 Outcome models

Following on from the treatment models, Tables 2.4 to 2.6 (pp. 30–35) present the regression outputs for the outcome models. The results are mostly consistent with previous work in this area (for example, Groot and Maassen van den Brink, 2000; Green and McIntosh, 2007; Hensen et al., 2009; Beckhusen et al., 2013; Li and Miller, 2013). For example, there is some evidence that older graduates are less likely to experience education–job mismatch, as are those who hold Australian permanent residency status, are qualified in health or education, have a full-time appointment in professional services, or are located in non-metropolitan locations (including both inner regional and distant areas). As expected, having a non-English-speaking background increases the likelihood of mismatch, similar to those who are working in manufacturing, trade and logistics, administrative services or recreation and other services. In contrast to existing literature suggesting that having worked during the final year of study is associated with higher odds of mismatch (Carroll and Tani, 2011), our analysis indicates that the work experience is not a significant determinant. This finding suggests that those who worked during the final year of studies tend to experience education–job mismatch mainly because they are less spatially flexible and mobile after graduation. As we controlled for post-graduation migration choice, the influence of work experience was diminished.

While prior studies tend to concentrate on the alignment between education level and employment (that is, qualification mismatch), this chapter examines three different forms of education–job mismatch, and the regression outcomes reveal an interesting result. Certain groups within the graduate population are at greater risk of experiencing all three forms of education–job mismatch. Those who are employed in manufacturing, trade and logistics, administrative services, health care or recreation and other services are associated with a higher chance of undergoing field-of-study, qualification and skills mismatches. In contrast, health graduates, full-time workers and those who take up jobs in professional services industry or in distant areas are consistently less susceptible to these mis-matches. There is also some evidence that working in the public sector or for not-for-profit organisations reduces the odds of experiencing the three forms of mismatch, suggesting that these sectors have a stricter screening procedure than private companies during the recruitment of employees.

The influence of post-graduation migration across labour-market regions, however, fluctuates over time and varies for the three forms of mismatch. The regression output reveals that spatial flexibility and mobility lower the chance of working in jobs that misalign with areas of expertise; however, the results are only statistically significant for the years 2010 and 2012. A similar effect is also observed for the case of skills mismatch in 2011. More surprising, perhaps, is the evidence that post-graduation migration significantly increases the likelihood of experiencing qualification mismatch in 2008. Nonetheless, these impacts are considered marginal, with estimated coefficients ranging between 0.015 and 0.028.

The differing effect of migration on the three forms of mismatch may relate to the spatial distribution of employment opportunities available in the Australian labour market. For example, jobs related to management and commerce tend to congregate in Sydney, which is deemed the com-mercial and financial locus of the country (Thrift, 1986; Rolfe, 2013), while Queensland is more specialised in mining and agricultural industries (ABS, 2013b). Accordingly, migration is important or even necessary in order to remain in their areas of expertise. In contrast, occupations of varying levels are likely to be more evenly distributed across space and therefore the role of migration is less important. The fluctuating influence over time is argued to be, at least in part, a result of the 2008 GFC. The financial crisis is likely to have counteracted and neutralised the impact of migration on field-of-study and skills mismatches between 2008 and 2009.

The marginal effect of migration on education–job mismatch is possibly due to the fact that DEOGs do not relocate in response to employment opportunities, but echo the settlement patterns of long-standing migrant communities in Sydney and Melbourne (Rowe et al., 2013; Tang et al., 2016). While social networks within the migrant communities may provide assistance in finding jobs (MacDonald and MacDonald, 1964; Portes and Sensenbrenner, 1993), major urban centres are often characterised by intense job competition and higher incidence of education–job mismatch (Beckhusen et al., 2013). Additionally, the tendency to settle in these met-ropolitan locations is sometimes associated with path dependence, which is also known as herd effects (Bauer et al., 2002; Epstein, 2008). In this case, DEOGs tend to lack social networks, which have been shown to be critical in securing employment during the recent economic downturn (Beets and

Table 2.4   Outcome models, field-of-study mismatch[a]

	Field-of-study mismatch				
	2008	2009	2010	2011	2012
Personal characteristics					
Age	0.022	−0.034	−0.047	−0.097**	−0.011
Age²	0.000	0.001	0.001	0.002**	0.000
Female	−0.215***	−0.014	−0.200***	−0.160**	−0.144**
Non-English-speaking background	−0.025	−0.047	0.004	−0.044	−0.045
Australian permanent resident	0.032	−0.081	−0.001	−0.112	−0.058
Educational characteristics					
Field of study[b] (base: creative arts and services[c])	–	–	–	–	–
Natural and physical sciences	0.001	0.027	−0.288	0.120	0.344
Information technology	0.012	0.134	0.150	0.246	0.176
Engineering and related technologies	−0.442**	−0.329	−0.198	0.081	0.097
Architecture and building	−0.214	−0.583*	−0.297	0.293	−0.467
Agriculture, environment and related studies	−0.150	−0.351	0.370	0.332	0.265
Health	−1.142***	−1.195***	−1.266***	−1.078***	−1.179***
Education	−0.839***	−0.436*	−0.643***	−0.628**	−0.338
Management and commerce	−1.065***	−0.981***	−1.071***	−0.861***	−0.689***
Society and culture	−0.924***	−0.789***	−0.784***	−0.631***	−0.544***
Post-graduate degree	0.093	0.013	0.007	0.063	0.190***
Worked during the final year of study	0.099	0.046	0.052	−0.011	0.022
Employment characteristics					
Full-time employment	−0.515***	−0.396***	−0.520***	−0.508***	−0.548***
Studying while working	0.162*	0.160*	0.139*	0.006	0.008

Employment sector (base: private sector)	–	–	–	–	–
Public sector	-0.129	-0.354***	-0.285***	-0.184*	-0.126
Not-for-profit organisation	-0.200	-0.205	-0.325*	-0.255	-0.103
Industry[b] (base: telecommunications)	–	–	–	–	–
Natural resources	-0.173	0.059	-0.102	0.101	-0.078
Manufacturing, trade and logistics	0.367**	0.532***	0.542***	0.511***	0.271*
Construction and utilities	0.203	0.143	0.131	0.095	-0.250
Professional services	-0.205	-0.239	-0.223	-0.197	-0.336*
Financial services	0.205	0.036	0.099	0.211	-0.156
Administrative services	0.526***	0.690***	0.720***	0.790***	0.498**
Education	0.062	0.182	0.186	0.503**	-0.091
Health care	0.348*	0.425**	0.545**	0.559***	0.357*
Recreation and other services	1.415***	1.584***	1.418***	1.447***	1.365***
Employment location (base: major cities)	–	–	–	–	–
Inner regional areas	0.243	0.134	0.128	-0.094	-0.172
Distant areas[d]	-0.165	-0.072	-0.244	-0.051	-0.331*
Migrated after graduation	-0.010	0.005	-0.021*	0.015	-0.018*
Observations	6,265	7,165	6,630	7,021	7,312

Notes:

a. The table reports the results of probit treatment effects models estimated using inverse-probability-weighted regression adjustment estimator with robust standard errors.

b. The categorisation of field of study conforms to the Australian Standard Classification of Education 2001, while industry of employment follows the Australian and New Zealand Standard Industrial Classification 2006.

c. Includes creative arts and food, hospitality and personal services.

d. Includes outer regional, remote and very remote areas.

Significance: ***1 per cent, **5 per cent, *10 per cent.

Table 2.5   Outcome models, qualification mismatch[a]

	Qualification mismatch				
	2008	2009	2010	2011	2012
Personal characteristics					
Age	−0.034	−0.068	−0.084*	0.069	0.044
Age^2	0.000	0.001	0.001	−0.001*	−0.001
Female	0.048	−0.039	0.126*	0.077	0.054
Non-English-speaking background	0.108	0.050	0.116	0.147*	0.068
Australian permanent resident	−0.132*	−0.094	−0.229***	−0.049	−0.173*
Educational characteristics					
Field of study[b] (base: creative arts and services[c])	–	–	–	–	–
Natural and physical sciences	0.045	0.286	0.367	0.450*	0.182
Information technology	0.358*	0.259	0.414*	0.404**	0.150
Engineering and related technologies	−0.213	−0.093	0.251	0.215	0.206
Architecture and building	0.100	0.833***	0.420	0.609**	−0.191
Agriculture, environment and related studies	0.385	−0.139	0.330	0.470	0.462
Health	−0.828***	−0.573***	−0.609***	−0.526***	−0.792***
Education	−0.362	0.038	−0.253	−0.255	−0.090
Management and commerce	0.386**	0.514***	0.532***	0.545***	0.422**
Society and culture	0.143	0.508**	0.283	0.277	0.329*
Post-graduate degree	−0.050	−0.023	0.001	−0.064	−0.072
Worked during the final year of study	−0.011	−0.049	0.025	0.017	0.022

Employment characteristics					
Full-time employment	-0.793***	-0.660***	-0.756***	-0.802***	-0.849***
Studying while working	0.023	0.104	-0.126	0.022	-0.034
Employment sector (base: private sector)					
Public sector	-0.083	-0.253***	-0.193*	-0.267***	-0.189**
Not-for-profit organisation	0.018	-0.157	0.048	-0.322*	-0.370**
Industry[b] (base: telecommunications)	-	-	-	-	-
Natural resources	-0.355	-0.034	-0.352	-0.023	-0.291
Manufacturing, trade and logistics	0.878***	1.004***	0.875***	0.838***	0.739***
Construction and utilities	0.137	0.319	0.141	0.111	0.032
Professional services	-0.471***	-0.499***	-0.476***	-0.395**	-0.506***
Financial services	0.174	0.144	0.432**	0.320*	0.444**
Administrative services	0.546***	0.705***	0.379*	0.606***	0.680***
Education	-0.280	-0.537***	-0.349*	-0.493***	-0.523***
Health care	0.084	0.073	0.057	0.226	0.284*
Recreation and other services	1.240***	1.212***	1.231***	1.380***	1.269***
Employment location (base: major cities)					
Inner regional areas	-0.188	-0.013	-0.171	-0.072	-0.344**
Distant areas[d]	-0.591**	-0.682***	-0.504**	-0.297*	-0.185
Migrated after graduation	0.015***	0.001	-0.002	0.006	0.000
Observations	6,265	7,165	6,630	7,021	7,312

Notes:
a. The table reports the results of probit treatment effects models estimated using inverse-probability-weighted regression adjustment estimator with robust standard errors.
b. The categorisation of field of study conforms to the Australian Standard Classification of Education 2001, while industry of employment follows the Australian and New Zealand Standard Industrial Classification 2006.
c. Includes creative arts and food, hospitality and personal services.
d. Includes outer regional, remote and very remote areas.
Significance: ***1 per cent, **5 per cent, *10 per cent.

Table 2.6   *Outcome models, skills mismatch*[a]

	Skills mismatch				
	2008	2009	2010	2011	2012
Personal characteristics					
Age	0.019	-0.009	-0.029	0.008	0.016
Age^2	0.000	0.000	0.001	0.000	0.000
Female	-0.024	0.025	-0.073	-0.138**	-0.107*
Non-English-speaking background	0.057	-0.108	0.090	-0.102	-0.056
Australian permanent resident	-0.083	-0.040	-0.035	0.036	-0.057
Educational characteristics					
Field of study[b] (base: creative arts and services[c])	–	–	–	–	–
Natural and physical sciences	-0.120	0.298	0.079	-0.093	0.278
Information technology	-0.199	0.134	0.208	-0.057	-0.032
Engineering and related technologies	-0.260	0.180	0.384*	-0.152	0.216
Architecture and building	-0.392	0.024	-0.457	0.108	-0.059
Agriculture, environment and related studies	-0.103	-0.159	0.139	-0.189	-0.098
Health	-0.630**	-0.417*	-0.475*	-0.712***	-0.554**
Education	-0.118	-0.024	0.186	-0.447*	0.041
Management and commerce	-0.325*	0.059	-0.012	-0.299*	-0.093
Society and culture	-0.073	0.020	0.143	-0.275	0.150
Post-graduate degree	0.097	0.128*	0.145*	0.053	0.067
Worked during the final year of study	0.061	0.032	0.036	-0.011	0.022
Employment characteristics					
Full-time employment	-0.565***	-0.373***	-0.492***	-0.509***	-0.624***
Studying while working	0.165*	0.100	0.073	0.063	-0.041

34

Employment sector (base: private sector)					
Public sector	−0.079	−0.098	−0.332***	−0.205*	−0.208*
Not-for-profit organisation	−0.243	−0.230	−0.561***	−0.228	−0.217
Industry[b] (base: telecommunications)	–	–	–	–	–
Natural resources	0.169	0.401	−0.044	−0.017	0.192
Manufacturing, trade and logistics	0.515***	0.477***	0.614***	0.285*	0.649***
Construction and utilities	−0.209	0.114	−0.031	−0.229	−0.321
Professional services	−0.189	−0.334*	−0.076	−0.346*	−0.008
Financial services	0.039	0.057	0.289	−0.099	0.292
Administrative services	0.417*	0.606***	0.790***	0.205	0.796***
Education	−0.306	−0.025	0.013	−0.367*	0.148
Health care	0.063	−0.036	0.424*	−0.157	0.334
Recreation and other services	0.651***	0.808***	0.845***	0.554***	0.992***
Employment location (base: major cities)	–	–	–	–	–
Inner regional areas	−0.258	0.023	−0.109	−0.359*	−0.096
Distant areas[d]	−0.373	−0.245	−0.484**	0.166	−0.161
Migrated after graduation	−0.019	−0.001	−0.013	−0.028**	−0.012
Observations	5,668	6,883	6,357	6,756	7,119

Notes:
a. The table reports the results of probit treatment effects models estimated using inverse-probability-weighted regression adjustment estimator with robust standard errors.
b. The categorisation of field of study conforms to the Australian Standard Classification of Education 2001, while industry of employment follows the Australian and New Zealand Standard Industrial Classification 2006.
c. Includes creative arts and food, hospitality and personal services.
d. Includes outer regional, remote and very remote areas.
Significance: ***1 per cent, **5 per cent, *10 per cent.

Willekens, 2009; OECD, 2009). This may help explain the increased chance of experiencing qualification mismatch in 2008.

2.6 CONCLUSIONS

While the overseas graduate population gradually expanded following the introduction of a new graduate visa scheme in late 2007, evidence suggests that these graduates tend to experience great difficulties in integrating into the Australian labour market. This chapter attempts to explain their inferior post-graduation employment outcomes in relation to spatial flexibility and mobility across labour-market regions. The regression modelling reveals that post-graduation migration has marginal impact on reducing the likelihood of experiencing field-of-study and skills mismatches over the period 2008–12. In contrast, there is some evidence that relocation potentially increased the chance of having qualification mismatch during the 2008 GFC. The minimal influence is at least in part a result of their tendency to follow migrant communities and congregate in highly competitive metropolitan labour markets, Sydney and Melbourne in particular, where the graduates may or may not have the social networks important for job search during the financial crisis.

In light of the growing overseas graduate population, it is important to gain a better understanding of their study-to-work transition and their early career performance in the Australian labour market. While this chapter provides some insights into the case of education–job mismatch, further research is now required to help improve their experience in the country after graduation. Future work may look into the relationship between spatial flexibility and full-time (or part-time) employment as well as the importance of social networks for these graduates to secure appropriate jobs in the Australian labour market. It is also interesting to explore how the effect of post-graduation migration changes when using different combinations of the three forms of education–job mismatch. Taken together, the results of this research will help develop skills policies that better harness the labour, skills and knowledge of this important source of human capital.

ACKNOWLEDGEMENTS

We wish to acknowledge Graduate Careers Australia for their co-operation and the supply of the data on which this chapter is based. Graduate Careers Australia cannot accept responsibility for any inferences or conclusions derived from the data by third parties.

NOTES

*   *Corresponding author:* email: z.tang@uq.edu.au.
1. In this study, we employed the Australian Statistical Geography Standard Remoteness Structure to capture the variation of labour-market condition across the urban hierarchy. Due to small overseas graduate population in outer regional, remote and very remote regions, we collapsed these categories into a single group termed 'distant areas'.
2. The treatment effects model will only estimate correctly if the Conditional Mean Independence assumption holds, that is, the potential outcomes are mean independent of the treatment. In this chapter, it is plausible to make this assumption given the large set of explanatory variables observed in our migration choice model (Wooldridge, 2002).
3. Our analysis does not explicitly control for income level when estimating the migration choice model as there is some evidence that income level does not have a significant influence on the migration and locational choices of DEOGs who remained in Australia after graduation (Tang et al., 2014).
4. To be doubly robust, both IPWRA and AIPW require the Overlap assumption, that is, each individual could receive any treatment level. This assumption holds for all models included in our analysis.

REFERENCES

Abreu, M., Faggian, A. and McCann, P. (2015), 'Migration and inter-industry mobility of UK graduates', *Journal of Economic Geography*, vol. 15, no 2, pp. 353–385.

ABS (Australian Bureau of Statistics) (2010), *Australian Statistical Geography Standard (ASGS): Volume 1 – Main Structure and Greater Capital City Statistical Areas, July 2011*, cat. no 1270.0, Canberra: Australian Bureau of Statistics.

ABS (Australian Bureau of Statistics) (2013a), *ANZSCO – Australian and New Zealand Standard Classification of Occupations, 2013, Version 1.2*, cat. no 1220.0, Canberra: Australian Bureau of Statistics.

ABS (Australian Bureau of Statistics) (2013b), *Agriculture*, available at: http://www.abs.gov.au/websitedbs/c311215.nsf/web/agriculture (accessed 1 August 2014).

ABS (Australian Bureau of Statistics) (2015), *Labour Force, Australia*, cat. no 6202.0, Canberra: Australian Bureau of Statistics.

Allen, J. and Velden, R. (2001), 'Educational mismatches versus skill mismatches: effects on wages, job satisfaction, and on-the-job search', *Oxford Economic Papers*, vol. 53, no 3, pp. 434–452.

Arkoudis, S., Hawthorne, L., Baik, Chi, Hawthorne, G., O'Loughlin, K., Leach, D. and Bexley, E. (2009), *The Impact of English Language Proficiency and Workplace Readiness on the Employment Outcomes of Tertiary International Students*, Canberra: Department of Education, Employment and Workplace Relations.

Baert, S., Cockx, B. and Verhaest, D. (2013), 'Overeducation at the start of the career: stepping stone or trap?', *Labour Economics*, vol. 25, pp. 123–140.

Battu, H., Belfield, C.R. and Sloane, P.J. (1999), 'Overeducation among graduates: a cohort view', *Education Economics*, vol. 7, no 1, pp. 21–38.

Bauer, T., Epstein, G. and Gang, I.N. (2002), 'Herd effects or migration networks? The location choice of Mexican immigrants in the U.S.', IZA Discussion Paper No 551, Bonn: Institute for the Study of Labor.

Beckhusen, J., Florax, R.J.G.M., Poot, J. and Waldorf, B.S. (2013), 'Attracting global talent and then what? Overeducated immigrants in the United States', *Journal of Regional Science*, vol. 53, no 5, pp. 834–854.

Beets, G. and Willekens, F. (2009), 'The global economic crisis and international migration: an uncertain outlook', Research note to European Commission Demography Network of the European Observatory on the Social Situation and Demography, The Hague: Netherlands Interdisciplinary Demographic Institute.

Bell, M. and Brown, D. (2006), 'Who are the visitors? Characteristics of temporary movers in Australia', *Population, Space and Place*, vol. 12, no 2, pp. 77–146.

Birrell, B. and Healy, E. (2008), 'Migrant accountants: high number, poor outcomes', *People and Place*, vol. 16, no 4, pp. 9–22.

Birrell, B., Healy, E., Betts, K. and Smith, F. (2011), 'Immigration and the resources boom mark 2', Research report, Melbourne: Centre for Population and Urban Research, Monash University.

Bonin, H., Eichhorst, W., Florman, C., Hansen, M.O., Skiöld, L., Stuhler, J., Tatsiramos, K., Thomasen, H. and Zimmermann, K.F. (2008), 'Geographic mobility in the European Union: optimising its economic and social benefits', IZA Research Report No 19, Bonn: Institute for the Study of Labor.

Borjas, G.J., Bronars, S.G. and Trejo, S.J. (1992), 'Self-selection and internal migration in the United States', *Journal of Urban Economics*, vol. 32, no 2, pp. 159–185.

BTRE (Bureau of Transport and Regional Economics) (2004), 'Focus on regions no 2: education, skills and qualifications', Information paper no 51, Canberra: Bureau of Transport and Regional Economics, Department of Transport and Regional Services.

Büchel, F. and van Ham, M. (2003), 'Overeducation, regional labor markets, and spatial flexibility', *Journal of Urban Economics*, vol. 53, no 3, pp. 482–493.

Carrington, W. and Detragiache, E. (1998), 'How big is the brain drain?', IMF Working Paper 98/102, Washington, DC.

Carroll, D. and Tani, M. (2011), 'Labour market under utilisation of recent higher education graduates: new Australian panel evidence', Working paper, Bonn: The Institute for the Study of Labour.

Chiquiar, D. and Hanson, G. (2005), 'International migration, self-selection and the distribution of wages: evidence from Mexico and the United States', *Journal of Political Economics*, vol. 113, no 2, pp. 239–281.

Dolton, P. and Vignoles, A. (2000), 'The incidence and effects of overeducation in the U.K. graduate labour market', *Economics of Education Review*, vol. 19, no 2, pp. 179–198.

Epstein, G.S. (2008), 'Herd and network effects in migration decision making', *Journal of Ethnic and Migration Studies*, vol. 34, no 4, pp. 567–583.

Faggian, A., Corcoran, J. and Rowe, F. (2015), 'Evaluating the effects of Australian policy changes on human capital: the role of a graduate visa scheme', *Environment and Planning C*, doi: 10.1177/0263774X15614755.

Frenette, M. (2004), 'The overqualified Canadian graduate: the role of the academic program in the incidence, persistence, and economic returns to overqualification', *Economics of Education Review*, vol. 23, no 1, pp. 29–45.

Green, F. and McIntosh, S. (2007), 'Is there a genuine under-utilization of skills amongst the over-qualified?', *Applied Economics*, vol. 39, no 4/6, pp. 427–439.

Greenwood, M. and Hunt, G. (2003), 'The early history of migration research revisited', *International Regional Science Review*, vol. 26, no 1, pp. 3–37.

Groot, W. and Maassen van den Brink, H. (2000), 'Overeducation in the labor market: a meta-analysis', *Economics of Education Review*, vol. 19, no 2, pp. 149–158.

Guthrie, B. (2008), *Graduate Destination 2007*, Melbourne: Graduate Careers Australia.

Hawthorne, L. and To, A. (2014), 'Australian employer response to the study–migration pathway: the quantitative evidence 2007–2011', *International Migration*, vol. 52, no 3, pp. 99–115.

Hensen, M.M., De Vries, M.R. and Cörvers, F. (2009), 'The role of geographic mobility in reducing education–job mismatches in the Netherlands', *Papers in Regional Science*, vol. 88, no 3, pp. 667–682.

Iammarino, S. (2005), 'An evolutionary integrated view of regional systems of innovations: concepts, measures and historical perspectives', *European Planning Studies*, vol. 13, no 4, pp. 495–517.

Iammarino, S. and Marinelli, E. (2015), 'Education–job (mis)match and inter-regional migration: Italian university graduates' transition to work', *Regional Studies*, vol. 49, no 5, pp. 866–882.

ILO (International Labour Organization) (2004), *International Standard Classification of Occupations*, International Labour Organization, available at: http://www.ilo. org/public/english/bureau/stat/isco/index.htm (accessed 25 September 2015).

James, K. and Otsuka, S. (2009), 'Racial biases in recruitment by accounting firms: the case of international Chinese applicants in Australia', *Critical Perspectives on Accounting*, vol. 20, no 4, pp. 469–491.

Li, I.W. and Miller, P.W. (2013), 'Overeducation in the Australian graduate labor market: the roles of immigrant status and language background', in P. Jelinek (ed.), *Education in Australia: Cultural Influences, Global Perspectives and Social Challenges*, New York: Nova Science Publishers, pp. 1–38.

Lindley, J. and McIntosh, S. (2010), 'Is the over-education wage penalty permanent?', Sheffield Economic Research Paper Series no 2010004, Sheffield, UK: University of Sheffield.

MacDonald, J.S. and MacDonald, L. (1964), 'Chain migration ethnic neighbour-hood formation and social networks', *The Milbank Memorial Fund Quarterly*, vol. 42, no 1, pp. 82–97.

Mueller, C.F. (1982), *The Economics of Labor Migration: A Behavioural Analysis*, New York: Academic Press.

Nicholas, A. and Shah, C. (2014), 'Incentives for relocating to regional Australia: estimates using a choice experiment', Research report, Adelaide: National Vocational Education and Training Research Program.

OECD (Organisation for Economic Co-operation and Development) (2009), *International Migration Outlook 2009*, Paris: Organisation for Economic Co-operation and Development.

OECD (Organisation for Economic Co-operation and Development) (2011), *Education at a Glance 2011: OECD Indicators*, Paris: Organisation for Economic Co-operation and Development.

OECD (Organisation for Economic Co-operation and Development) (2014a), *International Graduates: An Underutilised Labour Source in Norway*, Paris: Organisation for Economic Co-operation and Development.

OECD (Organisation for Economic Co-operation and Development) (2014b), *Special Focus: Mobilising Migrants' Skills for Economic Success*, Paris: Organisation for Economic Co-operation and Development.

O'Sullivan, S.J.H. (2013), 'Rural restructuring and rural in-migration patterns in Ireland', PhD Thesis, Limerick: University of Limerick.

Pekkala, S. and Tervo, H. (2002), 'Unemployment and migration: does moving help?', *The Scandinavian Journal of Economics*, vol. 104, no 4, pp. 621–639.

Peykov, P. (2004), 'Immigrant skilled workers: should Canada attract more foreign students?', SIPP Public Policy Paper no 27, Saskatchewan Institute of Public Policy, University of Regina.

Portes, A. and Sensenbrenner, J. (1993), 'Embeddedness and immigration: notes on the social determinants of economic action', *American Journal of Sociology*, vol. 98, no 6, pp. 1320–1350.

Quintini, G. and Broecke, S. (2014), 'The roles of skills in early labour market outcomes and beyond', in M. Keese (ed.), *OECD Employment Outlook 2014*, Genova: Organisation for Economic Co-operation and Development, pp. 211–260.

Reitz, J.G., Curtis, J. and Elrick, J. (2014), 'Immigrant skill utilization: trends and policy issues', *Journal of International Migration and Integration*, vol. 15, no 1, pp. 1–26.

Rolfe, M. (2013), 'State of the states: New South Wales', *The Conversation*, available at: http://theconversation.com/state-of-the-thestates-new-south-wales-17348 (accessed 7 April 2014).

Rowe, F., Corcoran, J. and Faggian, A. (2013), 'Mobility patterns of overseas human capital in Australia: the role of a "new" graduate visa scheme and rural development policy', *Australian Geography*, vol. 44, no 2, pp. 177–195.

Rowe, F., Corcoran, J. and Bell, M. (2014), 'Labour market outcomes and educational and occupational pathways of young movers starting off in regional Victoria', Technical report 4 prepared for State Government of Victoria, Queensland Centre for Population Research, School of Geography, Planning and Environmental Management, The University of Queensland, Australia.

Rowe, F., Corcoran, J. and Bell, M. (2016), 'The returns to migration and human capital accumulation pathways: non-metropolitan youth in the school-to-work transition', *The Annals of Regional Science*, doi: 10.1007/s00168-016-0771-8.

Rumberger, R.W. (1987), 'The impact of surplus schooling on productivity and earnings', *Journal of Human Resources*, vol. 22, no 1, pp. 24–50.

Sloane, P.J. (2003), 'Much ado about nothing? What does the over-education literature really tell us?', in F. Büchel, A. deGrip and A. Mertens (eds), *Overeducation in Europe: Current Issues in Theory and Policy*, Cheltenham, UK and Northampton, MA: Edward Elgar, pp. 11–45.

Smith Family, The (2014), 'Young people's successful transition to work: what are the pre-conditions?', Research report, Sydney: The Smith Family.

Stasiulis, D.K. (1990), *Multiculturalism and the Economic Agenda in Australia: Adult E.S.L., Overseas Skills Recognition and Anti-Racist Strategies*, Ottawa: Policy and Research, Multiculturalism Sector.

Tang, A.Z.R., Rowe, F., Corcoran, J. and Sigler, T. (2014), 'Where are the overseas graduates staying on? Overseas graduate migration and rural attachment in Australia', *Applied Geography*, vol. 53, pp. 66–76.

Tang, A.Z.R., Rowe, F., Corcoran, J. and Sigler, T. (2016), 'Spatial mobility patterns of overseas graduates in Australia', in T. Wilson, E. Charles-Edwards and M. Bell (eds), *Demography for Policy and Planning: Australian Case Studies*, Cham, Switzerland: Springer, pp. 175–195.

Tang, A.Z.R., Rowe, F., Corcoran, J. and Faggian, A. (forthcoming), 'The changing fortunes of overseas graduates in Australia: the case of Chinese and Indian graduates', in J. Poot and M. Roskruge (eds), *Population Change and Impacts in Asia and the Pacific*, Singapore: Springer.

Thrift, N. (1986), 'The internationalisation of producer services and the integration of the Pacific basin property market', in M. Taylor and N. Thrift (eds), *Multinationals and the Restructuring of the World Economy: The Geography of Multinationals*, Oxon, UK: Routledge, pp.142–192.

Trevelyan, J.P. and Tilli, S. (2010), 'Labour force outcomes for engineering graduates in Australia', *Australasian Journal of Engineering Education*, vol. 16, no 2, pp.101–122.

Van Ham, M. (2001), 'Workplace mobility and occupational achievement', *International Journal of Population Geography*, vol. 7, no 4, pp.295–306.

Van Ham, M., Hooimeijer, P. and Mulder, C.H. (2001a), 'Urban form and job access: disparate realities in the Randstad', *Journal of Economic and Social Geography*, vol. 92, no 2, pp.231–246.

Van Ham, M., Mulder, C.H. and Hooimeijer, M. (2001b), 'Spatial flexibility in job mobility: macrolevel opportunities and microlevel restrictions', *Environment and Planning A*, vol. 33, no 5, pp.921–940.

Wolbers, M. (2003), 'Job mismatches and their labour market effects among school-leavers in Europe', *European Sociological Review*, vol. 19, pp.249–266.

Wooldridge, J. (2002), *Econometric Analysis of Cross Section and Panel Data*, London: MIT Press.

3.   Graduate migration in Canada

K. Bruce Newbold

3.1   INTRODUCTION

There is a strong positive relationship between the size of a metropolitan area and the proportion of its population with a university degree, with large metropolitan areas home to larger shares of the university educated (Brown et al. 2010). In the Canadian context, about one in five persons living in large urban areas (places with a population of 500,000 and greater) aged fifteen and older has a university degree (Brown and Newbold 2011). This proportion falls to about one in seven for medium metropolitan areas (populations between 100,000 and 499,999), and just one in ten for small metropolitan areas (populations less than 10,000; ibid.).

Earlier work by Brown et al. (2010) established that Canada's largest cities both attract (through domestic migration and immigration) and generate degree holders (*in situ* growth). Large metropolitan centres, therefore, benefit from the infusion of human capital that enhances economic growth. Internal migration of recent graduates is also a significant source of human capital growth for mid-size Canadian cities, particularly in the years immediately after post-secondary graduation as individuals typically move for labour-market (employment) reasons (Ferguson et al., 2007; Gottlieb and Joseph, 2006; Partridge et al. 2007; Partridge and Rickman, 2003; Storper and Scott, 2009). Smaller urban centres and rural areas are typically associated with the out-migration of degree holders and more limited immigration (Brown and Newbold 2011). Migration also plays a positive role in achieving a good education–job match (Borjas et al., 1992; Costa and Kahn, 2000; Helsley and Strange, 1990).

The relative roles of the components of degree-holder growth (domestic migration, immigration, and *in situ* growth) vary across metropolitan areas (Brown and Newbold, 2011). In some cases, such as the university town of Kingston, Ontario, *in situ* growth dominates relative to growth through immigration or domestic migration, particularly for younger labour-force members. However, this human capital is often lost to out-migration shortly after graduation. Other places, such as Toronto, Vancouver,

Montreal and Ottawa (the large Canadian cities with populations greater than 1 million) are more likely to attract degree holders from elsewhere. But where are they drawing these migrants from? Amongst recent graduates, who is more likely to move? What is the outcome of the migration? Does it lead to employment, a good education–job match, further education or another migration?

While multiple studies (for example, Corcoran et al., 2010; Faggian et al., 2006; 2007; Faggian and McCann, 2009a; 2009b; Venhorst et al., 2011) have explored graduate mobility in the United Kingdom, Australia, Europe and the United States, there is little literature that considers migration patterns in Canada. Given the lack of evidence concerning the migration behaviour of recent graduates in the Canadian context, this chapter provides an exploratory analysis of the migration behaviours of recent university graduates by examining the migration behaviours of students following graduation from post-secondary institutions while controlling for socio-demographic factors and various factors reflecting employment and education. It adds to the literature in two ways. First, following Faggian et al. (2006), particular attention is paid to the type of post-graduate migration, distinguishing between repeat migrants (including return migrants) and first-time migrants who move post graduation. Second, it examines the differences in migration by type of degree, distinguishing post-secondary degree types including certificates and diplomas, which are typically granted by vocationally oriented colleges, and degrees such as bachelor's, master's or PhDs, which are typically granted by universities.

The remainder of the chapter is organized as follows. Section 3.2, following a review of the literature, discusses the data and methods in Section 3.3, before considering the analytical results in Section 3.4, including a discussion of both descriptive and multivariate results. Section 3.5 provides some conclusions.

3.2 BACKGROUND: MIGRATION, EDUCATION AND EMPLOYMENT

Since the mid 2000s, the migration literature has increasingly focused on concepts of human capital formation, employment, and migration. This includes the analysis of why human capital concentrates in some metropolitan areas and not others (Brown and Scott, 2012; Brown et al., 2010; Sjaastad, 1962). It is well established that the better educated are more likely to migrate, reflecting their better ability to collect and synthesize information on alternative locations and to afford the financial costs of relocating. It is therefore not surprising that university attendance is typically associated with high levels of mobility (Clark and Cosgrove, 1991; Faggian and McCann, 2009a). Students are, for example, first faced with the choice of where to go to university, a decision that will be influenced by location, university accessibility, cost, program availability, reputation, parental education, academic performance and academic engagement, amongst other factors (Drolet, 2005; Finnie, 2012; Finnie et al., 2005; Newbold and Brown, 2015). At the end of the university career, a second migration decision is typically made with the migration and destination decisions of recent graduates potentially shaped by income and employment opportunities, as well as place amenities at alternative locations (Brown and Scott, 2012; Glaeser and Gottlieb, 2006; Storper and Scott, 2009).

On average, people follow jobs (Brown and Scott, 2012; Partridge and Rickman, 2003) and migration addresses skill shortages. While the international literature has tended to focus on post-graduation migrations associated with job search and employment, complex post-graduation migration patterns have been observed (Sage et al., 2013), including migrations in and out of the parental home, migrations to employment, and migrations onward to other educational opportunities. Migrations to a parental home offer the advantages of security and lower financial costs. Recent graduates, particularly those with specialized skills and degrees, will be attracted to locations that offer labour-market opportunities (Venhorst et al., 2011), with larger cities offering thicker labour markets, greater employment opportunities, higher wages, and opportunities for greater wage growth (Ahlin et al., 2014; Brown and Scott, 2012; Newbold and Brown, 2012).

Although labour-market characteristics are important attractors of graduates, the complexity of migration amongst recent graduates is revealed by the different types of student and graduate migrations (Faggian et al., 2006; 2007), including repeat migrants, return migrants, university stayers, late migrants, and non-migrants (stayers), with these same categories used in the following analysis. Echoing the broader return and onward migration literature (Newbold and Bell, 2001; Newbold and Cicchino, 2007), *return* migrants are students who move away from home to attend university and then return to their origin region after graduation to enter the labour force. *Repeat* migrants, similar to the onward migrants found within the broader literature (see, for example, Newbold and Bell, 2001), are students who move away from their home region to attend university and then migrate onward to a new region to start employment. *University stayers* include those who migrate out of their home region to attend university, but who remain in that region after graduation. *Late migrants* are students who do not move to attend university, but who migrate after graduation to start employment. *Non-migrants* (stayers) are students who did not move either to attend university or after graduation.

The migration of recent graduates may be further complicated by the type of degree, with potential differences between individuals who obtain a certificate or diploma, a bachelor's degree, or more than a bachelor's degree. Typically, universities grant degrees (for example, bachelor's, master's or PhDs) while community colleges in Canada have typically offered vocationally or technically oriented programs and grant diplomas and certificates. Given regional differences in the demand for particular types of jobs across the country, the type of education is likely to influence the likelihood of migration. Since the mid 2000s, for example, inter-provincial movement of workers has been driven largely by resources and employment needs in Alberta and other resource-rich destinations. Such areas have seen growth in the resource sector driving migration of people in the trades sector, such as welders, plumbers and pipefitters. In an analysis of the labour-market migration in Canada, Turcotte and Weeks (2014) observed that those with the highest education had the highest rates of inter-provincial migration (7 per cent), while migration rates amongst individuals engaged in 'infrastructure trades' (post-secondary graduates whose major field of study was in construction trades, mechanics and repair, precision production, or heavy equipment machinery/crane operation) was 4 per cent, and 'other trades' had an inter-provincial migration rate of 3 per cent. Not surprisingly, Alberta was the primary destination for infrastructure workers, while demand for university-educated individuals would be greater in places in larger metropolitan places such as Toronto, Ontario, Montreal, Quebec, and Vancouver, British Columbia (ibid.). Consequently, the current analysis considers both the type of degree obtained as well as the type of migration amongst recent graduates in Canada.

3.3 DATA AND METHODS

Analysis draws upon Statistics Canada's 2013 National Graduates Survey (NGS), a nationally representative survey of graduates of the 2009–10 class from Canadian public post-secondary education institutions. With an unweighted sample size of approximately 28,700, the NGS focuses on post-secondary degree holders (that is, college certificate, bachelor's, master's or PhDs) – a definition that is consistent with the literature and other measures of human capital. While national in scope, the NGS considers movement only at the inter-provincial scale, and there is insufficient information to interpret migration flows at the sub-provincial scale. Clearly, analysis of graduate migration at the provincial scale is limited in that it misses the large volume of migrations between institutions within a province, as well as further insights into the development, attraction and retention of human capital at the scale of metropolitan areas. Similarly, the provincial scale lacks clarity in the definition of some of the migrations. For instance, students who return to their home province after graduation would be counted as 'return' migrants, but may in fact be migrating 'onward' to a different region within their origin province from where they left, ideas that are reflected in the work by Newbold and Bell (2001). Nevertheless, the scale of analysis reflects a long-term consideration of provincial migration, and there is broad interest among provincial governments and educational institutions in terms of inter-provincial movement of students for educational purposes (see, for example, Lawrance, 2009), with implications for recruitment, program delivery and development. Further, long-distance migrations across provincial borders can be conceived of as implying greater commitment to the move.

The analysis consequently focuses on inter-provincial migrants (see Figure 3.1), reflecting the geographic scale upon which the NGS collected data. It distinguishes between repeat migrants, return migrants, university stayers, late migrants, and non-migrants (stayers), with all migrations referenced to their home and destination provinces. Inclusion in the analysis is restricted to individuals aged 20–29, capturing those who are most likely completing their education and entering the workforce. The sample was further restricted to exclude individuals who moved across provincial boundaries in order to attend university. As such, the sample is typically capturing individuals returning to their origin or migrations associated with employment. Such restrictions reduced the sample size to approximately 10,000 observations.

Research methods draw upon complementary descriptive and multivariate techniques. To assess the magnitude of migration, in- and out-migration rates by migrant type and degree type (certificate/diploma, bachelor's, or greater than bachelor's) were calculated. Following the descriptive analysis, logistic regression was used to evaluate the determinants of each type of migration. Dependent variables included all migrants, repeat migrants, return migrants, and late migrants, relative to non-migrants. Throughout the analysis, weights developed by Statistics Canada for use in analysing the NGS are incorporated, and reporting standards are congruent to the standards enforced by Statistics Canada.

To evaluate the determinants of migration, a set of covariates are included in the regressions. Specifically, variables capturing socio-demographic effects include age, gender, degree type (certificate and diploma, bachelor's degree, or more than a bachelor's degree – that is, master's or PhD), immigrant status (Canadian by birth or immigrant), and self-reported visible minority status (visible minority or not). Since age is measured as a

Figure 3.1   Map of Canada and its provinces

47

continuous variable, an additional age-squared variable is included in the model to capture the well-known non-linear effects of age on the likelihood of migration. All other variables are entered into the models as a set of dummy variables.

It is expected that the various socio-demographic effects, including educational attainment, immigrant status, or visible minority status, influence the likelihood of migration consistent with findings from the broader literature (see, for example, Amirault et al., 2013; Brown and Scott, 2012; Finnie, 2004; Newbold and Liaw, 1995). For example, individuals with higher levels of education (and particularly those with more than a bachelor's degree) should be more likely to migrate than those with a certificate or diploma, reflecting potentially larger labour-market opportunities as well as the ability to better gather and synthesize information related to employment opportunities. Immigrants and individuals who are members of the visible minority community are less likely to make an inter-provincial migration than native-born Canadians (Newbold, 1996; Turcotte and Weeks, 2014), given potential responses to labour-market effects and the role of ethnic communities that provide links to employment (Li, 2009; Waldinger, 1996).

A second set of variables captures information related to educational and post-educational careers, including field of study (that is, education, humanities, social science, business, physical sciences, engineering, health, and math and computers) along with whether the individual was a full- or part-time student during their studies. The expectation is that full-time students would be more likely to move, while part-time students may be less mobile given that they have already developed ties to potential employers. Two sets of variables capture the post-graduation employment experience, including whether the job held at the time of the survey was related to the certificate, diploma or degree received, with the expectation that individuals whose jobs are more related to their education would be less likely to migrate. In addition, a variable capturing employment status (at the time of the survey) indicates whether the position was full-time or not. A final set of dummy variables captures the region (or province) of the educational institution (Atlantic provinces, Quebec, Ontario, Prairies, Alberta, and British Columbia).

3.4   RESULTS

Table 3.1 reports the migration rates (%) by degree type. Echoing work by Faggian et al. (2006; 2007), the five different types of graduate migration are observed. Stayers, or students that did not move to attend university

Table 3.1   Type and proportion of migration before and after studies in 2009–10: aged 20–29

	Cert./dip.	Bachelor's	Bachelor's+	Total
Stayer	94.3	86.2	80.3	89.3
Return to province of birth	1.7	5.2	7.9	3.9
Pre-graduate migration	1.4	2.8	4.6	2.4
Post-graduate migration (repeat)	0.1	1.1	1.7	0.7
Late migration	2.4	4.8	5.5	3.8

Notes: Individuals not attending university and reporting 1st post-graduation job. Bachelor's+ includes MA, MSc, MBA and PhD degrees.

or following graduation, represent the largest proportion of the sample by far (89.3 per cent). Both returns to the home province and late migrations (post-graduate migrations) represented nearly 4 per cent of migration flows amongst recent graduates (3.9 per cent and 3.8 per cent, respectively). Repeat migrations reflect the smallest proportion of moves (0.7 per cent).

Important differences in the rates of migration are also noted with respect to the type of post-secondary education. In general, certificate and degree holders were the least likely to make an inter-provincial migration, with 94.3 per cent staying in the region of their institution post gradua-tion. Conversely, graduates holding more than a bachelor's degree (that is, master's, MBA, PhD) were the most likely to make an inter-provincial migration and were more likely to engage in any of the different types of migration, including returning to their province of birth (7.9 per cent). Conversely, certificate and diploma holders were the least likely to migrate either before or after university.

Table 3.2 focuses on differences between migrants and non-migrants and whether migrations are associated with permanent positions, along with the relative relationship between the job and their degree. In this instance, all post-graduate migrations are defined as migrants, as sample size precluded further disaggregation by the type of migrant. The first two columns reflect the proportion of permanent employment positions obtained post graduation amongst migrants and non-migrants. While there was no statistical difference across all types of education (85.2 per cent and 85.6 per cent for stayers and migrants, respectively), individuals with a certificate or diploma were somewhat more likely to have a perma-nent position if they migrated as compared to their non-migrant coun-terparts (91.9 per cent and 86.7 per cent, respectively), perhaps reflecting differential demands for skilled trades across the provinces. Amongst those with a university education, however, there was no difference

Table 3.2   Permanent employment positions and relationship between degree and employment (%): inter-provincial migrants, aged 20–29, 2009–10

	Permanent		Close		Not at all close	
	Migrant	Stayer	Migrant	Stayer	Migrant	Stayer
Cert./dip.	91.9	86.7	60.5	66.5	27.6	16.4
Bachelor's	85.5	84.5	56.8	59.9	23.7	17.9
Bachelor's+	81.5	82.1	70.6	73.9	6.5	6.3
Total	85.6	85.2	61.5	65.0	19.5	15.5

Notes: Individuals not attending university and reporting 1st post-graduation job.
Bachelor's+ includes MA, MSc, MBA and PhD degrees.

between migrants and non-migrants in the proportion of individuals with a permanent position.

The last four columns reflect how close the job is to the degree for post-graduate migrants, with 'close' and 'not at all close' highlighted. Non-migrants were more likely to indicate that their position was more closely related to their degree as compared to migrants, with the greatest difference amongst certificate and diploma holders (66.5 per cent versus 60.5 per cent). For university degree holders, the difference in employment proximity was nearly equal. Conversely, amongst those indicating that there was no relationship 'at all' between their degree and first employment position, only a small proportion of individuals with more than a bachelor's degree indicated a discrepancy (6.5 per cent and 6.3 per cent for migrants and non-migrants, respectively). However, with 27.6 per cent of migrants and 16.4 per cent of non-migrants indicating that their job was unrelated to their degree, there was greater disparity in the work–degree fit amongst the certificate- and degree-holders group.

We can also gain some insight into the reasons for *not* moving (Table 3.3). Although sample size did not allow further disaggregation by the type of migration, satisfaction with the current location was the most predominant reason for not moving that was cited by respondents (50.4 per cent). However, the proportion of certificate- and degree-holders identifying this reason was somewhat higher (54.5 per cent) as compared to those whose education exceeded a bachelor's degree ('bachelor's+'). Family ties were the second-most important reason for not moving (39 per cent). Interestingly, individuals holding a certificate or diploma were less likely to indicate that family was a factor for not moving as compared to those with a bachelor's degree (34.8 per cent and 40.3 per cent, respectively). Other explanations for not migrating included social/cultural/linguistic effects,

Table 3.3   Reasons for not moving (%) by level of education: aged 20–29, 2009–10

	Family	Soc./cult./ linguistic[a]	Cost	No work	Satisfied	Other
Cert./dip.	34.8	3.8	2.3	0.6	54.5	4.0
Bachelor's	40.3	5.3	1.7	2.2	47.3	3.2
Bachelor's+[b]	47.5	3.6	0.4	1.2	44.6	2.7
Total	38.7	4.3	1.8	1.3	50.4	3.5

Notes:
a. Soc./cult./linguistic = social, cultural and linguistic reasons.
b. Bachelor's+ includes MA, MSc, MBA and PhD degrees.

costs of moving, and lack of work, although these explanations only accounted for less than 10 per cent of reasons for not moving.

Turning to the multivariate analysis, Table 3.4 reports the results of the logistic regression analyses. Four models are presented, including models for all inter-provincial migrants, post-graduation migrants, return migrants, late university migrants (post-graduation), and repeat migrants. Overall, results are largely consistent across the four models. For instance, the socio-demographic variables behave as expected, with individuals holding a degree greater than a bachelor's being more likely to migrate than individuals holding just a bachelor's. Moreover, both groups were more likely to migrate than certificate- or diploma-holders. Visible minority status also influenced migration, with individuals identifying as a visible minority less likely to migrate than non-visible minority individuals. Although it was expected that being an immigrant would reduce the likelihood of an inter-provincial migration, there was no statistical difference between Canadian citizens and immigrants. Likewise, age and age-squared were not statistically significant. While it is unclear why age did not have an impact on the likelihood of migration, it may be that the relatively narrow age range (20–29) precludes any significant age-related effects to be observed. Contrary to evidence elsewhere in the literature that suggests female graduates are more likely to migrate post graduation (Faggian et al., 2007), gender showed inconsistent results across the four models, seemingly dismissing arguments of gender imbalance in the labour market or coupled migrations as suggested by Faggian et al. (ibid.). Instead, the primary motivations for migration likely lie beyond sex and age, and include other factors which are discussed below.

Turning to education and employment effects, individuals who were full-time students were also more likely to migrate, suggesting that part-time

Table 3.4 *Logistic regression results: graduate inter-provincial migration by type, aged 20–29*

	All		Return		Late		Repeat	
	B	p	B	p	B	p	B	p
Intercept	-4.12	<0.0001	-6.18	<0.0001	-3.75	<0.0001	-8.97	<0.0001
Socio-demographic								
Male	0.097	0.2430	0.53	<0.0001	-0.27	0.0401	-0.46	0.0630
Visible minority	-0.44	0.0002	-0.85	<0.0001	-0.04	0.8103	-0.05	0.8658
Age	0.02	0.3907	0.03	0.3206	0.01	0.8426	0.05	0.4897
Age^2	-0.01	0.4826	-0.02	0.0820	0.01	0.3269	-0.17	0.5905
Citizenship (ref: Canadian)								
Immigrant	0.02	0.8608	-0.15	0.4735	0.07	0.7230	0.35	0.3148
Student status (ref: Part Time)								
Full-time	0.46	0.0052	1.40	<0.0001	-0.20	0.3190	0.88	0.0971
Education (ref: certificate or degree)								
Bachelor's	1.30	<0.0001	1.42	<0.0001	0.97	<0.0001	2.37	<0.0001
Bachelor's+	1.89	<0.0001	1.90	<0.0001	1.63	<0.0001	3.25	<0.0001
Field of study (ref: other)								
Education	-1.24	<0.0001	-1.17	0.0002	-1.22	0.0002	-1.84	0.0235
Humanities	-0.64	<0.0001	-0.88	0.0003	-0.77	0.0019	0.23	0.5972
Social science	-0.75	<0.0001	-0.55	0.0055	-1.09	<0.0001	-0.46	0.2803
Business	-0.68	<0.0001	-0.49	0.0097	-0.74	0.0002	-1.57	0.0025
Physical science	-0.95	<0.0001	-0.73	0.0038	-1.33	<0.0001	-0.79	0.1409
Math & comp.	-0.32	0.2157	-0.51	0.1782	-0.08	0.8110	-0.99	0.3355
Engineering	-0.38	0.0100	-0.41	0.0464	-0.52	0.0199	0.38	0.4024
Health	-0.42	0.0056	-0.26	0.2147	-0.61	0.0060	-0.35	0.4565

	Coef.	p	Coef.	p	Coef.	p	Coef.	p
Job related to degree (ref: other)								
Closely	-0.46	<0.0001	-0.40	0.0063	-0.37	0.0176	-1.26	0.0004
Somewhat	-0.47	0.0034	-0.41	0.0693	-0.42	0.0874	-0.71	0.1171
Not at all	0.01	0.9616	0.48	0.0129	0.68	0.0304	-0.91	0.0940
Employment status (ref: not working)								
Permanent	0.21	0.0153	0.04	0.7305	0.24	0.0669	0.84	0.0010
Region of institution (ref: Ontario)								
Atlantic	2.15	<0.0001	1.92	<0.0001	2.31	<0.0001	2.90	<0.0001
Quebec	-0.70	<0.0001	-0.81	<0.0001	-0.49	0.0149	-1.26	0.0240
Prairies	0.97	<0.0001	0.39	0.1115	1.43	<0.0001	1.40	0.0004
Alberta	0.91	<0.0001	1.05	<0.0001	0.77	0.0002	0.63	0.1347
BC	0.95	<0.0001	0.90	<0.0001	1.01	<0.0001	0.95	0.0100
N	10,602		9,780		9,684		9,264	
Rho-squared	0.164		0.162		0.130		0.261	
Log-likelihood	987.896		552.051		375.389		277.153	

Note: Shaded cells indicate significance at $p < 0.05$.

students had developed greater ties to employment opportunities during their educational career. No single field of study was associated with a greater likelihood of migrating across provincial boundaries. Instead, field of study either decreased the likelihood of migration or had no statistical impact on migration. However, individuals who indicated that their current employment was closely or somewhat related to their education were less likely to migrate. Permanent employment increased the likelihood of migrating, although whether permanency triggered the migration or occurred after migration is unknown.

Finally, region or province of the educational institution impacted migration propensities. Relative to Ontario, individuals who attended a post-secondary institution in the French-speaking province of Quebec were less likely to make an inter-provincial migration, reflecting broader migration trends including the greater propensity for French-speaking migrants to move only within Quebec (Lachapelle and Lepage, 2010). Conversely, students who had attended institutions in other provinces and regions were more likely to migrate inter-provincially relative to students who attended university in Ontario, with individuals attending universities in Atlantic Canada more likely to move following the completion of their education than students elsewhere in Canada, likely reflecting more limited employment options in the region.

Despite the broad similarities across the models, there are some differences, including visible minority status and student status, which are not significant (at the $p < 0.05$ level) for late and repeat migrations. In addition to differences by field of study and province or region of the educational institution, the relationship between job and degree also varied. While having an education that was closely related to their job consistently reduced the likelihood of migration, cases where there was no relationship significantly increased the likelihood of both return and late migrations.

3.5   CONCLUSIONS

This chapter has explored the inter-provincial migration behaviours of recent university graduates. In particular, it has examined differences in the types of migrations by recent graduates (that is, return, repeat and late migrations), along with the level of education, differentiating between individuals with a certificate or diploma, bachelor's degree, or more than a bachelor's. Overall, the results are largely consistent with the broader determinants of migration as observed within the literature, with the level of human capital an important determinant of migration. For example, irrespective of the type of migration, individuals with higher levels of education were found to be more likely to migrate following graduation, illustrated by the significant differences in migration propensities across the three educational levels. Given differences in skills and qualifications, and ultimately employment opportunities between the types of education, it is not surprising that differences in migration propensities exist.

In terms of other socio-demographic effects, visible minority status decreased the likelihood of any post-graduate migration as well as return migrations. While gender did not have a significant impact on any migration and repeat migration, males were more likely to engage in a return migration and less likely to make a late migration. However, neither immigrant status nor age were associated with migration as is commonly observed within the literature, although this may reflect the age interval (20–29) selected for inclusion in this chapter.

Migrations, particularly long-distance inter-provincial migrations, were also influenced by educational and employment-related effects. While field of study did not significantly increase the likelihood of migration, migrations were strongly motivated by employment both during the educational career and afterward: part-time students were less likely to migrate, potentially reflecting their ties to the labour force. In terms of employment effects, individuals whose job aligned with their degree were less likely to migrate, while individuals who felt that their job did not align with their degree were more likely to migrate, with subtleties between the educational levels captured both in the descriptive and logistic analyses.

While return migrations were the most common type of migrations and repeat migrations the least common, the covariates associated with each type of inter-provincial migration did not vary markedly across the models. In other words, there was no single factor that appeared to distinguish return migrations from other migrations. More than likely, the prevalence and determinants of return migrations reflect broader trends noted elsewhere in the return migration literature (that is, Newbold and Bell, 2001), including the importance of home and access to opportunities at home. For recent graduates, a migration away from home may have reflected preferences to attend a particular university or to live away from home, or the need for those in more rural and remote locations of Canada to access educational opportunities (Turcotte, 2006). Following graduation, returns to the parental home, or close to the parental home, can ease the transition between university and employment through local knowledge and connections into the labour force, echoing the idea of 'boomerang children' (Beaupré et al., 2008; Turcotte, 2006).

Finally, the results of this work suggest that if we are to understand the distribution of human capital, we need to look carefully at the immediate post-education migration patterns and their motivations. Overall, the results suggest that labour-market opportunities, and particularly the presence (or absence) of employment after graduation, are significant determinants of inter-provincial migration. In the absence of employment, individuals are more likely to return home or not to move at all. Consequently, knowledge of labour-market opportunities is critical as an enticement for early career migrations, particularly for regions that are keen to attract new workers given existing labour-market shortages. Echoing Brown and Scott (2012), the results therefore suggest that degree-holders are willing to move longer distances and, given the role of employment, are more likely to move to locations that are specialized in their industry, a conclusion that is consistent with skilled workers seeking out thick labour markets.

REFERENCES

Ahlin, L., Andersson, M. and Thulin, P. (2014), 'Market thickness and the early labour market career of university graduates: an urban advantage?', *Spatial Economic Analysis*, 9(4), 396–419.

Amirault, D., de Munnik, D.S. and Miller, S. (2013), 'Explaining Canada's regional migration patterns', *Bank of Canada Review*, Spring, 16–28.

Beaupré, P., Turcotte, P. and Milan, A. (2008), 'Junior comes back home: trends and predictors of returning to the parental home', *Canadian Social Trends*, Statistics Canada, Catalogue No 11-008.

Borjas, G.J., Bronars, S.G., and Trejo, S.J. (1992), 'Self-selection and internal migration in the United States', *Journal of Urban Economics*, 32, 159–185.

Brown, W.M. and Newbold, K.B. (2011), 'Human capital and cities: are university degree holders home grown or imported?', *Public Sector Digest*, Spring, 38–42.

Brown, W.M. and Scott, D.M. (2012), 'Human capital location choice: accounting for amenities and thick labor markets', *Journal of Regional Science*, 52, 787–808.

Brown, W.M., Newbold, K.B. and Beckstead, D. (2010), 'Growth and change in human capital across the Canadian urban hierarchy, 1996–2001', *Urban Studies*, 14(7), 1571–1586.

Clark, D.E. and Cosgrove, J.C. (1991), 'Amenities versus labor market opportunities: choosing the optimal distance to move', *Journal of Regional Science*, 32, 349–365.

Corcoran, J., Faggian, A. and McCann, P. (2010), 'Human capital in remote and rural Australia: the role of graduate migration', *Growth and Change*, 41(2), 192–220.

Costa, D.L. and Kahn, M.E. (2000), 'Power couples: changes in the location choice of the college educated, 1940–1990', *The Quarterly Journal of Economics*, 115(4), 1287–1315.

Drolet, M. (2005), 'Participation in post-secondary education in Canada: has the role of parental education and income changed over the 1990s?', Statistics Canada Cat. # 11F0019MIE – 243, Ottawa, ON: Statistics Canada.

Faggian, A. and McCann, P. (2009a), 'Universities, agglomerations and graduate human capital mobility', *Tijdschrift voor economische en sociale geografie*, 100, 210–223.

Faggian, A. and McCann, P. (2009b), 'Human capital, graduate migration and innovation in British regions', *Cambridge Journal of Economics*, 33, 317–333.

Faggian, A., McCann, P. and Sheppard, S. (2006), 'An analysis of ethnic differences in UK graduate migration behaviour', *Annals of Regional Science*, 40, 461–471.

Faggian, A., McCann, P. and Sheppard, S. (2007), 'Some evidence that women are more mobile than men: gender differences in UK graduate migration behaviour', *Journal of Regional Science*, 47, 517–539.

Ferguson, M., Kamar, A., Olfert, M.R. and Partridge, M. (2007), 'Voting with their feet: jobs versus amenities', *Growth and Change*, 38, 77–110.

Finnie, R. (2004), 'Who moves? A logit model analysis of inter-provincial migration in Canada', *Applied Economics*, 36, 1759–1779.

Finnie, R. (2012), 'Access to post-secondary education: the importance of family culture', *Children and Youth Service Review*, 34(6), 1161–1170.

Finnie, R., Lascelles, E. and Sweetman, A. (2005), 'Who goes? The direct and indirect effects of family background on access to post-secondary education', Statistics Canada Cat. # 11F0019MIE – 226, Ottawa, ON: Statistics Canada.

Glaeser, E. and Gottlieb, P.D. (2006), 'Urban resurgence and the consumer city', *Urban Studies*, 43, 1275–1299.

Gottlieb, P.D. and Joseph, G. (2006), 'College-to-work migration of technology graduates and holders of doctorates within the United States', *Journal of Regional Science*, 46, 627–659.

Helsley, R.W. and Strange, W. (1990), 'Matching and agglomeration economies in a system of cities', *Regional Science and Urban Economics*, 20(2), 189–212.

Lachapelle, R. and Lepage, J.-F. (2010), *Languages in Canada 2006 Census*, Cat. no CH3-2/8-2010, Ottawa: Statistics Canada.

Lawrance, J. (2009), 'Inter-provincial post-secondary student mobility: a review of data sources from a British Columbia perspective', Report prepared for the British Columbia Council on Admissions and Transfer, available at: www.bccat.ca.

Li, W. (2009), *Ethnoburb: The New Ethnic Community in Urban America*, Honolulu, HI: University of Hawaii Press.

Newbold, K.B. (1996), 'Internal migration of the foreign-born in Canada', *International Migration Review*, 30(3), 728–747.

Newbold, K.B. and Bell, M. (2001), 'Return and onwards migration in Canada and Australia: evidence from fixed interval data', *International Migration Review*, 35(4), 1157–1184.

Newbold, K.B. and Brown, W.M. (2012), 'Testing and extending the escalator hypothesis: does the pattern of post-migration income gains in Toronto suggest productivity and/or learning effects?', *Urban Studies*, 49(15), 3438–3456, doi: 10.1177/0042098012443859.

Newbold, K.B. and Brown, W.M. (2015), 'The urban–rural gap in university attendance: determinants of university participation among Canadian youth', *Journal of Regional Science*, 55(4), 585–608.

Newbold, K.B. and Cicchino, S. (2007), 'Inter-regional return and onwards migration in Canada: evidence based on a micro-regional analysis', *Canadian Journal of Regional Science*, 30(2), 211–226.

Newbold, K.B. and Liaw, K.L. (1995), 'Return and onward migration in Canada, 1976–81: an explanation by personal and ecological variables', *The Canadian Geographer*, 39(1), 16–29.

Partridge, M.D. and Rickman, D.S. (2003), 'The waxing and waning of U.S.

regional economies: the chicken–egg of jobs versus people', *Journal of Urban Economics*, 53, 76–97.
Partridge, M., Olfert, M.R. and Alasia, A. (2007), 'Canadian cities as regional engines of growth: agglomeration and amenities', *Canadian Journal of Economics*, 40, 39–68.
Sage, J., Evandrou, M. and Falkingham, J. (2013), 'Onwards or homewards? Complex graduate migration pathways, well-being, and the "parental safety net"', *Population, Space and Place*, 19, 738–755.
Sjaastad, L. (1962), 'The costs and returns of human migration', *Journal of Political Economy*, 70(5), 80–93.
Storper, M. and Scott, A.J. (2009), 'Rethinking human capital, creativity and urban growth', *Journal of Economic Geography*, 9, 147–167.
Turcotte, M. (2006), 'Parents with adult children living at home', *Canadian Social Trends*, Statistics Canada, Catalogue No 11-008.
Turcotte, M. and Weeks, J. (2014), 'The migration of infrastructure tradespersons', Statistics Canada, Catalogue No 75-006-X.
Venhorst, V., Van Digjk, J. and Van Wissen, L.J.G. (2011), 'An analysis of trends in spatial mobility of Dutch graduates', *Spatial Economic Analysis*, 6, 57–82.
Waldinger, R. (1996), *Still the Promised City? New Immigrants and African-Americans in Post-Industrial New York*, Cambridge, MA: Harvard University Press.

4. Graduate over-education and spatial mobility in Italy

Simona Iammarino and Elisabetta Marinelli*

4.1 INTRODUCTION

Graduates' entry into the labour market is a critical mechanism through which public investment in higher education reveals its returns: the returns to investment in human capital depend on the use that graduates can make of their education in the labour market, that is, on the degree of their education–job match.

A crucial question is whether university graduates' education–job match or mismatch – the latter commonly indicated as over-education – vary across regions within countries, leading to different returns to investments in higher education across space. Following the seminal work of Büchel and van Ham (2003), recent contributions have shown that geographical characteristics are likely to affect labour-market outcomes such as match or over-education. At the same time, the literature on technological change has long posited that an alignment between the local stage of socio-economic development and the quality of local human capital is a necessary condition for the latter to generate regional economic growth (see, for example, Nelson and Phelps, 1966; von Tunzelmann, 2009). The rationale behind this view depends on the assumption that graduates remain within the region where the investment in learning and education was carried out, or that gaps between the local demand and supply of human capital are met by adequate migration flows.

Despite the strong links between the literature on university education and regional development, the spatial dimension of graduates' knowledge use and their sub-national mobility remains under-explored. This chapter addresses this issue, focusing on the case of Italy, and testing whether inter-regional mobility has an impact on education–job match in the early stages of the graduate's professional career.

The chapter is organised as follows. Section 4.2 provides the background of the study; Section 4.3 introduces the data, defines the indicators of education–job match and over-education, and presents some descriptive statistics; Section 4.4 describes the econometric strategy; Section 4.5 discusses the empirical findings; and Section 4.6 concludes and summarises the main results.

4.2 BACKGROUND OF THE STUDY

The vast literature on education–job (mis)match and over-education has been stimulated by the observation that generalised increases in education levels have not always been mirrored by rises in skills use and remuneration (Freeman, 1976; see also Sloane, 2003 and McGuinness, 2006 for excellent reviews). Although in Rosen (1972) over-education emerges as a rather transitory phenomenon – as workers accept jobs requiring less education than the level that they actually possess to gain experience and improve their chances of a more suitable occupation in the future – the debate on the nature and persistence of education–job mismatch is still far from conclusive, with disconcerting evidence particularly with respect to university graduates (for example, Dolton and Vignoles, 2000; McGuinness, 2003; McGuinness and Wooden, 2009).

There are several reasons why understanding education–job (mis)match in relation to university graduates is important (Boudarbat and Chernoff, 2010). At the micro level, it is well established that an inadequate alignment between acquired and required competences is associated with worse employment conditions, such as for instance lower salary (for example, Battu et al., 2000; Heijke et al., 2003; Di Pietro and Urwin, 2006; Robst, 2007; Dolton and Silles, 2008) and employee dissatisfaction (for example, Garcia-Espejo and Ibanez, 2006; Iammarino and Marinelli, 2011; Green and Zhu, 2010). At the organisation or firm level, on the other hand, over-education is reflected in lower productivity and higher labour turnover (for example, Wolbers, 2003).

The literature that has tried to disentangle the determinants of graduate over-education at the micro level has found that this condition is more common in part-time or temporary jobs, in which graduates may often find themselves at the beginning of their career – the so-called *waiting room effect* (Dekker et al., 2002); along the same lines, other empirical contributions indicate that over-education decreases with tenure within a job (Groot and Maassen van der Brink, 2000). Scholars have also shown that graduates' education–job match depends on the field of study (Boudarbat and Chernoff, 2010; Venhorst and Cörvers, 2011) and, although the results are more mixed, on study performance measured by final grades (Battu et al., 1999; Biggeri et al., 2001; van der Klaauw and van Vuren, 2010). Furthermore, over-educated employees tend to earn lower wages and be less professionally gratified than their non-over-educated co-workers (see, for all, Sicherman, 1991).

On the basis of the high heterogeneity of graduates' conditions, some recent studies have pointed to the distinction between two different components of over-education: the first can be related to the mismatch of the formal qualification, while the second refers to the under-utilisation of skills and competencies acquired through the university experience. These two components are conceptually and empirically different (see, for various interpretations, Allen and van der Velden, 2001; Chevalier, 2003; Green and McIntosh, 2007; Green and Zhu, 2010) and have been used in the attempt to disentangle the different degrees of mismatch, some deemed more serious than others.

Resulting from this debate on the developmental role of universities (for example, Rosenberg and Nelson, 1994; Etzkowitz and Leydesdorff, 1997; Morgan, 1997; Salter and Martin, 2001; Mowery and Sampat, 2005; Gulbrandsen et al., 2011), growing emphasis has been put on the alignment between the skills demanded and the skills produced in a territory. Indeed, the impact of graduates on economic performance and knowledge creation depends on the level of social, technological and economic development of the region where they are employed (for example, Nelson and Phelps, 1966; Vandebussche et al., 2006; Faggian and McCann, 2009; von Tunzelmann, 2009; Rodriguez-Pose and Tselios, 2010; Kraber and Flöther, 2012; Consoli et al., 2013; Crescenzi et al., 2013).

Whilst the importance of education–job match at the individual and systemic levels has been recognised as critical to learning and knowledge-creation processes (Healy and Morgan, 2009), more needs to be done to understand how space shapes these phenomena (for example, Hensen et al., 2009; Croce and Ghignoni, 2011; Ramos and Sanromà, 2011; Venhorst and Cörvers, 2011). In this respect, studying the link between mobility and education–job match can shed light on how spatial conditions, by affecting the opportunity to apply skills and knowledge, generate virtuous dynamics of accumulation, creation and diffusion of knowledge. Indeed, human capital outflows from regions that lag behind are largely motivated by the graduates' desire to apply knowledge and competences acquired during their university study (for example, Faggian and McCann, 2006; Marinelli, 2011; 2013).

Italy is a particularly interesting case study. Not only is the country renowned for its marked sub-national socio-economic disparities (amongst a vast literature, see Vaccaro, 1995; Viesti, 2003; Iammarino, 2005; Barca, 2006; Svimez, 2009), but in recent years, these geographical differences have been accompanied by an increasing internal brain-drain. Since the mid 1990s the Mezzogiorno regions have experienced substantial outflow of graduates (for example, Piras, 2005; 2006; D'Antonio and Scarlato, 2007), particularly towards more innovative and dynamic regions that offer wider and better opportunities to apply competences and skills (Marinelli, 2011; Dotti et al., 2014). An additional factor that makes Italy an interesting case is that, whilst the typical Italian dualism is not reflected in university educational attainment (for example, Piras, 2005; 2006; di Liberto, 2008), there are large differences in the employment opportunities open to graduates from different parts of the country (for example, Checchi and Peragine, 2005; Coniglio and Peragine, 2007).

Against this background, this chapter focuses on the empirical investigation of two research questions: first, whether internal spatial mobility across regions impacts on education–job match and over-education in the early stages of graduates' careers; and second, whether such a link differs according to the geographical area the graduates are moving from and towards.

4.3   DATA AND INDICATORS

4.3.1   Dataset

The chapter uses the *Indagine sull'Inserimento Professionale dei Laureati* (ISTAT, 2010). The survey investigates the entrance of graduates into the labour market three years after they completed their studies: we use the 7th edition of the survey, carried out in 2007 and which includes 2004 graduates. At the time, the Italian system was in transition from the old *Laurea degree* (a longer degree comprising bachelor's and master's) to the new system aligned with the Bologna process, based on bachelor's and master's at two different stages. The focus here is exclusively on graduates from the old system: they account for 167,886 of the total population of 260,070 Italian graduates in 2004, and for 26,570 of the *Indagine*'s sample of 47,300.

The *Indagine* is characterised by a one-stage stratification by gender, university and type of degree. Each of the surveyed individuals is attributed a sampling weight which allows us to build indicators representative at the level of nation, field of study and, most importantly for the objective of the present work, region of study and current region of residence and employment.

4.3.2   Education–Job (Mis)match: Indicators

Different indicators and methods of measuring education–job match have been applied in the literature. According to Verhaest and Omey (2006), three categories of indicators can be identified: (i) those based on a professional job-analyst's definition of the skills or educational requirements for each occupation, labelled as 'objective' measures; (ii) those based on the 'subjective' assessment (that is, the graduate's or the employer's) of the job's educational requirements; (iii) those based on the distance between the worker's education and the mean or modal education level of her/his occupational group, labelled as the 'empirical method'.[1]

The indicators used here fall into the second category of subjective or self-reported measures. In particular, we use – both separately and in conjunction – information on (a) the formal educational requirements of the employer (referred to in the literature as Indirect Self-Assessment), and (b) the graduates' self-assessment with respect to the competences and skills required to perform their job (Direct Self-Assessment). According to Wald and Fang (2008) this type of measure has the advantage of being job-specific. However, as it is subjective, it may be biased by the individual's attitudes, for instance when the graduate wishes to increase the standing of the job (Hartog, 2000; Sgobbi and Suleman, 2013).

The *Indagine* asks graduates the following question related to the employers' educational requirement (Indirect Self-Assessment):

1a. Was the laurea degree formally required by the employer to apply for the job?

As for the Direct Self-Assessment, the question from the survey is:

1b. Is the laurea degree effectively necessary to carry out the job?

Both questions generate a yes/no variable. However, whilst question 1a gives insights into the qualification required, question 1b provides information on the graduate's perception of the use of her/his competences and skills acquired through university education. We employ a combined indicator, building on Allen and van der Velden (2001), Chevalier (2003), Ungaro and Verzicco (2005), and Iammarino and Marinelli (2011), incorporating the crucial distinction between qualification and competencies/skills utilisation. We obtain a matrix of four possible education–job (mis)matches, as shown in Table 4.1.

Following the literature, match and over-education are defined as *real* when the opinion of the graduate on the effective need of her/his qualifications is coherent with the perception of the formal requirement of the job. A *real match* (*real over-education*) therefore arises when the graduate believes (does not believe) that her/his education level is effectively needed in the job, and when the degree was also (was not) a formal requirement of the

Table 4.1   The matrix of education–job (mis)match

		Was the degree effectively necessary to carry out the job?	
		YES	NO
Was the degree formally required?	YES	**REAL MATCH:** matched qualification, full skill utilisation	**APPARENT OVER-EDUCATION:** matched qualification, skill under-utilisation
	NO	**APPARENT MATCH:** over-qualification, full skill utilisation	**REAL OVER-EDUCATION:** over-qualification, skill under-utilisation

employer. Whenever the opinion of the graduate and the employer's condition differ, on the other hand, *apparent match* (*apparent over-education*) arises. Specifically, when a graduate feels that the degree is needed to perform her/his work, though the employer did not formally require it, the graduate is experiencing *apparent education–job match*. Conversely, when the graduate is in a job for which the degree was formally required but is perceived unnecessary she/he is experiencing *apparent over-education*.

Of the two typologies of the matrix above that correspond to overqualification (that is, those for which, according to the Indirect Self-Assessment, the degree was *not* formally required by the employer), only the situation in which the graduate is both over-qualified and over-skilled represents what the literature has indicated as *real over-education*; the other category is instead indicated as *apparent match*, as it implies a full skills utilisation. Conversely, *apparent over-education* is the category where graduates have a matched qualification but their competences and skills are perceived as under-utilised: these graduates may be hired by employers who want to benefit from a highly qualified labour force even in low-skilled and low-salary jobs (a phenomenon already discussed for Italy by Di Pietro and Urwin, 2006). On the other hand, *apparently matched* graduates may be frustrated with their economic treatment, because employers are labelling the occupation as 'non-graduate' in order to pay lower wages, but employees perceive their skills as necessary to perform the job.

These four typologies can be ordered in the following way: *real over-education* indicates the lowest (or worst) degree of education–job match, followed by *apparent over-education, apparent match* and a *real match.*[2] An ordinal variable of education–job (mis)match is thus created, comprising the following levels:

1. Real over-education
2. Apparent over-education

3. Apparent match
4. Real match

4.3.3 Descriptive Statistics

Inter-regional migrants are defined as graduates whom, three years after graduation, are residing in a region different from the one in which they studied, and represent about a quarter of Italian graduates: such a proportion is similar across the three classical Italian macro-regions (north, centre, and south or Mezzogiorno).

As Table 4.2 shows, whilst nearly 25 per cent of total migrants move from the south to the centre or north of the country (9.6 per cent and 14.9 per cent respectively), the proportion of those who leave the north for the centre or the south is less than 15 per cent in total; it should be noted that nearly 27 per cent of total migrants are intra-north. The proportion of total migrants that leave the centre for another macro-region is slightly above 19 per cent (8.9 per cent for the north and 10.2 per cent for the south).

Table 4.3 highlights the remarkable differences in employment rates among the three macro-regions. In the south only 59.8 per cent of graduates are employed, as compared to 83.4 per cent in the north and 72 per cent in the centre. Although employment opportunities are significantly lower in the Mezzogiorno regions, the proportion of graduates with favourable education–job match is slightly higher in the south than in the other parts of Italy, whilst the shares are lower for over-education (both real and apparent). Overall, those experiencing real over-education (real match) according to our composite indicator are 18.3 per cent (61 per cent) in the south, versus 21.7 per cent (55.3 per cent) in the centre and 20.2 per cent (58.3 per cent) in the north.

Finally, Table 4.4 compares stayers, migrants and south-to-centre/ north migrants across the main indicators of education–job (mis)match. Remarkably, the values for graduates migrating after university from the south to work in other regions are higher across all indicators except

Table 4.2 Graduate migration flows by macro-area

Origin	Destination		
	North	Centre	South
North	26.9%	7.4%	7.2%
Centre	8.9%	5.8%	10.2%
South	14.9%	9.6%	9.1%

Table 4.3 Employment rate and indicators of education–job (mis)match by macro-area

	% empl. rate	% degree necessary for job (q.1b)	% degree formally required (q.1a)	% real over-education	% apparent over-education	% apparent match	% real match
North	83.4%	68.5%	69.5%	20.2%	11.3%	10.3%	58.3%
Centre	72.0%	67.4%	66.2%	21.7%	10.9%	12.1%	55.3%
South	59.8%	72.6%	70.0%	18.3%	9.1%	11.7%	60.9%

Table 4.4 Education–job (mis)match indicators by mobility category

	% degree necessary for job (q.1b)	% degree formally required (q.1a)	% real over-education	% apparent over-education	% apparent match	% real match
Stayers	68.5%	68.1%	20.7%	10.2%	12.2%	56.9%
All other migrants	70.4%	70.7%	19.1%	9.6%	12.9%	57.4%
South to centre/north migrants	75.4%	72.3%	15.9%	8.7%	11.8%	63.6%

for over-education (both real and apparent), indicating an overall better education–job match for these southern migrants as compared to other migrants and stayers.

4.4 ECONOMETRIC STRATEGY

In exploring our research questions we need to take into account two possible biases:

1. the endogenous relationship between mobility behaviour and employment;
2. the issue of self-selection into employment.

As a long scholarly debate has explored whether migration is the cause or the consequence of employment and other labour-market outcomes (see Hoogstra et al., 2011 for a meta-review), we take such an issue into account in our methodology. As for self-selection, the degree of education–job (mis)match is observable only for those graduates who are actually employed (see, among others, Buchel and van Ham, 2003; Jauhiainen, 2011; Devillanova, 2013). Thus, if unobserved factors affecting the outcome (in the case here, the education–job (mis)match) are correlated with unobserved factors affecting the selection process (that is, whether graduates are employed or not), standard regression techniques deliver inconsistent estimators (Heckman, 1979).

To tackle both issues we apply the methodology devised by Arendt and Holm (2006), which is an extension of the Heckman correction (Heckman, 1979).[3] Specifically, we follow three logical steps. First, we estimate an equation explaining the migration decision, and on this we calculate the Inverse Mills Ratio (IMR),[4] which becomes an explanatory variable for the employment equation, accounting for the endogeneity between the latter and migration. Second, we estimate the employment equation, and calculate its own IMR, which then becomes one explanatory variable of the third step, to account for self-selection between employment and education–job match. Finally, we estimate the education–job match equation.

As the software STATA allows for estimating probit and ordered probit with sample selection, empirically the three steps are collapsed into two stages, as follows:

1. Stage 1: we estimate the migration equation and calculate the IMR;
2. Stage 2: we run both ordered (Miranda and Rabe-Hesketh, 2006) and binary probit with sample selection. These models estimate two

equations simultaneously: one selection equation, which accounts for the probability of the graduate to be employed; and one outcome equation, where the level of education–job match is estimated.

To assess whether there is a selection bias we look at the parameter ρ, which measures the correlation between the error terms of the two equations: when ρ is significantly different from zero, then the Heckman selection model is appropriate. When ρ is not significantly different from zero, we estimate only the outcome equation, including the IMR from the migration equation among the independent variables.

As mentioned above, we need to specify three equations, explaining (i) migration, (ii) employment status, and (iii) education–job match, respectively. In the first equation we estimate the probability of being a migrant versus being a stayer (Migr), where migrant is defined as a graduate whom, three years after graduation, is residing in a different region from the one in which she/he studied (conversely a graduate who has remained in the same region of study is classified as a stayer).[5,6] Our selection equation explains graduates' employment status (a binary variable, expressing whether the graduate is employed or not). Finally, the outcome equation explains the education–job (mis)match – expressed as an ordinal variable with four levels as described in Section 4.3.2 above.

The three equations are specified as follows:

Migr = *f*(Field1, Mark, High_school_mark, Prev_degree, Study_migr, Erasmus, Work, Study_father, Uni_city, Uni_regio)

Employment = *f*(Migr, Field2, PERSONAL, CURR_EDU, Macro_Region, Uni_city, IMR)

Edu-job match = *f*(Mobility, Field2, Mark, ATTITUDE, JOB, Female, IMR).

The complete list of variables and their descriptions for all three equations is reported in Table 4.5.

4.5   RESULTS

Looking at our core research issue – the impact of inter-regional migration on education–job match – Table 4.6 shows the results of the ordered logit regressions for our four models.[7]

First of all, in line with the empirical evidence on the overall positive

Table 4.5   List of variables included in the migration equation, selection and outcome equations

ATTITUDE	A vector of variables that capture the graduates' attitude towards their field of studies. It includes: <ul><li>Interest: a dummy variable that identifies those graduates who chose their degree because they were interested in the topic</li><li>Job prospects: a dummy variable that identifies those graduates who chose their degree because of the job prospects it offered</li></ul>
CURREDU	A vector of variables capturing those graduates currently engaged in further education. It includes: <ul><li>PhD: the graduate is currently enrolled in a PhD programme</li><li>Training: the graduate is currently enrolled in a training/internship</li><li>Otheredu: the graduate is currently enrolled in other qualifications/courses</li></ul>
Edu-job match	Ordered indicator of education–job (mis)match based on Table 4.1. It is the dependent variable of the outcome equation
Employment	Binary variable identifying graduates who are employed vs those unemployed. It is the dependent variable of the selection equation
Erasmus	A binary variable capturing whether the graduate participated in international mobility programmes, such as Erasmus, during the degree
Female	A dummy variable identifying the gender of the graduate (also in PERSONAL in the selection equation)
Field1	Captures the fields of study of the graduate and it is a covariate in the migration equation: <ul><li>Humanities (base category)</li><li>Economics and statistics</li><li>Social and political sciences</li><li>Law</li><li>Sciences</li><li>Engineering</li><li>Architecture</li><li>Medicine</li><li>Sports</li></ul>
Field2	Captures the broad field of study and includes five groups, which collapse the nine fields of Field1 (in parenthesis): <ul><li>Sports (base category)</li><li>Humanities</li><li>Social sciences (economics and statistics, social and political sciences, and law)</li></ul>

(continues overleaf)

Table 4.5   (continued)

Field2	• Hard and technical sciences (sciences, engineering and architecture)
	• Medicine
High_school_M	Captures the high-school graduation mark and is expressed on a scale from 36 to 60
IMR	The Inverse Mills Ratio, derived from the migration equation
JOB	A vector of job-specific characteristics and includes:
	• Previous_job: a dummy variable that identifies graduates who had job experience before the current employment
	• Self_emp: a dummy variable that identifies graduates who are self-employed
	• Seniority: number of years the graduate has been in the job (from 0 to 3, as this question is asked exclusively to graduates who started their job after graduating and the *Indagine* targets graduates three years after the end of their studies)
	• Salary: monthly salary of graduates expressed in euros
Macro_Region	A categorical variable identifying whether the graduate obtained their university degree in the north (the base category), centre or south
Mark	A continuous variable that expresses the graduation mark of the graduate (in the Italian system from 70 to 110 *cum laudem*, the latter coded 111)
Migr	A binary variable which distinguishes migrants (those who live in a different region from the one in which they graduated) from stayers (those who live in the same region of graduation). It is the dependent variable of the migration equation and one of the covariates in the selection equation. For the education–job match equation, we adopt a more complex indicator (mobility) accounting for the direction of migration
Mobility	A categorical variable which distinguishes between migrants from the south to the centre and north of Italy, and the rest of inter-regional migrants (that is, either within each macro-region or between the centre and the north, or from there to the south). Specifically it distinguishes between:
	• Stayers (the base category, those who remain in the same region in which they studied)
	• Migr_Italy: those who live in a different region from that of graduation, excluding south-to-centre/north migrants (Migr_StoCN)
	• Migr_StoCN: those who left a region of the south to move to a region in the centre-north

Table 4.5 (continued)

	As we run separate models for Italy and its three macro-areas, this latter variable is then split into the following: ○ Migr_StoN: those who left a region of the south to move to a region of the north ○ Migr_StoC: those who left a region of the south to move to a region of the centre ○ Migr_StoS: those who left a region of the south to move to another region of the south
PERSONAL	A vector of variables capturing personal characteristics of graduates, including: • Age: age of the graduate expressed in years • Female: a dummy variable that identifies female graduates • Par_uni: a dummy variable that captures the social background of the graduate by identifying whether she/he has at least one parent with university education
Prev_degree	A categorical variable that captures whether the graduate had other university titles before her/his graduation in 2004
Study_migr	A dummy variable that identifies whether the graduate attended university in the same region as she/he was residing in before starting university
Study_father	An ordered variable, inserted in the regression as a continuous one, capturing the level of education of the father, with the following values: no title, elementary school, middle or vocational school, high school or high vocational school; university degree or doctorate
Uni_city	A binary variable that identifies graduates from the largest nine cities of Italy: Torino, Genova, Milano, Bologna, Firenze, Roma, Napoli, Bari and Palermo
Work	A categorical variable that identifies whether the graduate worked during her/his studies. It can take three values: 1. Occasional work – the base category 2. Continuous work 3. Never worked

effects of spatial mobility, the results indicate that, for the country as a whole, inter-regional migration increases both the probability of being employed and the probability of a better education–job match. Interestingly, migrating from the Mezzogiorno's regions towards the centre-north of the country (Migr_StoCN) raises the likelihood of achieving a good education–job match relative to stayers and other migrants. It has to be noted that in our sets of regressions the cut-offs across the four categories of the education–job matrix represented in Table 4.1 are all

Table 4.6   *Regression results: order logit equations with ordered dependent variable in the outcome equations (education–job (mis)match, 4 levels)*

	Italy	North	Centre	South[a]
Outcome equations				
Migr_Italy	0.117***	0.167***	0.146	0.371*
	(3.11)	(3.07)	(1.64)	(1.76)
Migr_StoCN	0.195***	–	–	–
	(3.16)	–	–	–
Migr_StoN	–	0.364***	–	–
	–	(4.77)	–	–
Migr_StoC	–	–	0.0858	–
	–	–	(0.81)	–
Migr_StoS	–	–	–	0.0227
	–	–	–	(0.10)
Humanities	−0.261***	−0.264***	−0.285	−0.0270
	(−3.43)	(−2.74)	(−1.26)	(−0.10)
Soc Sciences	−0.337***	−0.328***	−0.144	−0.588**
	(−4.86)	(−3.88)	(−0.66)	(−2.34)
Hard Sciences	0.261***	0.235***	0.415*	0.556**
	(3.81)	(2.79)	(1.87)	(2.18)
Medicine	1.451***	1.531***	1.356***	2.487***
	(12.60)	(8.45)	(4.46)	(6.30)
Mark	0.0171***	0.0150***	0.0205***	0.0289***
	(7.93)	(5.34)	(4.28)	(3.59)
Interest	0.165***	0.158***	0.252**	0.216
	(3.68)	(2.63)	(2.57)	(1.39)
Job_prospects	0.176***	0.208***	0.306***	−0.0723
	(4.37)	(3.78)	(3.52)	(−0.52)
Previous_job	−0.132***	−0.112**	−0.134*	−0.321***
	(−3.97)	(−2.45)	(−1.82)	(−2.88)
Self_emp	0.417***	0.428***	0.376***	0.817***
	(9.83)	(7.10)	(4.62)	(5.32)
Seniority	−0.0103	−0.0496**	0.0476	0.0192
	(−0.64)	(−2.23)	(1.46)	(0.37)
Salary	0.000136***	0.000136***	0.0000763	0.000148
	(4.27)	(2.82)	(1.20)	(1.36)
Female	0.000675	0.0194	−0.0586	−0.0310
	(0.02)	(0.44)	(−0.89)	(−0.29)
IMR	–	–	–	0.366**
	–	–	–	(2.01)
Selection equations (employment)				
Migr	0.195***	0.0364	−0.0487	–
	(4.38)	(0.39)	(−0.28)	–
Humanities	0.227***	0.437***	0.336	–
	(2.61)	(3.63)	(1.45)	–
Soc Sciences	−0.121	−0.0872	0.211	–
	(−1.63)	(−0.84)	(0.99)	–

Table 4.6   (continued)

	Italy	North	Centre	South[a]
Hard Sciences	0.405***	0.282***	0.668***	–
	(5.23)	(2.65)	(2.98)	–
Medicine	−0.938***	−1.089***	−0.615***	–
	(−11.21)	(−8.93)	(−2.79)	–
Par_uni	−0.0492	−0.152**	−0.0561	–
	(−1.07)	(−2.31)	(−0.52)	–
Age	0.00317	−0.00515	0.00795	–
	(0.39)	(−0.50)	(0.37)	–
Female	−0.260***	−0.276***	−0.238***	–
	(−7.69)	(−5.14)	(−3.23)	–
PhD	−1.556***	−1.703***	−1.435***	–
	(−21.88)	(−16.79)	(−10.23)	–
Training	−0.831***	−0.931***	−1.002***	–
	(−14.17)	(−9.80)	(−7.87)	–
Other_Edu	−0.398***	−0.391***	−0.435***	–
	(−6.62)	(−4.50)	(−3.18)	–
Centre	−0.413***	−0.0169	−0.0163	–
	(−7.60)	(−0.13)	(−0.08)	–
South	−0.605***	−0.0301	0.267	–
	(−16.35)	(−0.24)	(1.59)	–
Uni_city	0.00955	0.132**	−0.0446	–
	(0.27)	(2.52)	(−0.59)	–
IMR	0.149***	0.0703	−0.109	–
	(3.82)	(1.30)	(−1.34)	–
_cons	0.914***	1.285***	0.628	–
	(4.11)	(4.43)	(1.05)	–
Auxiliary parameters				
cut1	1.217***	0.970***	1.997***	2.208**
	(5.30)	(3.29)	(3.73)	(2.39)
cut2	1.575***	1.339***	2.337***	2.803***
	(6.86)	(4.53)	(4.37)	(3.03)
cut3	1.891***	1.631***	2.663***	3.400***
	(8.23)	(5.51)	(4.98)	(3.68)
load	0.391***	0.655**	1.781***	–
	(3.14)	(2.21)	(3.75)	–
Rho	0.257 ***	0.387***	0.617***	0.127
	(0.071)	(0.122)	(0.039)	(0.114)
N	26,570	12,093	5,929	3,005

Notes: a. In the 'south' model, the r was not significant and thus the results of a simple ordered logit are reported.
t statistics in parentheses; * $p < 0.10$, ** $p < 0.05$, *** $p < 0.01$.

highly statistically significant and with coefficients of remarkable magnitude (bottom of Table 4.6), supporting our choice to rank the matching according to ordinal degrees of importance, from real over-education to real match.

This national-level result, however, tends to average out the effects of different geographical peculiarities. In the regression for the north, whilst migrants and stayers have, *ceteris paribus*, the same chance of being employed (that is, Migr is not significant in the selection equation), migrants are more likely overall to improve their education–job match. Furthermore, as in the case of Italy as a whole, migrants from the south (Migr_StoN) are more likely than all the other graduates (both stayers and other migrants) to achieve a good match as the coefficient is highly significant and of notable magnitude. Conversely, in the regression for the central regions the results at the national level are neither confirmed in the employment equation nor in the outcome equation: inter-regional mobility of graduates seems to have no impact on employability, or on the education–job match. Although the results for the south have to be interpreted with caution, as self-selection into employment appears not to be significant (non-significant ρ) and we only report the outcome equation, some positive effect of overall inflows of migrants from the rest of Italy in the Mezzogiorno is exerted on the probability of a better match.

In the outcome equation, graduates in medicine and science are more likely to experience a good education–job match, independent of geography. In contrast, graduates in humanities and social sciences always have negative coefficients, which turn out to be highly significant in the regressions for Italy and the north, indicating that graduates in such fields are less likely to achieve a good education–job match (graduates in sport constitute the base category).

Graduates who chose their degree out of interest and because of its job prospects tend to have a better match (the coefficients of Interest and Job_prospects are positive and significant in all equations but for that of the south). Graduates with a higher grade are found to be more likely to be matched in all four models.

Job-specific characteristics impact considerably on over-education. Those who are self-employed are always better matched than the rest, conceivably demonstrating the rewarding role of entrepreneurship in terms of skill application across geographical areas. The opposite is true for graduates who had previous job experience, who seem less likely to achieve a good education–job match independently from geography: this might hint at a worse capacity of integration in the labour markets than those who had to work before and/or during their university studies. The coefficient for salary is, as expected, positive, whereas seniority does not seem to impact on education–job match, and in fact it shows a negative and significant role in the north regression. Finally, gender has no effect on education–job match, whilst it plays a strong role in determining employability.

4.6 CONCLUSIONS

The aim of this chapter was to empirically test whether or not inter-regional migration has an impact on the education–job matches at the early stages of graduates' careers. Our findings confirm, for the national model, previous empirical literature on the positive role that inter-regional migration exerts on decreasing the probability of real over-education – that is, the combination of both over-qualification and under-utilisation of the graduate's skills and capabilities. However, remarkable differences emerge when looking at the sub-national dimension. In the north, where regional economic and innovation systems are the most dynamic, migration significantly increases the likelihood of achieving a good education–job match. Yet this is not the case for migrants to the centre, which, in spite of the weight of the capital region in terms of employment in the public sector, is an area associated with a lower level of over-education (Devillanova, 2013).

In the traditional role of 'vector of regional convergence' assigned to labour mobility by classical economics, the north emerges as a net winner as it not only gains from public investment in higher education made in other regions of the country, but it is also able to ensure a more productive use of such an investment than other areas. We conclude that the positive effect of spatial mobility on education–job match needs further investigation, particularly by assuming geographically specific research perspectives. A better understanding of the profiles needed at the territorial level has critical implications for public policies targeting the gap between the demand and the supply of competences and skills, especially in light of the rising competition from global markets which has made even more apparent the vulnerability of the Mezzogiorno's productive systems.

ACKNOWLEDGEMENTS

The authors gratefully acknowledge funding from the European Community's Seventh Framework Programme (FP7/2007–2013) under grant agreement no 266959.

This chapter is based on Iammarino and Marinelli (2015), copyright © Regional Studies Association, reprinted by permission of Taylor and Francis Limited, www.tandfonline.com on behalf of Regional Studies Association.

The empirical results of this chapter have previously been published in Iammarino and Marinelli (2014).

NOTES

*   The content of this chapter does not reflect the official opinion of the European Commission. Responsibility for the information and views expressed herein lies entirely with the author.
1.   For a discussion of the limitations of education–job match indicators, see Sloane (2003) and Sgobbi and Suleman (2013).
2.   In placing *apparent over-education* below *apparent match* in the ordered scale, we have assumed that the graduate's judgement on skills use is more relevant than the employer's assessment. This choice is supported in the results by strongly significant coefficients for the cut-off points. Nevertheless, in our robustness tests (not reported here) we have collapsed the two categories and the key results of the analysis remain stable.
3.   Current routines available in STATA do not allow for self-selection and endogeneity simultaneously in ordered models. It is thus necessary to use an approximation; hence we extend the approach of Arendt and Holm (2006) – who focus on a binary dependent – to our ordered dependent variable.
4.   The IMR is the ratio of the probability density function to the cumulative distribution function of a distribution.
5.   This definition of inter-regional mobility is clearly limited, as it does not distinguish those who moved to return to their home region – having studied somewhere else – from the rest. Unfortunately, the *Indagine* does not allow the performance of such a distinction; however, in one of our robustness checks we take this aspect into account, following the methodology devised in Marinelli (2013).
6.   Different specifications where explored: the final choice was based on indicators of goodness of fit, such as the Pseudo-$R2$ (0.3007) and the percentage of correctly predicted cases (83.7 per cent).
7.   The results of the migration equation are not reported here, as this stage is only instrumental to our main selection and outcome regressions. Results are available on request from the authors.

REFERENCES

Allen, J. and van der Velden, R. (2001), 'Educational mismatches versus skill mismatches: effects on wages, job satisfaction and on-the-job search', *Oxford Economic Papers*, 53(3), 434–452.

Arendt, J.N. and Holm, A. (2006), 'Probit models with binary endogenous regressors', CAM Working Paper, 2006-06.

Barca, F. (2006), *Italia Frenata, Paradossi e Lezioni della Politica per lo Sviluppo*, Rome: Donzelli.

Battu, H., Belfield, C.R. and Sloane, P. (1999), 'Overeducation among graduates: a cohort view', *Education Economics*, 7(1), 21–38.

Battu, H., Belfield, C.R. and Sloane, P. (2000), 'How well can we measure graduate overeducation and its effects?', *National Institute Economic Review*, 171, 82–93.

Biggeri, L., Bini, M. and Grilli, L. (2001), 'The transition from university to work: a multilevel approach to the analysis of the time to obtain the first job', *Journal of the Royal Statistical Society: Series A* (Statistics in Society), 164(2), 293–305.

Boudarbat, B. and Chernoff, V. (2010), 'The determinants of education–job match among Canadian university graduates', Scientific Series, Ciranos Working Paper 14-2010.

Büchel, F. and van Ham, M. (2003), 'Overeducation, regional labor markets and spatial flexibility', *Journal of Urban Economics*, 53(3), 482–493.

Checchi, D. and Peragine, V. (2005), 'Regional disparities and inequality of opportunity: the case of Italy', IZA Discussion Papers 1874, Bonn: Institute for the Study of Labor.

Chevalier, A. (2003), 'Measuring overeducation', *Economica*, 70, 509–531.

Coniglio, N. and Peragine, V. (2007), 'Giovani al Sud: tra Immobilità Sociale e Mobilità Territoriale', in Coniglio, N. and Peragine, V. (eds), *Primo Rapporto Banche e Mezzogiorno*, Bari: Banca Carime–University of Bari.

Consoli, D., Vona, F. and Saarivirta, T. (2013), 'Analysis of the graduate labour market in Finland: spatial agglomeration and skill–job match', *Regional Studies*, 47(10), 1634–1652, doi: 10.1080/00343404.2011.603721.

Crescenzi, R., Gagliardi, L. and Percoco, M. (2013), 'Social capital and the innovative performance of Italian provinces', *Environment and Planning A*, 45(4), 908–929.

Croce, G. and Ghignoni, E. (2011), 'Overeducation and spatial flexibility in Italian local labour markets', MPRA working paper no 29670, October.

D'Antonio, M. and Scarlato, M. (2007), 'I Laureati del Mezzogiorno: una Risorsa Sottoutilizzata o Dispersa', Quaderni SVIMEZ, Roma: SVIMEZ.

Dekker, R., de Grip, A. and Heijke, H. (2002), 'The effects of training and over-education on career mobility in a sequential labour market', *International Journal of Manpower*, 23(2), 106–136.

Devillanova, C. (2013), 'Over-education and spatial flexibility: new evidence from Italian survey data, *Papers in Regional Science*, 92(3), 445–464.

Dolton, P.J. and Silles, M.A. (2008), 'The effects of overeducation on earnings in the graduate labour market', *Economics of Education Review*, 27, 125–139.

Dolton, P. and Vignoles, A. (2000), 'The incidence and effects of overeducation in the UK graduate labour market', *Economics of Education Review*, 19, 179–198.

Dotti, N.F., Fratesi, U., Lenzi, C. and Percoco, M. (2014), 'Local labour market conditions and the spatial mobility of science and technology university students: evidence from Italy', *Review of Regional Research*, 34(2), 119–137.

Etzkowitz, H. and Leydesdorff, L. (1997), *Universities and the Global Knowledge Economy: A Triple Helix of University–Industry–Government Relations*, London: Pinter.

Faggian, A. and McCann, P. (2006), 'Human capital flows and regional knowledge assets: a simultaneous equation approach', *Oxford Economic Papers*, 58(3), 475–500.

Faggian, A. and McCann, P. (2009), 'Human capital, graduate migration and innovation in British regions', *Cambridge Journal of Economics*, 33(2), 317–333.

Freeman, R.B. (1976), *The Overeducated American*, New York: Academic Press.

Garcia-Espejo, I. and Ibanez, M. (2006), 'Education–skill matches and labour achievements among graduates in Spain', *European Sociological Review*, 22(2), 141–155.

Green, F. and McIntosh, S. (2007), 'Is there a genuine under-utilization of skills amongst the over-qualified?', *Applied Economics*, 39(4), 427–439.

Groot, W. and Maassen van den Brink, H. (2000), 'Overeducation in the labor market: a meta-analysis', *Economics of Education Review*, 19, 149–158.

Gulbrandsen, M., Mowery, D. and Feldman, M. (2011), 'Introduction to the special section: heterogeneity and university–industry relations', *Research Policy*, 40, 1–5.

Hartog, J. (2000), 'Mismatch and earnings: where are we, where should we go', *Economics of Education Review*, 19, 131–147.

Healy, A. and Morgan, K. (2009), 'Spaces of innovation: learning, proximity and the ecological turn', Utrecht University, Papers in Evolutionary Economic Geography (PEEG), No 0918.

Heckman, J. (1979), 'Sample selection bias as a specification error', *Econometrica*, 47, 153–161.

Heijke, H., Meng, C. and Ris, C. (2003), 'Fitting to the job: the role of generic and vocational competencies in adjustment and performance', *Labour Economics*, 10, 215–229.

Hensen, M.M., De Vries, M.R. and Cörvers, F. (2009), 'The role of geographic mobility in reducing education–job mismatches in the Netherlands', *Papers in Regional Science*, 88(3), 667–682.

Hoogstra, G., van Dijk, J. and Florax, R. (2011), 'Determinants of variation in population–employment interaction findings: a quasi-experimental meta-analysis', *Geographical Analysis*, 43(1), 4–37.

Iammarino, S. (2005), 'An evolutionary integrated view of regional systems of innovation: concepts, measures and historical perspectives', *European Planning Studies*, 13(4), 495–517.

Iammarino, S. and Marinelli, E. (2011), 'Is the grass greener on the other side of the fence? Graduate mobility and job satisfaction in Italy', *Environment and Planning A*, 43, 2761–2777.

Iammarino, S. and Marinelli, E. (2014), 'Education–job (mis)match and inter-regional migration: Italian university graduates' transition to work', *Regional Studies*, doi: 10.1080/00343404.2014.965135.

Iammarino, S. and Marinelli, E. (2015), 'Education–job (mis) match and inter-regional migration: Italian university graduates' transition to work', *Regional Studies*, 49(5), 866–882.

ISTAT (2010), *Indagine Campionaria sull'Inserimento Professionale dei Laureati*, Rome: ISTAT.

Jauhiainen, S. (2011), 'Overeducation in the Finnish regional labour markets', *Papers in Regional Science*, 90(3), 578–588.

Klaauw, B. van der and A. van Vuuren (2010), 'Job search and academic achievement', *European Economic Review*, 54, 294–316.

Kraber, S. and Flöther, C. (2012), 'Here today, gone tomorrow? Regional labour mobility of German university graduates', *Regional Studies*, doi: 10.1080/00343404.2012.739282.

Liberto, A. di (2008), 'Education and Italian regional development', *Economics of Education Review*, 27, 94–107.

Marinelli, E. (2011), 'Graduates on the move: knowledge flows and Italian regional disparities – migration patterns of 2001 graduates', PhD thesis, London School of Economics and Political Sciences.

Marinelli, E. (2013), 'Sub-national graduate mobility and knowledge flows: an exploratory analysis of onward and return migrants in Italy', *Regional Studies*, 47(10), 1618–1633.

McGuinness, S. (2003), 'Graduate overeducation as a sheepskin effect: evidence from Northern Ireland', *Applied Economics*, 35, 597–608.

McGuinness, S. (2006), 'Overeducation in the labour market', *Journal of Economic Surveys*, 20(3), 387–418.

McGuinness, S. and Wooden, M. (2009), 'Overskilling, job insecurity and career mobility', *Industrial Relations: A Journal of Economy and Society*, 48(2), 265–286.

Miranda, A. and Rabe-Hesketh, S. (2006), 'Maximum likelihood estimation of endogenous switching and sample selection models for binary, ordinal, and count variables', *Stata Journal*, 6(3), 285–308.

Morgan, K. (1997), 'The learning regions: institutions, innovation and regional renewal', *Regional Studies*, 31(5), 491–503.

Mowery, D.C. and Sampat, B.N. (2005), 'The Bayh–Dole Act of 1980 and university–industry technology transfer: a model for other OECD governments?', *Journal of Technology Transfer*, 30, 115–127.

Nelson, R.R. and Phelps, E.S. (1966), 'Investments in humans, technology diffusion and economic growth', *The American Economic Review*, 56(1/2), 69–75.

Pietro, G. di and Urwin, P. (2006), 'Education and skills mismatch in the Italian graduate labour market', *Applied Economics*, 38(1), 79–93.

Piras, R. (2005), 'Il Contenuto di Capitale Umano dei Flussi Migratori Interregionali: 1980–2002', *Politica Economica*, 21, 461–491.

Piras, R. (2006), 'I Movimenti Migratori Interregional per Titolo di Studio: una Stima dei Tassi Migratori ed un'Analisi dei Flussi', *Studi di Emigrazione*, 43, 153–170.

Ramos, R. and Sanromà, E. (2011), 'Overeducation and local labour markets in Spain', IZA DP No 6028, October.

Robst, J. (2007), 'Education and job match: the relatedness of college major and work', *Economics of Education Review*, 26, 397–407.

Rosenberg, N. and Nelson, R. (1994), 'American universities and technical advance in industry', *Research Policy*, 23, 323–348.

Salter, A.J. and Martin, B.R. (2001), 'The economic benefits of publicly funded basic research: a critical review', *Research Policy*, 30, 509–532.
Sgobbi, F. and Suleman, F. (2013), 'A methodological contribution to measuring skills (mis)match', *The Manchester School*, 81(3), 420–437.
Sicherman, N. (1991), 'Overeducation in the labor market', *Journal of Labor Economics*, 9(2), 101–122.
Sloane, P.J. (2003), 'Much ado about nothing? What does the over-education literature really tell us?', in Büchel, F., deGrip, A. and Mertens, A. (eds), *Overeducation in Europe: Current Issues in Theory and Policy*, Cheltenham, UK and Northampton, MA: Edward Elgar, pp. 11–48.
Svimez (2009), 'Rapporto sull'economia del Mezzogiorno 2008', Bologna: Il Mulino.
Tunzelmann, N. von (2009), 'Regional capabilities and industrial regeneration', in Farshchi, M., Janne, O. and McCann, P. (eds), *Technological Change and Mature Industrial Regions: Firms, Knowledge and Policy*, Cheltenham, UK and Northampton, MA: Edward Elgar, pp. 11–28.
Ungaro, P. and Verzicco, L. (2005), 'Misura e Analisi del Rendimento dei Titoli di Studio Superiori nella Fase di Primo Inserimento nel Mondo del Lavoro', Paper presented at the XX Convegno Nazionale di Economia del Lavoro, Rome, 22–23 September.
Vaccaro, R. (1995), *Unità Politica e Dualismo Economico in Italia: 1861–1993*, Padova: Cedam.
Vandenbussche, J., Aghion, P. and Meghir, C. (2006), 'Growth, distance to frontier and composition of human capital', *Journal of Economic Growth*, 11(2), 97–127.
Venhorst, V.A. and Cörvers, F. (2011), 'Entry into working life: spatial mobility and job match quality of higher educated graduates', Mimeo, Faculty of Spatial Science, University of Groningen.
Verhaest, D. and Omey, E. (2006), 'The impact of overeducation and its measurement', *Social Indicators Research*, 77(3), 419–448.
Viesti, G. (2003), *Abolire il Mezzogiorno*, Bari: Laterza.
Wald, S. and Fang, T. (2008), 'Overeducated immigrants in the Canadian labour market: evidence from the workplace and employee survey', *Canadian Public Policy*, 34(4), 457–479.
Wolbers, M.H.J. (2003), 'Job mismatches and their labour-market effects among school-leavers in Europe', *European Sociological Review*, 19(3), 249–266.

FURTHER READING

Boudarbat, B. and Montmarquette, C. (2009), 'Choice of fields of study of university Canadian graduates: the role of gender and their parents' education', *Education Economics*, 17(2), 185–213.
Green, F. and Zhu, Y. (2010), 'Overqualification, job dissatisfaction, and increasing dispersion in the returns to graduate education', *Oxford Economic Papers*, 62, 740–763.
Rodriguez-Pose, A. and Tselios, V. (2010), 'Returns to migration, education and externalties in the European Union', *Papers in Regional Science*, 89(2), 411–434.

Rosen, S. (1972), 'Learning and experience in the labour market', *Journal of Human Resources*, 7(3), 326–342.

Tunzelmann, N. von and Wang, Q. (2007), 'Capabilities and production theory', *Structural Change and Economic Dynamics*, 18, 192–211.

5. Constrained choice? Graduate early career job-to-job mobility in core and non-core regions in the Netherlands

Viktor A. Venhorst*

5.1 INTRODUCTION

Recent higher-education graduates have been central to recent advances in the literature as a result of their relatively high levels of spatial mobility and expected impacts on regional economies. For graduation cohort after graduation cohort, the years surrounding the time of completion of a final higher-education degree entail a substantial likelihood of spatial mobility. Studies for Australia, the United States and various European countries have demonstrated this, reporting that destinations rich in labour-market opportunities are favoured by graduates (Biagi et al., 2011; Venhorst et al., 2011). Despite this pattern, mobility rates differ by departure region, specialization, gender and quality of graduate (Abreu et al., 2012; Busch and Weigert, 2010; Corcoran et al., 2010; Faggian et al., 2007; 2013a; 2013b; Franklin, 2003; Haapanen and Tervo, 2012; Winters, 2011). Attraction and retention of recent graduates is not only driven by current regional circumstances, but also helps shape these regional circumstances (Venhorst, 2016; Winters, 2011). Moreover, between graduates, there are substantial differences in the economic returns to spatial mobility (Abreu et al., 2014; Venhorst and Cörvers, 2015).

In the context of the Netherlands, however, Venhorst et al. (2013) demonstrate that the migration window closes relatively quickly – within a few years after graduation – as a result of changes in other life-course domains, such as the formation of households. The presence of a partner and children may be of fundamental influence on the flexibility of a recent graduate to switch jobs, and the pathways selected whilst doing so. These factors may also serve to reduce the extent of spatial job mobility for graduates who are somewhat further into their careers. This in turn may put more emphasis on the structure of the local or regional economy and the degree of relatedness of its industries, as graduates seek for better matches or career development on the regional labour market. If the labour market is sparse, this could lead to a need to employ more far-reaching job-switch strategies, potentially involving combinations of residential, job and sectoral mobility. Moreover, recent cohorts of university students and graduates, like the middle class more generally, seem to exhibit a renewed interest in city life (Boterman et al., 2010; Venhorst et al., 2013). Cities provide job opportunities for both partners, which lessens the necessity of further spatial mobility at the household level. Likewise, access to other cities with ample density, size or a favourable skill structure might, in the Dutch polycentric context, provide similar opportunities.

In this chapter, we investigate the effect of the graduate's household situation, in relation to the residential location, on the way job-to-job mobility is shaped in the medium to longer term after leaving a higher-education institution (HEI). It commences in Sections 5.2 through 5.5 with a discussion of the recent literature on residential and job mobility, and highlights the constraints, opportunities, and personal and regional circumstances associated with residential mobility. This literature has focused predominantly on the spatial mobility of recent graduates and mainly studies the migration of graduates within three years of receiving their degree. In this chapter, we investigate job-switch strategies of graduates in core and non-core regional labour markets, using a longitudinal registry dataset which allows us to track graduates up to eighteen years after leaving their HEI. From this source, labour-market dynamics over this period are mapped, with patterns illustrating that all dynamics decrease substantially within a few years after HEI departure and that residential mobility is relatively unlikely to occur in combination with other labour-market dynamics. We proceed to model strategies – that is, sector, workplace or residential mobility, or a combination thereof – for a sample of graduate job-switchers, in Sections 5.6 and 5.7. We then conclude and provide policy recommendations in Section 5.8.

5.2 JOB-TO-JOB MOBILITY AND THE OPPORTUNITY SPACE

We borrow the conceptualization from Hidalgo et al. (2007): to structure our thinking on how improved matching follows pathways determined by skill level, experience and motivation. Hidalgo et al. (ibid.) explain that economies grow by upgrading the products they produce and export. Upgrades from one product variety to the next follow pathways determined by technology, capital, institutions, and also the skills required to make that step. Hidalgo et al. (ibid.) define the 'product space' as a network of related product varieties. They find that key economies, producing sophisticated products, are active in the densely connected core of this product network. This provided such economies with ample opportunities to diversify. Countries producing less-sophisticated products occupy the less-connected periphery. The key thought is that countries have to traverse towards the well-connected centre in order to develop, but do so by using infrequently travelled connections: making it through as a developing economy is unlikely. Countries that occupy the product-space core continue to do so. Low-productive countries remain active in the peripheral areas of the product space. The authors conclude that success is unlikely because *ex ante* identification of a successful route towards the well-connected core, via potential target products, is difficult.

Returning to labour-market mobility of individual workers moving towards better matches, we note that these pathways may also be shaped by constraints or flexibility presented by the private household domain and regional factors. Successful transitions out of continued inactivity or bad labour-market matches happen infrequently, and become less likely with duration in such circumstances. Less-successful workers can be thought of as operating in jobs located at the ill-connected periphery of the regional labour-market opportunity space, or in jobs that are regarded as a bad match in terms of other aspects, such as low income or long commuting distances. Likewise, these workers might not be in the network to begin with. It may be difficult to reach the well-connected jobs in the opportunity-space core, given regional and individual characteristics, as they might present constraints to either the sectoral, workplace or residential mobility that would have been necessary.

In this study we operationalize job-to-job mobility as a combination of sectoral mobility and work-location spatial mobility. The benefit of finding work nearby might be offset by the fact that job offers are in an industry which is poorly matched to the individual worker skill-set, or vice versa. Yet an additional consideration might come into play: residential mobility might be necessary to open up a wider array of job offers. In our approach, we assume that, when a worker considers a job switch, the worker decides simultaneously on these issues. Outcomes may differ between workers of different skill levels and in different phases of the life course. In what follows, we develop an understanding of the simultaneity in residential, workplace and sectoral mobility in job-to-job adjustments and the role of worker heterogeneity therein.

5.3   RESIDENTIAL AND WORKPLACE MOBILITY

In neoclassical economics, migration occurs in response to wage differences between regional labour markets. This disequilibrium model of migration, which essentially assumes that wage differences perfectly coincide with utility differences between locations, does not appear dominant in many contexts (Graves, 2014). Graves (ibid.) also notes that there is little convergence in wage rates and further suggests that an alternative view, concerning the broader concept of utility equilibrium across space, might be more useful in explaining labour-market equilibrium. In this view, wages and local rents can be understood as compensation for (un)favourable and untradeable characteristics of the region. This interchange between the labour market and other amenity characteristics of regions is central to a better understanding of the functioning of regional labour markets (Moretti, 2012).

Perhaps unsurprisingly in this light, the importance of migration as an adjustment mechanism has been found to be changing over time. Recent research by Partridge (2010) shows that since 2000 population development in the United States (US) has been more driven by amenities than by economic factors. Storper and Scott (2009) argue, however, that changes in US migration patterns have more to do with changes in economic structure, and the economic geography of sectors that are booming versus sectors that are in decline, rather than with micro-level changes in household residential preferences as suggested by Partridge (2010).

Next to spatial wage and utility differentials, the interplay between regional and individual characteristics may lead to self-reinforcing migration flows towards opportunity-rich regions. The endogenous growth model of Lucas (1988) and Romer (1986) suggests that regions that are rich in human capital may become increasingly attractive to other individuals with high human capital as a result of knowledge spill-overs. Globalization and shocks to the world economy have only served to increase the need to locate close to or within core regions: the transfer of tacit knowledge is a key driver in growth (McCann 2008; 2013). These core-region benefits do not only entail workplace-knowledge spill-overs but also consumption effects of a higher variety of tastes as groups flow into the city (Autor and Dorn, 2013, Venhorst, 2016).

In contrast, recent literature suggests that endogenous-worker-sorting in large agglomerations as described above constitutes only part of the story. Broersma and Van Dijk (2008) point to slower multi-factor productivity growth in the Netherlands in the economic core regions. Positive agglomeration advantages are over-ruled by negative congestion effects. The contribution of non-core regions to economic growth is increasing (Dijkstra et al., 2013). Bacolod et al. (2009) describe the allocation of skills across the urban hierarchy and note that large cores are more skilled than smaller cities, but not by a great margin.

This brings us to two additional, but related, issues. First, work and residential locations are often confounded in empirical studies. What makes a location opportunity-rich, in terms of labour-market outcomes, does not necessarily imply that residential qualities are high as well. Then, second, in countries such as the Netherlands, which can be characterized as predominantly polycentric (Burger et al., 2013) and have short inter-city commuting distances, work and residential considerations can indeed lead to differences in location outcomes whereby a degree of commuting is accepted in order to maximize individual and/or household utility. In such a spatial setting, distinguishing between workplace and residential location choices then becomes vitally important in understanding locational outcomes of a heterogeneous population of workers. In this study, we attempt to take this peculiarity into account by including both work- and residential-mobility, whilst controlling for characteristics of cities with which commuting-flow relationships exist, next to characteristics of one's own residential city.

5.4   THE LIFE COURSE, THE HOUSEHOLD AND LOCATION DECISIONS

Destination choice and migration propensities differ between age groups, with an aging population resulting in shifting migration balances for some regions, and a change in the responsiveness of the population to economic disparities. Gottlieb and Joseph (2006) and Whisler et al. (2008) demonstrate this underlying shift in preferences for a group of relatively homogeneous residents who are younger and more highly educated. Moreover, regions differ substantially in the degree to which they are able to attract and retain high-potential internal and international migrants. Agglomerations may have specific functions for migrants in different phases of their life course. Fielding (1992) uses the escalator region metaphor to describe how core cities serve to help individuals achieve career goals, after which they move onwards or retire to a non-core region. Champion (2012) shows that youngsters step off this escalator. Plane et al. (2005) notes that migration down the urban hierarchy is becoming more prevalent, as a result of changing composition of the population in favour of groups less oriented towards the urban core. This might explain part of the Partridge (2010) amenity migration argument.

Migration history has also been found to play a role in future spatial mobility: not only does past mobility lead to future mobility (DaVanzo, 1983), but such flows are often directed at locations which are familiar to the migrant. Venhorst (2013) demonstrates this for a sample of graduates from Dutch higher education.

Household composition, or the household career in a life-course context, is another important determinant of migration behaviour, with implications for sorting across regions. Hanson and Pratt (1988) call for a reconceptualization of the links between home and work. They argue for the need to develop frameworks which take into account the effect of home on work (that is, household characteristics that may stimulate or inhibit the opportunities in the local or wider labour market), the effect of work on home (characteristics of jobs and careers that affect residential choice, affecting opportunities for other household members) and the inter-relations between these two factors. In their 1992 paper, Hanson and Pratt apply such a framework in a qualitative study, finding that employers not only recruit locally with a keen eye to the local geography of attractive and not-so-attractive labour pools, but this, as a result, helps shape that local labour-market geography – a geography which is often gendered, as men and women differ in their extent and mode of spatial flexibility.

The extent of this process depends on household spatial mobility. A variety of studies have looked into the household location problem. Costa and Kahn (2000) note how 'power couples' (defined as two partners with higher education) tend to locate in central places, with ample opportunities for both partners. However, moving towards such a place might already be a difficulty. Brandén (2013) investigates the effect of both men's and women's education on couples' migration propensities. She finds that both have an effect, but that men's education has a more predominant effect on migration propensities than women's education. However, income and occupational characteristics are a key factor in this relationship, as are the different types of occupations held by men and women. Occupational characteristics have similar effects for men and for women. Eliasson et al. (2014) suggest that family migration is selective of relatively low-earning wives with unmeasured potential for high earnings. It is not only the level of education, but also the field of study that has been shown to affect migration propensities (Venhorst et al., 2010) and opportunities on the labour market (Abreu et al., 2012). Over time, the field of study may become less important to individual career development. To date, however, this longitudinal dimension of the specialization–spatial-mobility relationship has not been investigated.

If migration is prohibitive, a change in job location by one or both partners might be a feasible adjustment mechanism. Van Ommeren et al. (1998) show theoretically that, in the case of two-earner households, job mobility depends positively on the distance between the two workplaces. Residential mobility depends negatively on that distance. However, Van Ommeren et al. (1999) find no empirical evidence for the effect of workplace distances on job mobility. Clark and Davies Withers (1999) study the residential effects of a job change in a longitudinal framework. They show that job changes can act as a trigger for residential changes, but that this effect differs by tenure (that is, renters are affected, not home-owners) and family composition. Moreover, the timing of events is not strict, as foresight might lead to moves preceding job changes.

Overall, it can be said that migration is not a random event – rather, it is selective and persistent. But likewise, neither is workplace mobility, which has received less attention in the international literature. In the next section, we investigate these issues for our third job-switch avenue: sector mobility.

5.5   SECTOR MOBILITY AND RELATEDNESS

Neoclassical economics suggests that, in the wake of a negative shock leading to involuntary unemployment, the real wage rate will adjust downward to ensure clearing of the local labour market through higher demand and lower supply. However, depending on the characteristics of the shock as well as the peculiarities of the regional industrial structure and institutional factors, a wide variety of different outcomes is possible (McCann, 2013). If local employers translate the shock into negative expectations regarding local demand for final goods, labour demand may not expand even in the face of downward pressure on wages. This depends on the relative exposure of local firms to local demand conditions. Evidence has also been found for spill-over effects between sectors via the consumption patterns of skilled workers (Moretti, 2012).

In this context, job-to-job mobility may involve (forced) sector changes. Switching to another sector is facilitated if the destination sector is related, for example through similarities in skills required for occupations in the sector. Neffke and Henning (2013) identify skill-relatedness of industries using data from Sweden. Skill-relatedness was measured through inter-sectoral labour flows which are observed to be larger than expected based on relative sector size and wage differentials. Neffke and Henning (ibid.) develop their methodology with the specific purpose of predicting firm diversification patterns, choosing recession-neutral time periods and labour flows measured for workers aggregated across all phases of the life course or their career. It is not known, however, to what extent life-course patterns in mobility between sectors affect the outcomes: some pathways may not be opportunistic when workers are in certain phases of their life course or, likewise, their work careers. Like migration, sectoral mobility may show forms of persistence as well.

From this overview, it transpires that job-to-job mobility may be shaped differently by graduates who are exposed to different situations. The relevant factors appear to be one's experience in mobility, human capital characteristics and the household dimension. We expect that, relative to singles, graduates in households with (economically active) partners might be less inclined to apply job-to-job mobility strategies involving residential relocations. Furthermore, regional circumstances, such as good access to labour-market opportunities may serve to reduce the need for spatial mobility.

5.6   DATA AND METHOD

The analysis in this study is based on micro data from the Statistics Netherlands registries. Starting from the Dutch CRIHO[1] higher-education registry, where everyone who is enrolled at a Dutch HEI is entered, we derive duration of enrolment, discipline, age at graduation and final degree obtained. Around 70 per cent of those that were enrolled for at least two years also graduate from their programme. We also include students who failed to complete their final degree programme, but among this group about one-third did complete an earlier HEI programme. The registry provides us with information on the seventeen consecutive graduation cohorts between 1990 and 2006. These cohorts are then tracked using tax-office registries which provide us with net annual income, self-employment, social security benefits, sector of employment and firm-level information, and municipality registries which provide gender, nationality, location of residence, household composition and the identity of the partner, if present. For their partner, we record the main source of income and their education level.

We aim to disentangle a variety of dynamic effects: the effect of labour-market experience, period-specific economic shocks, cross-cohort changes in preferences and opportunities, and individual-level household dynamics need to be taken into account. Micro data from Statistics Netherlands are provided in a strict calendar-year-based format. These data were recoded from a calendar-year to a cohort format. Second, the researcher needs to decide on the time precision. Continuous time analyses typically allow the precise analysis of ordering of events. However, the theoretical basis for these types of analyses is often a difficulty. If agents are assumed to be forward-looking, priorities are not easily derived from exact ordering as events may be pre- or postponed in the light of expected future opportunities. Discrete time analysis offers sufficient precision in most applications and thus we employ this method as well, and compute transition events by comparing states from one year to the next.

The available tax office and municipality data span the calendar years 2000 to 2008. These provide an observation window of a maximum of nine years in which the mobility of individuals can be tracked. Restructuring the data from the calendar-year format to a graduation-cohort format allows us to distinguish between age, period and time to graduation patterns in the outcomes we observe. A graduate finishing her programme in 2004 is classified as being in graduation cohort 2004. We observe labour-market statuses, place of residence and other information from 2000 to 2008, or put differently, from the four years leading up to her HEI departure ($T = -4$) until four years after ($T = 4$) with 2004 labelled as $T = 0$ for this particular graduate. Graduates from older cohorts (graduating in the 1990s) are typically observed later in their labour-market career (up to $T = 18$, or eighteen years after HEI departure), whereas younger cohorts are mostly observed during their student phase ($T < 0$). Note that we reserve capital T for this variable and lower-case t for time notation of our time-varying variables. This is referred to as our time-to-graduation variable, and it measures the time spent in the labour market. In our models we enter time-to-graduation fixed effects, which serve the purpose of catching any unmodelled variation at these moments in time.

For this study we have taken a 10 per cent simple random sample of the original population of 1.1 million (former) students. For this sample, a person–period file was constructed where every record is a time-specific observation on a person, with persons appearing up to nine times – the maximum time span resulting from the tax-office and municipality registries. We used our data on the full population of graduates to construct Figures 5.1 through 5.3, which we will use to introduce the main patterns for this population of recent graduates. Then, from our 10 per cent sample, we have selected observations for graduates in employment at time t, but who were about to experience a job change between that time and $t + 1$. This results in our final analysis file with around 164,000 observations (job changes) experienced by about 75,000 unique individuals. Sample statistics are reported in Table 5.1 and are discussed below.

Figure 5.1 depicts the share of students and graduates in dependent employment. The x-axis contains the time relative to HEI departure, with $T = 0$ denoting the moment of HEI departure, often as a graduate. As can be seen, our data cover the period from seven years prior to eighteen years after HEI departure. From the figure it is clear that many students enter the labour market well before the time of graduation. These are usually

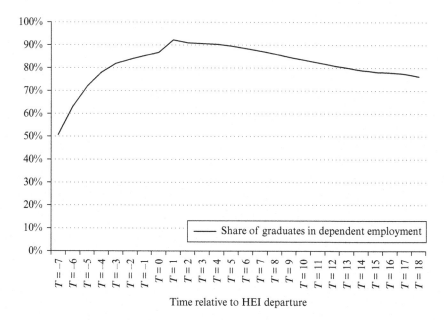

Time relative to HEI departure

Notes: Pooled cohort dataset, full sample. $N = 11.0$ million.

Source: Statistics Netherlands SSB, own computations.

Figure 5.1   *Share of higher-education graduates in dependent employment,
relative to time of graduation (*T = 0*).*

lower-paid and lower-qualified jobs (Venhorst et al., 2013). The percentage
of graduates in dependent employment peaks at around 90 per cent during
the year after graduation, only to decline steadily afterwards. This is due
mainly to the transition into self-employment, which is not studied further
in this chapter.

Labour-market entry and exit are therefore the driving forces behind the
overall pattern reported in Figure 5.1. However, most graduates already
active on the labour market experience substantial job-to-job mobility as
they find their way towards jobs better matched to their education profile.
Strategies of job changers may involve (i) a change of sector, (ii) a change
in workplace location, and (iii) a residential move. Mindful of our earlier
discussion, we have taken a sector change to imply a switch at the 2-digit
NACE[2] level in order to catch a change to a substantially different industry. The alternative is therefore a new job either in the same sector, or in
a different sector in the wider 2-digit NACE group. Such a switch then
reflects a change to a new and unrelated industry, which can be regarded

Table 5.1 Sample statistics

	Mean	Std. dev.	Min.	Max.
Endogenous regressors				
Change 2D sector *t* +1	0.568	–	0.000	1.000
Change work loc *t* +1	0.582	–	0.000	1.000
Change resid loc *t* +1	0.054	–	0.000	1.000
Sectoral and spatial mobility t *(ref = no mobility)*				
Change 2D sector *t*	0.283	–	0.000	1.000
Change work loc *t*	0.295	–	0.000	1.000
Change resid neighb within city *t*	0.152	–	0.000	1.000
Change resid city within labmreg *t*	0.084	–	0.000	1.000
Change resid labmreg within NUTS 2 *t*	0.051	–	0.000	1.000
Change resid NUTS 2 within NUTS 1 *t*	0.031	–	0.000	1.000
Change resid NUTS 1 within country *t*	0.012	–	0.000	1.000
Density				
Work city is very urban	0.378	–	0.000	1.000
Resid city is very urban	0.314	–	0.000	1.000
Characteristics of city of residence				
Resid in core labmreg	0.648	–	0.000	1.000
Tot pop size	1.823	2.208	0.009	7.431
Tot pop size, neighb cities	0.483	0.407	0.067	3.163
Workers share high-level job	0.226	0.100	0.014	0.668
Workers share high-level job sur area	0.203	0.030	0.020	0.358
Workers share scientific-level job	0.096	0.086	0.000	0.515
Workers share scient-level job sur area	0.066	0.016	0.002	0.171
Population share higher-educated	0.280	0.093	0.008	0.567
Population share higher-educated sur area	0.239	0.029	0.056	0.372
Other characteristics of city of residence				
Average firm size	1.107	0.349	0.272	2.339
Unemployment rate	0.054	0.021	0.014	0.156
Average housing value	1.005	0.240	0.500	2.763
Number of grads from local HEI	1.758	2.375	0.000	8.567
Number of grads from HEIs in surrounding cities	0.730	0.270	0.000	2.638
Sector specific employment growth over 1997–08	1.757	0.458	0.145	2.809
Household position and partner characteristics (ref = single)				
Partner primarily employed	0.403	–	0.000	1.000
Partner primarily self-employed	0.021	–	0.000	1.000
Partner primarily on benefits	0.042	–	0.000	1.000
Partner primarily student	0.025	–	0.000	1.000
Single	0.250	–	0.000	1.000
Lives with parents	0.189	–	0.000	1.000
Is a single parent	0.009	–	0.000	1.000

Table 5.1   (continued)

	Mean	Std. dev.	Min.	Max.
Couple without kids	0.311	–	0.000	1.000
Couple with kids	0.221	–	0.000	1.000
Partner education level low	0.093	–	0.000	1.000
Partner education level high	0.223	–	0.000	1.000

Other control variables (excl. 2-digit sector, work region, residential region dummies)

Study characteristics (ref = graduate, college, behavioural sciences)

	Mean	Std. dev.	Min.	Max.
University	0.318	–	0.000	1.000
Behavioural social sciences	0.173	–	0.000	1.000
Teaching	0.116	–	0.000	1.000
Agriculture	0.029	–	0.000	1.000
Natural sciences	0.021	–	0.000	1.000
Engineering	0.181	–	0.000	1.000
Healthcare	0.078	–	0.000	1.000
Economics	0.297	–	0.000	1.000
Law	0.045	–	0.000	1.000
Humanities	0.060	–	0.000	1.000
Graduated	0.713	–	0.000	1.000
Dropout with earlier HE degree	0.090	–	0.000	1.000
Dropout without earlier HE degree	0.197	–	0.000	1.000
Time spent in HE	4.810	2.187	1.000	28.000

Dem. charact. and household position (ref = single)

	Mean	Std. dev.	Min.	Max.
Female	0.496	–	0.000	1.000
Foreign	0.139	–	0.000	1.000
Age at graduation	23.545	3.356	16.000	65.000

Characteristics of current job

	Mean	Std. dev.	Min.	Max.
ln(Net total annual wage)	9.628	0.841	2.814	13.762
Commutes between labmregs	0.575	–	0.000	1.000

Main source of income (ref = current job)

	Mean	Std. dev.	Min.	Max.
Primarily employed	0.795	–	0.000	1.000
Primarily self-employed	0.003	–	0.000	1.000
Primarily on benefits	0.010	–	0.000	1.000
Primarily student	0.192	–	0.000	1.000

Time to graduation dummies (ref = T = −5)

	Mean	Std. dev.	Min.	Max.
$T = -5$	0.012	–	0.000	1.000
$T = -4$	0.019	–	0.000	1.000
$T = -3$	0.027	–	0.000	1.000

Table 5.1   (continued)

	Mean	Std. dev.	Min.	Max.
$T = -2$	0.040	–	0.000	1.000
$T = -1$	0.056	–	0.000	1.000
$T = 0$	0.086	–	0.000	1.000
$T = 1$	0.076	–	0.000	1.000
$T = 2$	0.074	–	0.000	1.000
$T = 3$	0.069	–	0.000	1.000
$T = 4$	0.067	–	0.000	1.000
$T = 5$	0.064	–	0.000	1.000
$T = 6$	0.062	–	0.000	1.000
$T = 7$	0.058	–	0.000	1.000
$T = 8$	0.055	–	0.000	1.000
$T = 9$	0.052	–	0.000	1.000
$T = 10$	0.048	–	0.000	1.000
$T = 11$	0.039	–	0.000	1.000
$T = 12$	0.032	–	0.000	1.000
$T = 13$	0.024	–	0.000	1.000
$T = 14$	0.019	–	0.000	1.000
$T = 15$	0.013	–	0.000	1.000
$T = 16$	0.007	–	0.000	1.000
Year of observation dummies (ref = 2000)				
2000	0.123	–	0.000	1.000
2001	0.121	–	0.000	1.000
2002	0.119	–	0.000	1.000
2003	0.107	–	0.000	1.000
2004	0.100	–	0.000	1.000
2005	0.175	–	0.000	1.000
2006	0.135	–	0.000	1.000
2007	0.120	–	0.000	1.000

Notes: Pooled cohort dataset, person–period file, job changers. $N = 164{,}354$.

Source: Statistics Netherlands, own computations.

as more costly and difficult to achieve. A change of work and residential locations is defined as a switch to a different labour-market region. In the Netherlands, this implies a switch between two of a total of 40 NUTS[3] 3 regions. Typically, residential mobility for non-labour-market considerations is confined within labour-market regions. This approach implies a significant data reduction as more elaborate and specific trajectories may be mapped out with the data available to us. However, these cut-offs are positioned to signal substantial changes. In Figure 5.2 we report the incidence of these strategies, focusing on combinations of events that

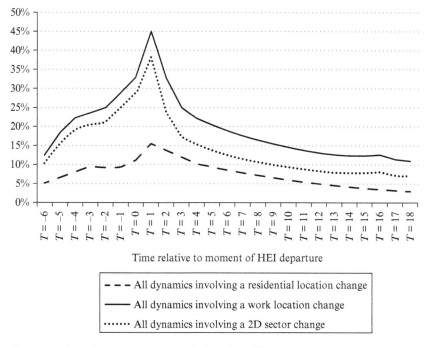

Time relative to moment of HEI departure

    - - - All dynamics involving a residential location change
    ——— All dynamics involving a work location change
    ······· All dynamics involving a 2D sector change

Notes: Pooled cohort dataset, full sample. $N = 9.2$ million.

Source: Statistics Netherlands SSB, own computations.

Figure 5.2   *Year-to-year labour-market dynamics among recent higher-education graduates, aggregate summary of main events of interest, relative to time of HEI departure* $(T = 0)$

include one or more of our three main strategies. As can be seen, the total of dynamics involving a residential change between labour-market areas peaks at around three years prior to HEI departure, with 10 per cent of all students experiencing migration at that time, as prospective graduates gradually make their way into their HEI cities to commence their studies. Residential mobility peaks at one year after HEI departure, when 15 per cent experience a move. Migration propensities decline steadily thereafter, until about 3 per cent per year, which is the rate for those who are eighteen years into their career. Workplace mobility occurs much more frequently, peaking at 45 per cent in the year following HEI departure, only to decline afterwards as well. Mobility between 2-digit sectors peaks at 38 per cent and rates decline rather more steeply than workplace mobility in the years following HEI departure.

In Figure 5.3 we provide a full overview of graduate labour market and migration dynamics over the period surround HEI departure, again based on our pooled cohort dataset. The Figure is based on the full population and was constructed by comparing labour market status, work- and residential locations from one year to the next for all individuals in our dataset. The categories depicted in the graph denote (combinations of) events which occurred in that given year. In this descriptive analysis we distinguish changes in sector of employment, workplace and residential mobility and labour-market entry and exit. Around the time of graduation ($T = 0$), dynamics are high, with many graduates experiencing a combination of events. The most important combination of events is a change of job to a different 2-digit sector, with the new job located in a different labour-market region. However, as time progresses, the 'event', or rather a lack thereof, *active in same job and with no other change* becomes the most frequent outcome indicating that stability becomes the norm for most within a couple of years of the moment of HEI departure. Other forms of dynamics keep occurring, though, in varying combinations. An increasing proportion of spells is observed for graduates who are *not in employment* from one year to the next. As was noted in our discussion of Figure 5.1, these are predominantly graduates who are self-employed and remain in self-employment (Koster and Venhorst, 2014).

In this study, we model strategies applied by job changers. Thus we do not study dependent employment, graduates entering and exiting the labour market, and those continuing in the same job. In Table 5.1, we present summary statistics for these job changers.[4] On average, for the entire period under study, around 57 per cent of job switchers observed included a 2-digit sector switch, 58 per cent involved a change of workplace, and a little over 5% identified a change of residential location. In this light, the incidence of residential changes is rather low. From Figure 5.3, it becomes clear that residential mobility is a relatively frequent occurrence, but not necessarily contemporaneous to labour-market dynamics.

These different strategies are inter-related and may or may not be applied together, and should be modelled as such. Pre-imposing a hierarchy in decision-making is difficult in this case. To do so would involve the estimation of a multinomial logit or probit model, involving outcomes which are effectively nested. In our case, this would lead to eight possible outcomes with the explanatory variables for seven outcomes needing to be interpreted against a reference outcome, on top of the relativity of the interpretation of within-outcome factors. This leaves interpretation intractable for most practical purposes, even after substantial data reduction. Instead, we therefore propose to model these strategies using

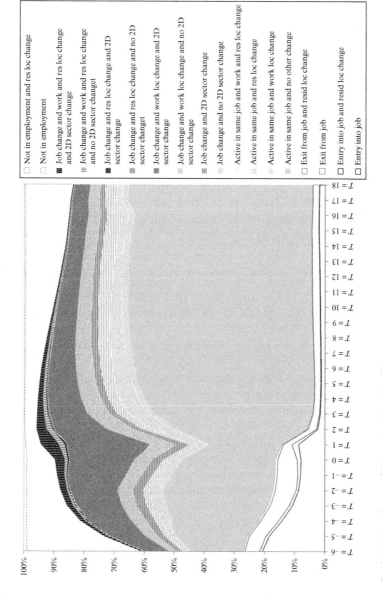

Legend:

- ⬚ Not in employment and res loc change
- ⬚ Not in employment
- ■ Job change and work and res loc change and 2D sector change
- ☰ Job change and work and res loc change and no 2D sector change†
- ⬛ Job change and res loc change and 2D sector change
- ▨ Job change and res loc change and no 2D sector change†
- ▨ Job change and work loc change and 2D sector change
- ▨ Job change and work loc change and no 2D sector change
- ☰ Job change and 2D sector change
- ☰ Job change and no 2D sector change
- ⬚ Active in same job and work and res loc change
- ⬚ Active in same job and res loc change
- ⬚ Active in same job and work loc change
- ⬚ Active in same job and no other change
- ☐ Exit from job and resid loc change
- ☐ Exit from job
- ☐ Entry into job and resid loc change
- ☐ Entry into job

Notes: Pooled cohort dataset, full sample. $N = 9.2$ million.

Source: Statistics Netherlands SSB, own computations.

Figure 5.3 *All year-to-year labour-market dynamics among recent higher-education graduates, relative to time of graduation ($T = 0$)*

97

linear probability models (LPMs) in a simultaneous equations system, estimated using 3SLS using Stata's reg3 command. (See Angrist, 2001 for a presentation of an IV set-up with dummy endogenous regressors; and Mendola and Carletto, 2012 for a 3SLS approach similar to our application.) An obvious drawback associated with LPMs is that predictions are not constrained to the [0,1] interval, as logit or probit predicted outcomes would have been. This implies that marginal effects should be interpreted locally as much as possible. Although this is a potential limitation, the advantages of reporting on a much more parsimonious model are strong.

We define an equation for sector change, workplace change and residential location change occurring between t and $t + 1$, sequentially. Each equation includes the other two elements as binary endogenous regressors. This approach allows us to arrive at direct estimates of the relevant marginal effects, which are directly comparable between equations. It takes inter-relations between different outcomes into account, by treating them as endogenous, and helps to quantify them (Zellner and Theil, 1962). The three equations are all of the following general specification:

$$Y_{i,t+1} = \beta_0 + \Sigma\beta_j Y_{j \neq i,t+1} + \Sigma\beta_i Y_{i,t} + \beta_c Core_t + \Sigma\beta_h D\&HH_{h,t} + \Sigma\beta_{ch}Core_t {}^* HH_{h,t} + \Sigma\beta_r RDen\&Size\&HC_{r,t} + \Sigma\beta_q Educ_q + \Sigma\beta_w CurJob_{w,t} + \Sigma\beta_a TtG_{a,t} + \Sigma\beta_p Cal_{p,t} + \Sigma\beta_k FE_{k,t} + \varepsilon_{i,t}$$

and include the following explanatory variables and controls. Individual subscripts are suppressed, and t is a time operator. Outcome $Y_{i,t+1}$ is a dummy variable indicating a 2-digit sector switch, workplace or residential location change. For each equation, the other outcomes $Y_{j\neq i,t+1}$ are included as dummy endogenous regressors. We control for job or residential switches in year t to check for persistence in mobility. Around one-third of our final sample of job changers also experience sector or workplace dynamics in the year leading up to the change under study. We enter information on demographic characteristics and the household structure. If a partner is present, we include information on their main source of income as well. Where relevant, these variables are time-varying. Around 50 per cent of our sample of job changes occurs to women, and 14 per cent to graduates with a non-Dutch nationality. The variable '*residing in a core labour-market area in the Netherlands (Core$_t$)*' is a dummy indicating residence in one of the twelve largest regional labour-market areas in the Netherlands in terms of total population and active labour force. This variable is entered directly and in an interaction with the household composition, as well as with the main source of income of the partner.

The reference category is a single resident living in non-core labour-market areas.

We also control for density of the workplace, where areas defined as urban have an average address density per square kilometre in excess of 2,500 units. We additionally control for variables regarding the residential city at time *t*, including density, total population and total population of adjacent cities, education structure and skill structure of the active labour force and population for the city of residence, and for cities within commuting distance. Although 65 per cent of observations occur within Dutch core labour-market regions, only about one-third actually occur in very urbanized workplaces (38 per cent) or residential (31 per cent) cities. This implies a substantial share of dynamics outside, but in the vicinity of, the highly urbanized areas. Given the suburbanized and polycentric Dutch geography, this is not surprising. All regional characteristics are based on Statistics Netherlands data, except the education structure of the incumbent active labour force, which was based on the matched employer–employee AVO[5] survey. We enter time-fixed dummies for the degree programme that was taken up. We control for characteristics of the job at time *t* (commuting between labour-market regions yes or no, log of total income, and the nature of main source of income).

To conclude, we enter time-to-graduation and calendar-year dummies in all models. These dummies serve to control for period-specific factors not picked up on by our time-varying regional control variables as well as small differences in registration techniques. Cohort membership is perfectly co-linear with time to graduation and calendar year and therefore is not entered into the analysis. We enter age at graduation as a time-fixed covariate to control for differing patterns between young and mature graduates. The 3SLS approach relies on a sufficient number of exogenous variables unique to each equation. To this end we enter sectoral, workplace and residential regional fixed effects to each respective equation.

5.7   RESULTS

In Table 5.2, we report the main coefficients from our 3SLS analysis of labour-market dynamics. The table contains three columns for the LPMs, describing *change of 2D sector t+1*, *change of work location t+1* and *change of residential location t+1*, respectively.

We find evidence for the inter-relatedness of these outcomes. A change of 2-digit sector and a change of workplace positively influence each other, implying that these strategies are applied in tandem. The coefficients are significant, but their effect sizes are not large. We

Table 5.2 3SLS model of labour-market dynamics

	Change 2D sector t+1		Change work loc t+1		Change resid loc t+1	
	B	Sig	B	Sig	B	Sig
Endogenous regressors						
Change 2D sector t+1	–	–	0.195	***	0.002	–
Change work loc t+1	0.100	***	–	–	-0.051	***
Change resid loc t+1	-0.569	***	-0.544	***	–	–
Sectoral and spatial mobility t (ref = no mobility)						
Change 2D sector t	0.184	***	-0.079	***	-0.005	**
Change work loc t	-0.076	***	0.144	***	0.008	***
Change resid neighb within city t	-0.018	***	-0.021	***	-0.040	***
Change resid city within labmreg t	0.005	–	-0.001	–	0.006	*
Change resid labmreg within NUTS 2 t	0.039	***	0.047	***	0.065	***
Change resid NUTS 2 within NUTS 1 t	0.001	–	0.021	*	0.005	–
Change resid NUTS 1 within country t	0.019	–	0.022	–	0.033	***
Household position and partner characteristics (ref = single)						
Partner primarily employed	-0.072	***	-0.085	***	-0.122	***
>> interaction 'resid in core labmreg'	0.036	***	0.035	***	0.058	***
Partner primarily self-employed	-0.077	***	-0.098	***	-0.133	***
>> interaction 'resid in core labmreg'	0.051	***	0.060	***	0.072	***
Partner primarily on benefits	-0.047	***	-0.054	***	-0.100	***
>> interaction 'resid in core labmreg'	0.020	–	0.025	*	0.051	***
Partner primarily student	-0.029	–	-0.055	***	-0.098	***
>> interaction 'resid in core labmreg'	0.009	–	0.026	–	0.053	***
Lives with parents	-0.048	***	-0.061	***	-0.103	***
>> interaction 'resid in core labmreg'	0.043	***	0.041	***	0.082	***

	(1)		(2)		(3)	
Is a single parent	−0.045	**	−0.031	–	−0.027	**
>> interaction 'resid in core labmreg'	0.037	–	0.018	–	0.035	***
Couple without kids	0.032	***	0.038	***	0.061	***
>> interaction 'resid in core labmreg'	0.004	–	0.005	–	0.003	–
Couple with kids	−0.001	–	−0.003	–	0.037	***
>> interaction 'resid in core labmreg'	0.014	–	0.028	***	0.020	***
Partner education level low	0.012	**	0.004	–	0.003	–
Partner education level high	0.005	–	0.007	*	0.007	***
Density						
Work city is very urban	0.000	–	−0.055	***	−0.007	***
Resid city is very urban	0.007	–	−0.003	–	−0.011	***
Characteristics of city of residence						
Resid in core labmreg	−0.035	***	−0.030	***	−0.080	***
Tot pop size	−0.001	–	0.000	–	0.001	–
Tot pop size, neighb cities	−0.003	–	−0.004	–	−0.001	–
Workers share high level job	−0.039	**	0.055	***	−0.031	***
Workers share high level job sur area	−0.065	–	0.128	*	0.015	–
Workers share scientific level job	0.066	**	0.033	–	0.067	***
Workers share scient level job sur area	0.122	–	−0.364	**	−0.027	–
Population share higher educated	0.046	**	0.022	–	0.011	–
Population share higher educated sur area	0.141	**	0.051	–	0.123	***
Average firm size	0.003	–	0.023	***	0.007	***
Unemployment rate	0.090	–	−0.029	–	0.071	–
Average housing value	−0.002	–	−0.004	–	0.003	–
Number of grads from local HEI	0.001	–	0.003	**	0.003	***
Number of grads from HEIs in surrounding cities	0.011	–	0.019	***	0.015	***
Sector specific employment growth over 1997–08	0.001	–	0.010	**	−0.003	–

(continues overleaf)

Table 5.2 (continued)

	Change 2D sector t+1		Change work loc t+1		Change resid loc t+1	
	B	Sig	B	Sig	B	Sig
Study characteristics (ref = graduate, college, behavioural sciences)						
University	0.030	***	0.021	***	0.019	***
Teaching	-0.029	***	-0.036	***	0.000	–
Agriculture	-0.007	–	-0.001	–	0.017	***
Natural sciences	0.005	–	-0.004	–	0.000	–
Engineering	0.005	–	0.011	**	0.006	***
Healthcare	-0.034	***	0.024	***	0.022	***
Economics	0.002	–	0.005	–	0.006	***
Law	-0.071	***	0.002	–	-0.001	–
Humanities	-0.005	–	-0.012	**	0.001	–
Dropout with earlier HE degree	-0.004	–	-0.005	–	-0.004	**
Dropout without earlier HE degree	-0.009	**	0.009	**	-0.004	**
Time spent in HE	0.001	–	0.002	***	0.000	–
Dem. charact. and household position (ref = single)						
Female	0.000	–	-0.011	***	0.006	***
Foreign	-0.005	–	0.008	**	-0.007	***
Age at graduation	-0.001	–	-0.002	***	-0.002	***
Characteristics of current job						
ln(Net total annual wage)	-0.038	***	-0.021	***	-0.003	**
Commutes between labmregs	-0.017	***	0.305	***	0.028	***
Main source of income (ref = current job)						
Primarily self-employed	0.033	–	-0.024	–	-0.007	–

	(1)		(2)		(3)	
Primarily on benefits	0.063	***	0.064	***	0.007	—
Primarily student	0.036	***	−0.008	—	0.003	—
Time to graduation dummies (ref = T = −5)						
T = −4	0.034	**	0.043	***	0.018	***
T = −3	0.017		0.034	***	0.003	—
T = −2	0.074	***	0.048	***	0.000	—
T = −1	0.094	***	0.074	***	0.007	—
T = 0	0.107	***	0.096	***	0.025	***
T = 1	0.048	***	0.059	***	0.003	—
T = 2	0.048	***	0.048	***	0.003	—
T = 3	0.034	***	0.038	***	−0.002	—
T = 4	0.031	**	0.025	**	−0.013	**
T = 5	0.025	*	0.019	—	−0.010	*
T = 6	0.017	—	0.018	—	−0.015	**
T = 7	0.010	—	0.008	—	−0.015	**
T = 8	0.013	—	−0.005	—	−0.024	***
T = 9	0.005	—	−0.007	—	−0.028	***
T = 10	0.009	—	−0.017	*	−0.028	***
T = 11	−0.001	—	−0.024	*	−0.034	***
T = 12	0.010	—	−0.035	**	−0.034	***
T = 13	−0.001	—	−0.041	***	−0.038	***
T = 14	−0.008	—	−0.051	***	−0.041	***
T = 15	0.007	—	−0.043	***	−0.040	***
T = 16	−0.029	—	−0.041	**	−0.044	***
Year of observation dummies (ref = 2000)						
2001	−0.017	***	−0.001	—	0.007	***
2002	−0.047	***	−0.033	***	−0.001	—

(continues overleaf)

Table 5.2 (continued)

	Change 2D sector $t+1$		Change work loc $t+1$		Change resid loc $t+1$	
	B	Sig	B	Sig	B	Sig
2003	-0.017	***	-0.004	–	0.001	–
2004	-0.007	–	0.012	**	0.006	*
2005	-0.071	***	-0.073	***	-0.002	–
2006	-0.030	***	0.001	–	0.004	–
2007	-0.033	***	-0.013	**	0.000	–
Constant	1.050	***	0.609	***	0.181	***
Fixed effects (all origin sector. labour market regions)						
2D sector fixed effects	YES		NO		NO	
Work location, labour-market region	NO		YES		NO	
Residential location, labour-market region	NO		NO		YES	
N	164,354		164,354		164,354	
R-sq	0.115		0.117		0.023	
chi2	29,597.62	***	33,161.05	***	7,256.972	***

Notes: * $p<0.1$, ** $p<0.05$, *** $p<0.01$. Pooled cohort dataset, person–period file, job changers.

Source: Statistics Netherlands SSB, own computations.

have seen in Figure 5.3 that a change of residential location overall is less likely to occur in combination with labour-market dynamics. As demonstrated in Table 5.2, when residential mobility occurs for job changers, it exerts a strong negative effect on the likelihood of the other two strategies being applied in that same year. This implies that either a residential change is applied to avoid having to engage in sectoral or workplace mobility, or that this change follows the other types. The positive effect of a change in workplace in the running year t on subsequent residential mobility seems to support this, however the effect of 2-digit sector mobility at time t on subsequent residential mobility is negative. A contemporaneous change of 2-digit sector at $t + 1$ has no effect on residential mobility.

We find evidence of persistence in mobility. Having engaged in sectoral or workplace mobility in year t increases the likelihood of applying this strategy again at time $t + 1$. However, the cross effects are negative. Sectoral mobility in year t makes workplace mobility at $t + 1$ less likely, and vice versa. Relative to not moving, we find positive effects of previous long-distance moves on the likelihood to move again. However, switching neighbourhoods within a city, presumably more driven by residential considerations, reduces the likelihood of further mobility. Moving medium distance – that is, between labour-market regions but within provinces – also makes sectoral and workplace mobility more likely.

Overall, sector and workplace mobility appear contemporarily interrelated, persistent, but also inter-temporally competing. For residential changes, labour-market motivations are mingled with residential demands. Those that engage in classic residential upgrading through short-distance moves are less likely to engage in strong changes in job characteristics, even within a sample of job changers. These findings suggest that there is a considerable heterogeneity among job switchers in terms of job-change strategies that they are able, or forced, to apply.

We also analysed interactions of the variable $Core_t$ with our dummies indicating household position and partner's main source of income. The results for these interacted variables are summarized in Figure 5.4. Relative to being single and living in a non-core area, all other household types with an (economically active) partner present exhibit lower mobility across the board. This is especially true for graduates with partners with *main source of income from employment* or *self-employment*. In particular, the effects of a partner on residential mobility are relatively strong. Controlling for education level and economic activity of a partner, we find that graduates who are part of a couple without children, living in non-core labour-market areas, are in fact more likely to engage in all forms of mobility than singles. Graduates who are part of a couple without children in core areas

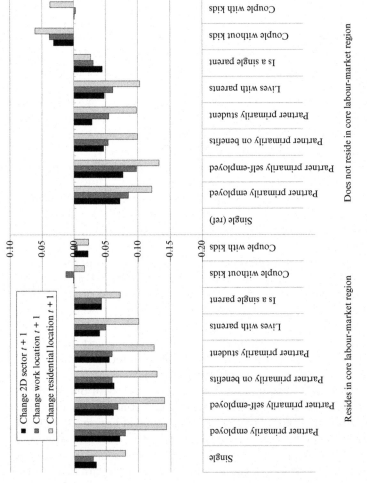

Notes: Pooled cohort dataset, person–period file, job changers.

Source: Statistics Netherlands SSB, own computations.

Figure 5.4 Marginal effects of household position and residential location in core and non-core labour-market areas

are slightly more likely to engage in workplace mobility. Moreover, we find that non-core couples with children present are also more likely to change residential locations than singles. The implication is that, even though lower spatial mobility rates for couples and families might be observed, this is not necessarily caused by the household composition *per se*. Rather, results suggest that this is related to the extent to which partners are economically active and thus bound to certain locations. Partners with higher levels of education have a positive effect on workplace and residential mobility.

In order to assess the role of one's position in the densely networked polycentric system of Dutch cities, we entered a variety of characteristics at the city level as well as for those cities which lie within commuting distance for a given graduate. If the workplace is situated in a very urbanized city, workplace mobility and residential mobility are found to be less likely. If the residential city is highly urbanized, this reduces the likelihood of further residential mobility. This is in line with other recent findings for the Netherlands which suggests that urban environments are increasingly popular, at least among existing inhabitants (Boterman et al., 2010; Venhorst et al., 2013).

Next to this, we enter a number of other controls for the residential city as well as the surrounding areas. Interestingly, we find no remaining effect for total population size of either the city of residence or the size of the surrounding municipalities. Among our remaining control variables, our results are generally in line with earlier literature. We find differences between graduates from different specializations, with, for example, lower sectoral mobility for elementary schoolteachers as well as healthcare and law professionals. Workplace mobility is low for teachers and humanities graduates, but high for engineers and healthcare graduates. Together with economics and agriculture graduates, for engineers and healthcare graduates this is also coupled with high residential mobility. Dropouts without an earlier degree from another program apply sectoral mobility less often, which may imply that they follow a within-sector learning-on-the-job strategy, which might also involve more workplace mobility.

Females are found to be more migratory but they exhibit less workplace mobility, findings which are in line with Faggian et al. (2007) and Hanson and Pratt (1992). Those currently in a job with higher income exhibit less mobility across the board, whereas graduates who are currently commuting between labour-market areas are more likely to experience both workplace and residential mobility. Graduates *on benefits* (mostly partial disability) as the main source of income are more likely to engage in sectoral and workplace mobility, but there is no effect on residential mobility.

The time-to-graduation dummies remain strongly significant. Controlling for a host of individual and regional factors has not rendered these dummies insignificant, which implies that the effect of the life-course position emanating from Figures 5.1 through 5.3 remains critically important over and above the general patterns outlined above.

5.8 CONCLUSIONS AND DISCUSSION

In this study we map out labour-market dynamics of graduates in Dutch HEIs. Registry data from Statistics Netherlands enables us to track a large sample of pooled graduation cohorts from seven years prior to eighteen years following graduation. We apply this data in a study of job-switch strategies by a sub-sample of graduate job changers.

Overall, the likelihood of labour-market dynamics varies strongly with the life phase in which we find graduates: the likelihood of changes occurring declines sharply within a few years of leaving the HEI. The policy window of opportunity, often cited as a rationale in the literature on migration of recent graduates appears to close very quickly, and stability becomes the norm relatively fast. This life-course or time-to-graduation effect remains important even after controlling for a host of individual and regional factors. We find that, like migration, job mobility in general is not a random event. It occurs in some cases repeatedly, to specific groups who appear to operate at the edges of the job-opportunity space. Generally, residing in core labour-market areas and dense cities substantially reduces workplace and residential mobility. There is no added effect of own or neighbouring city population size.

We find that sector and workplace mobility appear contemporarily positively inter-related, persistent, but also inter-temporally competing. Residential mobility appears somewhat disconnected from labour-market dynamics, in a direct sense. However, we do find evidence for contemporary and inter-temporal trade-offs. It appears that some wait for a match to come to fruition before changing residences. Distance moved plays an important role, with short-distance residential moves associated with lower mobility, rather than persistently higher mobility for all outcomes.

Mobility is higher across the board for graduates residing in non-core areas, with non-core singles found to be relatively mobile. However, our study serves to nuance earlier results on lower spatial mobility of multi-person households. We demonstrate that it is not the presence of a partner as such, but whether or not he or she is economically active, that lowers spatial mobility. On the one hand, the household may be bound by this activity. On the other hand, engaging in spatial workplace or residential mobility is less necessary if a working partner is present. Controlling for this, and contrary to what is often reported in migration literature, we find that couples without children, living in non-core areas, are more likely to exhibit residential mobility than singles. They are also more likely to engage in sectoral and workplace mobility. Non-core couples with children are also found to be more likely to engage in residential mobility than singles. This is an interesting avenue for further research. In this light, it is also interesting to note that we find that females are more migratory but that they exhibit less workplace mobility. The latter results appear in line with findings on gendered labour markets (Faggian et al., 2007; Hanson and Pratt, 1992).

The heterogeneity which transpires from our results implies that policy initiatives aimed at graduate retention or facilitation of smooth labour-market transition for this group have to be targeted precisely. Given the vital role of the economic activity of a partner, a retention or attraction policy should provide ample opportunities for both partners. There appears to be scope for targeting multi-person households in non-core areas. These households demonstrate relatively high propensities for spatial mobility. Also, we demonstrate that certain job-to-job switch strategies, such as sector switches within a given region for graduates with particular specializations, are less feasible depending on the skill profile of a graduate. A notable limitation to our data in this respect is the lack of information on occupations: switching to a similar occupation in a very different sector might provide a graduate with a relatively low-cost alternative strategy. Finally, we find that complex relationships exist between the job-to-job switch strategies as defined in this chapter. In particular, residential mobility more often than not is not directly related to work location and sectoral mobility. It is important to consider whether or not this is reflecting actual housing-market constraints on labour-market mobility, or whether graduates simply make forward-looking moves or wait until a switch has turned out to be a success. Clearly, depending on the strain on the local housing market, suitable policy measures may differ substantially between regions.

ACKNOWLEDGEMENTS

This research was partially funded by Platform31, the Hague, the Netherlands. The work greatly benefited from comments received during presentations at the meetings of the Western Regional Science Association and the North American Regional Science Council and comments received from two anonymous referees.

NOTES

*   Email: v.a.venhorst@rug.nl.
1. Central Register Enrolments Higher Education.
2. Nomenclature statistique des Activités économiques dans la Communauté Européenne.
3. Nomenclature of Units for Territorial Statistics.
4. The observations on person–period episodes without a job change occurring prove to be rather similar, in terms of background characteristics of the graduate experiencing them. This is not surprising, seeing as most graduates experience a job change at some point during our observation window.
5. Dutch Arbeidsvoorwaarden Onderzoek.

REFERENCES

Abreu, Maria, Roberta Comunian, Alessandra Faggian and Philip McCann (2012). 'Life is short, art is long': the persistent wage gap between bohemian and non-bohemian graduates, *Annals of Regional Science*, 49(2), 305–321.

Abreu, Maria, Alessandra Faggian and Philip McCann (2014). Migration and inter-industry mobility of UK graduates, *Journal of Economic Geography*, doi: 10.1093/jeg/lbt043.

Angrist, Joshua (2001). Estimation of limited dependent variable models with dummy endogenous regressors: simple strategies for empirical practice, *Journal of Business and Economic Statistics*, 19(1), 2–16.

Autor, David H. and David Dorn (2013). The growth of low-skill service jobs and the polarization of the US labor market, *American Economic Review*, 103(5), 1553–1597.

Bacolod, Marigee, Bernardo S. Blum and William C. Strange (2009). Skills in the city, *Journal of Urban Economics*, 65, 136–153.

Biagi, Bianca, Alessandra Faggian and Philip McCann (2011). Long and short distance migration in Italy: the role of economic, social and environmental characteristics, *Spatial Economic Analysis*, 6(1), 111–131.

Boterman, Willem R., Lia Karsten and Sako Musterd (2010). Gentrifiers settling down? Patterns and trends of residential location of middle-class families in Amsterdam, *Housing Studies*, 25(5), 693–714.

Brandén, Maria (2013). Couples' education and regional mobility: the importance of occupation, income and gender, *Population, Space and Place*, 19(5), 522–536.

Broersma, Lourens and Jouke Van Dijk (2008). The effect of congestion and agglomeration on multifactor productivity growth in Dutch regions, *Journal of Economic Geography*, 8, 181–209.

Burger, Martijn J., Erik J. Meijers and Frank G. Van Oort (2013). Regional spatial structure and retail amenities in the Netherlands, *Regional Studies*, doi: 10.1080/00343404.2013.783693.

Busch, Oliver and Benjamin Weigert (2010). Where have all the graduates gone? Internal cross-state migration of graduates in Germany 1984–2004, *Annals of Regional Science*, 44, 559–572.

Champion, Tony (2012). Testing the return migration element of the 'escalator region' model: an analysis of migration into and out of south-east England, 1966–2001, *Cambridge Journal of Regions, Economy and Society*, 5, 255–269.

Clark, William A. and Suzanne Davies Withers (1999). Changing jobs and changing houses: mobility outcomes of employment transitions, *Journal of Regional Science*, 39(4), 653–673.

Corcoran, Jonathan, Alessandra Faggian and Philip McCann (2010). Human capital in remote and rural Australia: the role of graduate migration, *Growth and Change*, 41(2), 192–220.

Costa, Dora and Matthew Kahn (2000). Power couples: change in the locational choice of the college educated, 1940–1990, *Quarterly Journal of Economics*, 115, 1287–1314.

DaVanzo, Julie (1983). Repeat migration in the United States: who moves back and who moves on? *The Review of Economics and Statistics*, 65(4), 552–559.

Dijkstra, Lewis, Enrique Garcilazo and Philip McCann (2013). The economic performance of European cities and city regions: myths and realities, *European Planning Studies*, 21(3), 334–354, doi: 10.1080/09654313.2012.716245.

Eliasson, Kent, Robert A. Nakosteen, Olle Westerlund and Michael A. Zimmer (2014). All in the family: self-selection and migration by couples, *Papers in Regional Science*, 93(1), 101–124.

Faggian, Alessandra, Philip McCann and Stephen Sheppard (2007). Some evidence that women are more mobile than men: gender differences in UK graduate migration behavior, *Journal of Regional Science*, 47(3), 517–539.

Faggian, Alessandra, Roberta Comunian, Sarah Jewell and Ursula Kelly (2013a). Bohemian graduates in the UK: disciplines and location determinants of creative careers, *Regional Studies*, 47(2), 183–200.

Faggian, Alessandra, Jonathan Corcoran and Philip McCann (2013b). Modelling geographical graduate job search using circular statistics, *Papers in Regional Science*, 92(2), 329–343.

Fielding, Anthony J. (1992). Migration and social mobility: South East England as an escalator region, *Regional Studies*, 26(1), 1–15.

Franklin, Rachel S. (2003). Migration of the young, single, and college educated: 1995 to 2000, Census 2000 Special Reports, U.S. Department of Commerce Economics and Statistics Administration, US Census Bureau.

Gottlieb, Paul D. and George Joseph (2006). College to work migration of technology graduates and holders of doctorates within the United States, *Journal of Regional Science*, 46(4), 627–659.

Graves, Philip E. (2014). Spatial equilibrium in the labor market, in Peter Nijkamp and Manfred Fischer (eds), *The Handbook of Regional Science*, Dordrecht, Heidelberg and New York: Springer, pp. 17–33.

Haapanen, Mika and Hannu Tervo (2012). Migration of the highly educated: evidence from residence spells of university graduates, *Journal of Regional Science*, 52(4), 587–605.

Hanson, Susan and Geraldine Pratt (1988). Reconceptualizing the links between home and work in urban geography, *Economic Geography*, 64(4), 299–321.

Hanson, Susan and Geraldine Pratt (1992). Dynamic dependencies: a geographic investigation of local labor markets, *Economic Geography*, 68(4), 373–405.

Hidalgo, César A., Bailey Klinger, Albert-László Barabási and Ricardo Hausmann (2007). The product space conditions the development of nations, *Science*, 317(5837), 482–487.

Koster, Sierdjan and Viktor A. Venhorst (2014). Moving shop: residential and business relocation by the highly educated self-employed, *Spatial Economic Analysis*, 9(4), 436–464.

Lucas, Robert E. (1988). On the mechanics of economic development, *Journal of Monetary Economics*, 22, 3–42.

McCann, Philip (2008). Globalization and economic geography: the world is curved, not flat, *Cambridge Journal of Regions, Economy and Society*, 1, 351–370.

McCann, Philip (2013). *Modern Urban and Regional Economics*, 2nd edn, Oxford: Oxford University Press.

Mendola, Mariapia and Calogero Carletto (2012). Migration and gender differences in the home labour market: evidence from Albania, *Labour Economics*, 19, 870–880.

Moretti, Enrico (2012). *The New Geography of Jobs*, New York: HMH Publishing.

Neffke, Frank and Martin Svensson Henning (2013). Skill-relatedness and firm diversification, *Strategic Management Journal*, 34, 297–316.

Ommeren, Jos van, Piet Rietveld and Peter Nijkamp (1998). Spatial moving behavior of two-earner households, *Journal of Regional Science*, 38(1), 23–41.

Ommeren, Jos van, Piet Rietveld and Peter Nijkamp (1999). Impacts of employed spouses on job-moving behaviour, *International Regional Science Review*, 22(1), 54–68.

Partridge, Mark (2010). The duelling models: NEG vs amenity migration in explaining US engines of growth, *Papers in Regional Science*, 89(3), 513–536.

Plane, David A., Christopher J. Henrie and Marc J. Perry (2005). Migration up and down the urban hierarchy and across the life course, *Proceedings of the National Academy of Sciences of the USA*, 102(43), 15313–15318.

Romer, Paul M. (1986). Increasing returns and long-run growth, *The Journal of Political Economy*, 94(5), 1002–1037.

Storper, Michael and Allen J. Scott (2009). Rethinking human capital, creativity and urban growth, *Journal of Economic Geography*, 9, 147–167.

Venhorst, Viktor A. (2013). Graduate migration and regional familiarity, *Tijdschrift Voor Economische En Sociale Geografie*, 104(1), 109–119.

Venhorst, Viktor A. (2016). Human capital spillovers in Dutch cities: consumption or productivity? *Annals of Regional Science*, doi: 10.1007/s00168-016-0754-9.

Venhorst, Viktor A. and Frank Cörvers (2015). Entry into working life: spatial mobility and the job match quality of higher-educated graduates, ROA Research Memorandum ROA-RM-2015/3, Maastricht, the Netherlands: Maastricht University School of Business and Economics.

Venhorst, Viktor A., Jouke van Dijk and Leo J.G. van Wissen (2010). Do the best graduates leave the peripheral areas of the Netherlands? *Tijdschrift Voor Economische En Sociale Geografie*, 101(5), 521–537.

Venhorst, Viktor A., Jouke van Dijk, and Leo J.G. van Wissen (2011). An analysis of trends in spatial mobility of Dutch graduates *Spatial Economic Analysis*, 6(1), 57–82.

Venhorst, Viktor A., Sierdjan Koster and Jouke van Dijk (2013). Geslaagd in de Stad, URSI Research Report 344, Faculty of Spatial Sciences, University of Groningen, the Netherlands.

Whisler, Ronald L., Brigitte S. Waldorf, G.F. Mulligan and David Plane (2008). Quality of life and the migration of the college–educated: a life–course approach, *Growth and Change*, 39(1), 58–94.

Winters, John V. (2011). Human capital, higher education institutions, and quality of life, *Regional Science and Urban Economics*, 41, 446–454.

Zellner, Arnold and Henri Theil (1962). Three stage least squares: simultaneous estimate of simultaneous equations, *Econometrica*, 29, 54–78.

6. Working while studying: does it lead to greater attachment to the regional labour market?

Mika Haapanen* and Hannu Karhunen**

6.1 INTRODUCTION

Extensive theoretical and empirical research indicates that highly educated individuals are more likely to migrate, as investments in human capital increase the expected returns on migration (see for example Greenwood, 1997, ch. 12). Recent empirical evidence has, however, shown that internal migration rates have fallen for the highly educated since the beginning of the 1990s in the United States[1] (Molloy et al., 2011; 2014). Figure 6.1

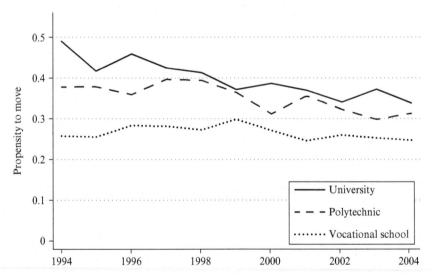

Source: Own calculations based on 7 per cent random sample.

Figure 6.1   Propensity to move within three years of graduation by level of education (in 1994–2004 in Finland)

shows a similar pattern for higher-education graduates in Finland. A falling trend in internal migration is also visible in Britain (short-distance migration, Champion and Shuttleworth, 2015), Australia, Canada and Switzerland (Bell and Charles-Edwards, 2013). It is not clear whether the decline in mobility originates in changes in individual behaviour or characteristics, or is connected to a wider shift in the labour market. Traditionally, high labour mobility is seen as a sign of labour-market dynamism (Borjas, 1999). Conversely, low labour mobility can potentially prolong recessions and reduce growth. Hence, it is important to understand the underlining factors that affect migration.

We argue that the decline in the migration of higher-education graduates might be related to changes in the labour market, and particularly to how much they work during their studies. The American Community Survey for 2011 indicates that around 70 per cent of college students worked part- or full-time while enrolled (Davis, 2012). In Finland, the magnitude of student employment is similar; over 60 per cent of university students are working during their studies despite the generous student-benefit system (OSF, 2016). As short-lived jobs before graduation can constitute a stepping stone to long-lasting jobs (Cockx and Picchio, 2012), work experience accumulated during the studies might attach youths to their study region. When students start to work, for example, to finance their education or to gain a higher standard of living, they begin to accumulate work-related human capital.[2] Occupational and industry-specific human capital is often needed to perform specialised tasks (Sullivan, 2010; Yamaguchi, 2012). If human capital is not easily taken to the new occupation or work, this accumulation can decrease migration due to the increased cost of moving. Yet the relationship between student work and migration is not fully understood.

The purpose of this chapter is to investigate how working while studying is related to geographical mobility after education in Finland. The analysis focuses on high school graduates who have completed their first university, polytechnic or vocational school degree in 1991–2004. Our first observation from Figure 6.1 is that the mobility of university and polytechnic graduates has declined in Finland since the first half of the 1990s. Surprisingly, the decline of migration rates coincides with a period in which the Finnish economy expanded significantly, even though periods of economic growth are normally understood to be associated with higher rates of labour mobility (Saks and Wozniak, 2011). This finding is worrisome; high labour mobility is believed to be important for economic development because it improves the allocation of labour across regions (for example, Blanchard et al., 1992).

Our main contribution is to show that working while studying is negatively related to graduate migration in Finland (even after controlling for a rich set of confounding factors). Thus, increases in working while studying can partly explain why the migration rates have declined for higher-education graduates in Finland. Second, policy-makers in Finland are actively looking for ways to speed up graduation, and new constraints on working while studying might form part of the policy toolkit. Our results imply that restrictions on working while studying could potentially lead to the increased out-migration of graduates from higher education, particularly from regions outside the Helsinki capital region. Third, we also document differences in the relationship by study region and prior mobility.

The rest of the chapter is organised as follows. Section 6.2 reviews the related literature. Section 6.3 gives general information on the higher-education system in Finland. Section 6.4 introduces the data and method. Section 6.5 presents descriptive evidence and estimation results. Section 6.6 discusses the findings and provides avenues for future research. Section 6.7 concludes.

6.2   LITERATURE REVIEW

The positive relationship between education and migration has been documented in the literature for many decades. Since early contributions by Sjaastad (1962) and Bowles (1970), this literature has expanded enormously, confirming that college and university graduates are more geographically mobile than their less-educated peers (see for example Malamud and Wozniak, 2012; Wozniak, 2010). Recently, scholars have shown growing interest in the migration of graduates from higher education. The literature has shown, for example, that gender (Faggian et al., 2007), ethnicity (Faggian et al., 2006), field of study (Venhorst et al., 2010), local labour-market conditions (Venhorst et al., 2011) and location of the educational institution (Groen, 2010; Haapanen and Tervo, 2012) are important for mobility (see also Abreu et al., 2015).

In addition, destination choices of graduates from higher education have been investigated. For example, Marinelli (2013) finds that return migrants (from study region to origin region) have a poorer academic performance and are less strongly attracted to highly innovative regions than onward migrants (see also Faggian et al., 2013). According to Ahlin et al. (2014), the attraction of urban regions among university graduates in Sweden is due to their thicker labour markets for skills: large cities increase employment probabilities and yield higher returns to human capital.

Nevertheless, very little is known about how students' work experience during the studies is related to their future geographical mobility. This observation is surprising because graduates are effectively transferring knowledge from the university sector to the labour market, and when they move, they further transfer this knowledge across regions (for example, Marinelli, 2013). Migration can also potentially mediate the effect of education on other labour-market outcomes, since migration is important for gaining returns from education investments. For example, di Cintio and Grassi (2013) find large wage gains from migrating after university graduation and smaller wage gains from migrating to study in a university, compared to those who remain in their current region.

6.2.1 How Does Working While Studying Affect Migration?

Theoretically, it is unclear whether working while studying should have a net positive or negative effect on graduate migration. On the one hand, working while studying expands local labour-market networks because the student's employer and fellow employees can share information about local jobs. The increased stability (for example, the lower risk of unemployment) is likely to reduce the propensity to move after graduation. Furthermore, those who work during their studies might disproportionately consist of students whose skills match well with the employment needs of the local industries, and vice versa. Therefore, the wage-opportunity cost of moving is relatively high for these matched workers and low for mismatched workers who might invest in migration as a means of improving their job matches (cf. discussion in Nakosteen et al. 2008, p. 772).

On the other hand, working while studying can also increase migration. A good employment history is an indicator of high productivity, which elicits job offers across the regions and thus increases a graduate's propensity to move. Migration also requires an initial outlay of financial resources. Graduates who have worked during their studies are better able to finance their migration efforts. However, because students in higher education are relatively wealthy in Finland and government support is generous (see Section 6.3), financial restrictions are unlikely to play a major role in the decision to move in Finland. In sum, the sign of the effect of working while studying on graduate migration is theoretically ambiguous, and empirically it remains an open question.

6.2.2 Other Labour-Market Outcomes

Although prior evidence on the relationship between working while studying and migration is lacking, a number of studies examine how employment during studying affects academic achievements and other labour-market outcomes after graduation. Working while studying is observed to prolong graduation, but it is less clear whether work harms students' grades (see for example Darolia, 2014; Nonis and Hudson, 2006). Avdic and Gartell (2015) show that Swedish student aid reform, which enhanced student employment during their studies, also decreased the pace of study among students from low socio-economic backgrounds. High-intensity work during studying is observed to slow academic progression in the United States (US) (Darolia, 2014), Italy (Triventi, 2014), France (Body et al., 2014), the United Kingdom (UK) (Jewell, 2014) and Finland (Häkkinen and Uusitalo, 2003). By contrast, student aid reforms that increased conditional financial aid in Germany (Glocker, 2011) and in Norway (Gunnes et al., 2013) enhanced on-time graduation.

Working while studying has been found to affect labour-market outcomes such as employment and earnings after graduation, but estimated effects vary by country, level of education and empirical approach. In the US, studies have shown that employment during high school can have a positive earnings effect (see the early survey by Ruhm, 1997), but this might be explained by individual selection and unobserved heterogeneity (for example, Hotz et al., 2002). Still, Molitor and Leigh (2005) find that in-school work experience is a significant determinant of earnings in the US, but that it is more important for two-year than four-year college students (see also Light 2001). Häkkinen (2006) finds that student employment has a positive effect on earnings right after graduation from university in Finland (19 per cent one year after graduation), but when she accounts for the effect on the duration of studies, the earnings effect is insignificant. Her results suggest that although working while studying can ease the transition from school to work, it has no long-term effect on earnings. Returns to student employment are also found to depend on what kind of jobs students have. Field-related employment during university studies has been found to result in lower unemployment risk and higher wages after graduation in Switzerland (Geel and Backes-Gellner, 2012) and in the UK (Jewell, 2014). In addition, Saniter and Siedler (2014) show that mandatory internships have a positive wage effect after graduation in Germany.

Moreover, a growing body of literature has investigated how different labour-market decisions can have profound long-term effects on youths' lives. The early career period is often 'chaotic'; changing jobs is common among youths (Neumark and Joyce, 2001; Ryan, 2001). The long-term outcomes depend on how young individuals succeed in these first labour-market years. For example, for graduates from universities of applied sciences, a poor match between education and job after graduation is found to lead to income penalty and worse job satisfaction (Diem, 2015). Unemployment at a young age or after graduation has a significant negative effect on future earnings (Doiron and Gørgens, 2008; Mroz and Savage, 2006; Oreopoulos et al., 2012; Wachter and Bender, 2006). In contrast, stability in the early career and a successful transition from school to work increases future labour-market activity (Neumark and Joyce, 2001) and adult earnings (Neumark, 2002). Migration is an often essential part of this transition.[3] Graduates choose a labour market at the beginning of their work life, and their mobility declines rapidly after they find a suitable job, establish a family and develop new social networks in the region (Gordon and Molho, 1995; Huff and Clark, 1978; Molho, 1995).

In sum, the literature on graduate migration and the effects of working while studying on other labour-market outcomes has expanded recently, but it is still unknown how work-related activities during studies are related to future mobility. Since working while studying can provide essential information on the local labour market before graduation, it is likely to be an important factor in determining whether the graduate stays in the study region. Gained work experience is a competitive advantage over graduates without experience, especially in the slow-growth regions, where employment opportunities are scarce.

6.3 INSTITUTIONAL SETTING: HIGHER EDUCATION IN FINLAND

After completing compulsory education, approximately 50 per cent of students in Finland will continue to high school, which lasts for three years and ends with a matriculation examination. High school gives qualifications for applying to institutions of tertiary education, that is, universities and polytechnics. Approximately 36 per cent of applicants to polytechnics and 29 per cent of applicants to universities are successful and commence studies (Statistics Finland, 2013). As entry to tertiary education is highly competitive, many students also complete vocational school after high school. Nonetheless, only 12 per cent of new vocational school students had a high school degree in 2012 (OSF, 2012). Degrees from vocational schools and colleges were more common for high-school graduates at the beginning of the 1990s than they are today because the vocational schooling system was more fragmented and no polytechnics existed in Finland. The polytechnics were formed gradually after 1991 by merging 215 vocational colleges and schools. This expanded the higher-education network to 26 polytechnics in addition to the pre-existing 15 universities. As illustrated by Figure 6.2, the universities are located in ten regions, whereas the networks of polytechnics and vocational schools cover the entire country.

In Finland, education is practically free at all levels, and students

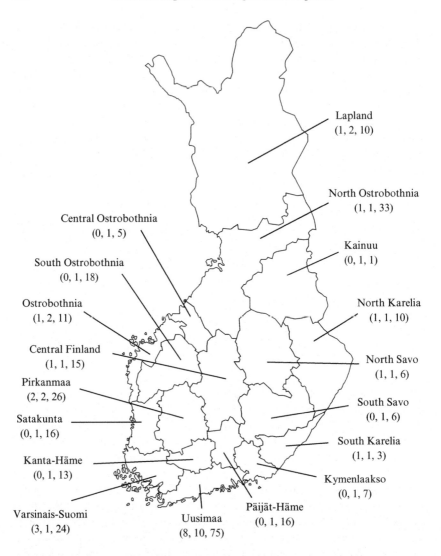

Note: Number of universities, polytechnics and vocational schools are given in parentheses below the name of the region.

Source: Statistics Finland, Education Statistics.

Figure 6.2   NUTS 3 regions and educational institutions in Finland in 2004

receive government support, which consists of three parts: direct allowances, housing benefits and government-guaranteed loans. After the student support system reform of 1992, subsidy levels and the rules guiding the use of entitlements have been relatively stable for the majority of students. From 1992 to 2012, government support for students in higher education has increased: direct monthly allowances from €264 to €298 (by 13 per cent), monthly housing benefits from €149 to €202 (by 36 per cent) and the maximum of government-guaranteed loans from €202 to €300 (by 49 per cent; see Ministry of Education and Culture, 2012). At the same time, living costs have increased by 40 per cent and the general income level by 93 per cent. Therefore, the financial incentives for working have increased over time because much of the increase in benefits has been in the government-guaranteed loans that Finnish students are reluctant to take.[4]

The support system allows students to earn substantial amounts during the academic year and still receive full student benefits. For example, in 1998–2007 students were allowed to earn €505 for each month they received full student benefits and/or housing benefits, and this earnings limit was €1,515 for each benefit-free month.[5] Thus, students who collect full benefits from the typical nine study months could still annually earn €9,090 without the need to repay the allowances.

6.4   DATA AND METHOD

Our analysis is based on the Longitudinal Census Files and the Longitudinal Employment Statistics Files constructed by Statistics Finland. These datasets are annually updated from the registers, and contain a large set of variables spanning 1987 to 2006, including information on, for example, high-school matriculation exam scores, spouses, parents and regions of residence. For this study, we use a 7 per cent random sample of individuals who were Finnish residents in 2001.

The analysis focuses on high-school graduates who have completed their first master's, polytechnic or vocational school degree in 1991–2004, that is, to fourteen cohorts of graduates.[6] Because we only know the matriculation exam results from 1990 onwards, we restrict the sample to individuals who completed high school in the period 1990–96 in our main analysis. We censor the later high-school cohorts to allow sufficient time for them to graduate from higher education within the study time-frame. We also exclude 124 individuals who were older than 25 when they graduated from high school to increase the homogeneity of the sample. After deleting a further 2,872 observations with incomplete data, we are left with 10,077 graduates from university, polytechnic or vocational school. On average, they were 25 years old at graduation.

We investigate the propensity to move within three years of graduation. First, students' NUTS[7] 3 region of residence is saved one year before graduation. Migrants are then defined as students who change their NUTS 3 region of residence (on an annual basis) at least once by the end of the second year after graduation. For example, a student who received a degree in 2000 will be classified as migrant if (s)he changed regions in 1999–2002. Thus, a non-migrant is someone who did not move between 1999 and 2002. This definition of migration is motivated by prior research showing that many graduates from higher education already move before graduation and that the propensity to move declines rapidly after graduation (Haapanen and Tervo, 2012).

Following Böckerman and Haapanen (2013), Haapanen and Tervo (2012) and Nivalainen (2004), we study long-distance migration between the nineteen Finnish NUTS 3 regions. Although short-distance migration is also common near the graduation year (for example, because of leaving student accommodation), we focus on migration between the NUTS 3 regions, which constitute distinct labour markets and cultural and geographic areas in Finland. We believe that this definition of migration gives a reliable measure of the graduate's decision to change the labour-market area and not just to commute over a longer distance. Robustness checks (available on request) show that our estimation results are similar when NUTS 4 classification (that is, 79 regions) is used instead.

We have constructed two measurements of work that are used to investigate the relationship between working while studying on migration. First, we define full-time work over a three-year period before the graduation year by using annual earnings, which are deflated using the consumer price index (base year 2000). Statistics Finland classifies an individual as a full-time worker for the year if his/her earnings exceed €8,409 (Statistics Finland, 2000). This definition of full-time work is also used by Böckerman et al. (2009). We apply this threshold using average annual earnings over the three-year period. Second, we define an individual as a part-time worker if his/her average earnings from the same period are less than €8,409 but more than €6,060. The lower threshold for part-time work is based on the rules related to student benefits discussed above. Students can earn a maximum of €505 per month and receive full student benefits each month (12 × €505 = €6,060). Results available on request indicate that our conclusions below are not sensitive to small changes in lower-bound limits for earnings.[8]

Since our dependent variable, migration, is binary, we use probit models to estimate how working while studying is related to graduate migration.

To allow for the relationship between working status and migration to vary according to the level of education, our models include a full set of interaction terms between the level of education and working status. The probit models also use a number of background variables to control for individual-specific heterogeneity (such as high-school grades to control for individual differences in ability). Table 6.1 displays the variables used in the models and their definitions and mean values.

Control variables are measured three years before graduation year or earlier. They are thus determined before our work measurements to avoid endogeneity problems. The control variables contain information on individual, family, parent and regional characteristics that have been linked to migration decisions in the prior literature. They include individual and household factors such as marriage (for example, Newbold, 2001), spouse's earnings (for example, Haapanen and Tervo, 2012), education in general (for example, Malamud and Wozniak, 2012), high qualifications (for example, Venhorst et al., 2010) and earlier migration behaviour (for example, DaVanzo, 1983), which all have an effect on graduate migration.

Although our models utilise a number of control variables, we cannot entirely exclude the possibility that some unobserved factor is affecting both student employment and migration decisions. Individuals make educational and locational choices according their own preferences and capabilities, which are practically impossible to observe. This self-selection problem can bias the estimation results despite the extensive use of individual and region-specific background variables. Thus, caution should be exercised when interpreting the results as (causal) effects of student work on future migration. The estimated parameters below reflect conditional correlations between the factors of interest.

6.5   RESULTS

6.5.1   Descriptive Analysis

We will first provide descriptive results on student employment and graduate migration before presenting our estimation results. Figure 6.3 illustrates the extent to which Finnish graduate cohorts worked over the three-year period before their graduation in 1994–2004. After a severe recession in the early 1990s, the share of students who worked full-time or part-time grew substantially. For example, in 1996, only 11 per cent of university graduates worked full-time before graduation, but in 2004, this had increased to 36 per cent. The change is similar in magnitude for polytechnic and vocational school graduates. Unfortunately, our data do not enable us to

Table 6.1   Description of variables and their mean values

Variable	Description	Mean
Dependent variable		
Migration	1 if individual changes NUTS 3 region of residence at least once during a period starting one year before the graduation year and ending two years after the graduation year, 0 otherwise	0.32
Working while studying		
Full-time work	1 if average annual earnings over €8,409 during 3-year period before graduation year, 0 otherwise	0.19
Part-time work	1 if average annual earnings €6,060–8,409 during 3-year period before graduation year, 0 otherwise	0.14
Less than part-time work	1 if average annual earnings less than €6,060 during 3-year period before graduation year, 0 otherwise	0.67
Level of education		
Master's degree	1 if graduated with master's degree, 0 otherwise	0.30
Polytechnic degree	1 if graduated with polytechnic degree (lower-degree-level tertiary education), 0 otherwise	0.26
Vocational school degree	1 if graduated with vocational school degree (upper-secondary-level education or lowest-level tertiary education), 0 otherwise	0.44
Control variables		
Age	Graduation age	25.08
Age^2	Graduation age squared	635.2
Female	1 if female, 0 otherwise	0.61
Swedish	1 if Swedish speaking minority, 0 otherwise	0.05
Married*	1 if married, 0 otherwise	0.06
Children*	1 if at least one child, 0 if no children	0.24
Female with children*	Interaction term (female × children)	0.16
Spouse's education*	0 if not married, 1 if comprehensive education, . . . , 5 if university education	0.55
Spouse's employment*	1 if spouse is employed, 0 otherwise	0.09
Spouse's income*	Annual income of spouse, €1,000	0.86
Home-owner*	1 if owns a flat or house, 0 otherwise	0.21
HS work experience	Sum of work months over 3-year period during high school	6.26
HS work experience^2	HS work experience squared	92.08
Math score	Matriculation exam score for math grades at the basic and advanced level from high school (1–10; 10 is the best)	3.27

Table 6.1   (continued)

Variable	Description	Mean
Language score	Matriculation exam score for the grade of the native language (1–5; 5 is the best)	2.39
Missing scores	1 if matriculation score(s) missing, 0 otherwise	0.33
Migrated for studies	1 if study region of higher education is not high school region (NUTS 3), 0 otherwise	0.20
Parent's region	1 if mother or father is living in the study region; otherwise	0.79
Unemployment rate*	Average unemployment rate for 20–34-year-old population in the NUTS 4 study region	18.55

Notes: Estimations also use NUTS 3 study region dummies and graduation year dummies for high school and the next degree. Study region refers to the region where the graduate receives his/her first degree after high school. Variables marked (*) are measured three years before the year of graduation. Earnings were deflated using consumer price index in 2000.

investigate whether students work for the same firm or industry before and after graduation. Successful employee–job or employee–industry matches before graduation could be a crucial factor in determining migration decisions in the future. Because we only observe the amount of work measured by annual earnings, it should be stressed that employed students can have multiple employers and employment spells during their studies. We cannot observe their importance with our data.

Increased student employment indicates that more students enter the labour markets before graduation. In Figure 6.4, we consider how graduates' propensity to move is related to their work experience during the studies. Again, each group of graduates (university, polytechnic and vocational school graduates) is displayed separately. Migration within three years of graduation is clearly less common for those who worked full-time before graduation. For example, approximately 19 per cent of university students who worked full-time and graduated in 2004 migrate, against 33 per cent among those who did not. Although this negative relationship between student employment and migration is relatively similar across the graduate groups, the decline in the migration rates is most noticeable for polytechnic and university graduates, as also illustrated by Figure 6.1.

6.5.2   Modelling

Our descriptive analysis revealed a negative relationship between working while studying and future mobility. Next we will investigate whether

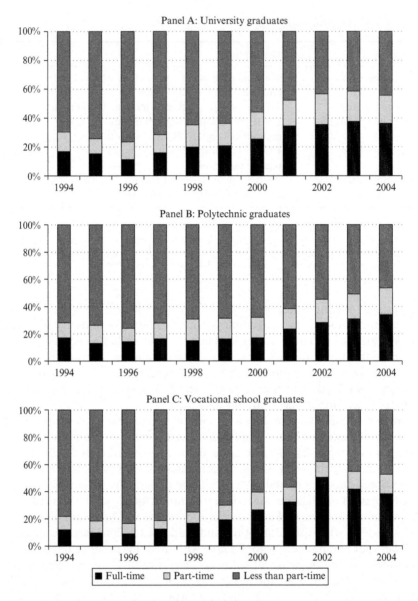

Note: No restrictions are placed on the matriculation year.

Source: Own calculations based on 7 per cent random sample.

Figure 6.3   Proportion of graduates working full-time, part-time, or less than part-time by level of education

Panel A: University graduates

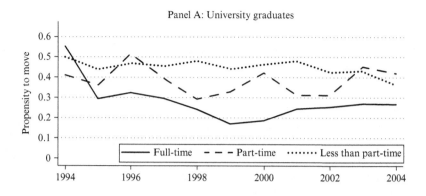

Panel B: Polytechnic graduates

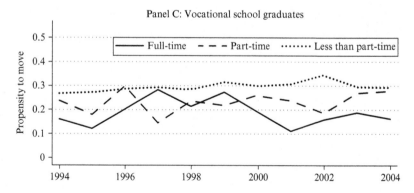

Panel C: Vocational school graduates

Note: No restrictions are placed on the matriculation year.

Source: Own calculations based on 7 per cent random sample.

Figure 6.4 Propensity to move within three years of graduation by prior work experience and level of education

this negative relationship holds even after controlling for confounding factors. First, Table 6.2 shows the baseline results for the entire country and regionally disaggregated results (Helsinki capital region vs the rest of the country). Then we show the relevance of the prior (school-to-school) mobility on the results. Throughout, we report average marginal effects on migration.[9]

The results for the entire country show, as expected, that the level of education is positively related to migration propensity (see column (1) in Table 6.2). The estimated average marginal effects indicate that university graduates with a master's degree have, on average, a 12 percentage-point higher propensity to migrate than vocational school graduates. The corresponding figure for the polytechnic graduates is 5 percentage points. Yet student employment is negatively related to migration propensity. Students who have worked full-time (part-time) are 7 (4) percentage points less likely to migrate than those who have not worked significantly prior to graduation (that is, the reference group). These findings suggest that better labour-market opportunities during studies significantly decrease migration later on.

As our probit model contains interaction terms between the level of education and working status, we can investigate how the relationship between student employment and migration varies with the level of education. Although students who work full-time have, on average, a 7 percentage-point lower propensity to move, the conditional marginal effects show that the negative relationship is particularly strong for university graduates (–12 per cent) and polytechnic graduates (–9 per cent) but not significant for vocational school graduates. Part-time work also hinders migration of polytechnic university graduates.

Migration decisions are likely to be differently determined in the Helsinki region than elsewhere in the country (cf. Haapanen and Tervo, 2012). The Helsinki region is the only metropolitan area in Finland, and approximately one-third of all economic activity occurs there. Therefore, columns (2) and (3) in Table 6.2 present the average marginal effects that have been estimated separately for sub-samples of students living inside and outside the Helsinki region. The results confirm our expectations. Having a master's (polytechnic) degree is related to only a 4 (0) percentage-point increase in migration propensity in the Helsinki region, whereas outside Helsinki, having a completed master's (polytechnic) degree is on average related to a 16 (7) percentage-point higher migration propensity than having a vocational school degree. This finding is in line with Haapanen and Tervo (2012): graduates from higher education tend to stay in the Helsinki region, where migration rates are lower than outside Helsinki. In our data, the average predicted migration rate is 12 per cent in the Helsinki region and 41 per cent elsewhere in the country.

Table 6.2   Average marginal effects on migration propensity by study region

Dependent variable: Migration (1/0)	Entire country	Study region is Helsinki	Study region is not Helsinki
	(1)	(2)	(3)
Level of education			
Master's degree[a]	0.119***	0.041**	0.159***
	(0.014)	(0.019)	(0.018)
Polytechnic degree[a]	0.049***	0.004	0.068***
	(0.012)	(0.016)	(0.015)
Working while studying			
Full-time work[b]	−0.070***	−0.038**	−0.095***
	(0.014)	(0.015)	(0.019)
Part-time work[b]	−0.039***	−0.052***	−0.030
	(0.014)	(0.016)	(0.019)
Conditional on master's degree			
Full-time work[b]	−0.118***	−0.068***	−0.134***
	(0.020)	(0.024)	(0.029)
Part-time work[b]	−0.047**	−0.077***	−0.017
	(0.022)	(0.027)	(0.030)
Conditional on polytechnic degree			
Full-time work[b]	−0.094***	−0.045*	−0.117***
	(0.022)	(0.024)	(0.031)
Part-time work[b]	−0.062***	−0.049*	−0.068**
	(0.024)	(0.028)	(0.031)
Conditional on vocational school degree			
Full-time work[b]	−0.022	−0.006	−0.057**
	(0.021)	(0.024)	(0.028)
Part-time work[b]	−0.020	−0.030	−0.016
	(0.022)	(0.024)	(0.030)
Log likelihood	−5,343	−999	−4,285
Pseudo *R*-squared	0.152	0.095	0.097
Average predicted migration rate	0.318	0.118	0.405
Number of observations	10,077	3,046	7,031

Notes: Average marginal effects (AMEs) are based on probit models that include main effects for the level of education and working status and the full set of interactions. All three models also contain the control variables described in Table 6.1. Marginal effects are computed as averages over all relevant observations. Conditional AMEs are computed only for the selected graduate population (for example, master's). *** $p < 0.01$, ** $p < 0.05$, * $p < 0.1$.
a.   Reference education is a vocational school degree (for example, 'full-time work' displays its AME on migration relative to working less than part-time for all graduates).
b.   Reference working status is less than part-time.

Table 6.2 shows that graduates who work full-time during their studies are more likely to stay in their study region than those who work less, but the negative relationship is stronger for those who live outside the Helsinki region (see columns (2) and (3)). There are many reasons why working while studying may have a smaller effect in the Helsinki region. The demand for student work is greater in the vicinity of the capital region, and high living expenditures, such as rent, can force students to work to finance their daily life. Elsewhere, rent and other living expenditures are more modest but jobs are also harder to find. Thus, local work experience might be appreciated by employers more outside the Helsinki region. It is also possible that other unobservable factors might explain the observed difference in the estimated relationship across the regions.

Finally, in Table 6.3, we have further divided the two regional samples according to graduates' prior mobility (stayers vs movers). In particular, stayers (movers) are defined as graduates whose study region is (not) the same as their high-school region. The results show that migration history does matter: average predicted migration rates across the four sub-samples (the bottom of Table 6.3) reveal that Helsinki region stayers are, on average, the least likely to move after graduation, whereas movers graduating outside Helsinki are the most migratory. As expected, movers are more geographically mobile after graduation than stayers in both regional samples. Nonetheless, both stayers and movers graduating from Helsinki are less mobile than graduates outside Helsinki.

For brevity, we only discuss the average marginal effects of working while studying on migration. Overall, results show that regardless of the sample, working is negatively (or insignificantly) related to graduate migration, but the level of education moderates the relationship. For graduates from vocational education, we do not find a significant (negative) relationship between working and graduate migration. The only exceptions are stayers outside Helsinki. For polytechnic graduates, working while studying notably decreases the migration propensity for the stayers but not for the movers. This result applies both to graduates from Helsinki and other regions. It is possible that polytechnic students who originate from the region are particularly well informed about possible job opportunities compared with students arriving from other regions. The reverse is true for university graduates: working while studying at a university slows down migration more for movers than for stayers in both types of regions. In sum, the level of education, prior mobility and type of region play a role in moderating the relationship between working while studying and graduate migration.

Table 6.3   *Average marginal effects on subsequent migration propensity by study region and prior migration status*

Dependent variable: Migration (1/0)	Study region is Helsinki		Study region is not Helsinki	
	(1) Stayer	(2) Mover	(3) Stayer	(4) Mover
Level of education				
Master's degree[a]	0.053**	−0.002	0.175***	0.082**
	(0.021)	(0.043)	(0.020)	(0.038)
Polytechnic degree[a]	0.012	−0.033	0.071***	0.038
	(0.016)	(0.042)	(0.017)	(0.039)
Working while studying				
Full-time work[b]	−0.041***	−0.035	−0.086***	−0.116***
	(0.016)	(0.038)	(0.021)	(0.041)
Part-time work[b]	−0.032**	−0.096**	−0.012	−0.094**
	(0.016)	(0.039)	(0.021)	(0.042)
Conditional on master's degree				
Full-time work[b]	−0.065***	−0.068	−0.090**	−0.201***
	(0.024)	(0.049)	(0.035)	(0.054)
Part-time work[b]	−0.028	−0.146***	0.036	−0.149**
	(0.031)	(0.048)	(0.035)	(0.059)
Conditional on polytechnic degree				
Full-time work[b]	−0.068***	0.002	−0.122***	−0.056
	(0.023)	(0.065)	(0.034)	(0.072)
Part-time work[b]	−0.068***	0.022	−0.077**	−0.000
	(0.024)	(0.086)	(0.034)	(0.079)
Conditional on vocational school degree				
Full-time work[b]	−0.011	−0.001	−0.064**	−0.050
	(0.024)	(0.075)	(0.031)	(0.075)
Part-time work[b]	−0.015	−0.103	0.000	−0.104
	(0.024)	(0.084)	(0.033)	(0.078)
Log likelihood	−570	−402	−3,506	−736
Pseudo *R*-squared	0.082	0.068	0.096	0.094
Average predicted migration rate	0.080	0.223	0.377	0.547
Number of observations	2,233	813	5,852	1,179

Notes: Stayers (movers) are individuals whose study region is (not) the same as their high-school region (NUTS 3). See also notes to Table 6.2.

6.6   DISCUSSION

This chapter has contributed to the prior literature studying the possible impacts that the intensity of work experience during studies has on student-level outcomes (cf. Darolia, 2014). Tertiary education takes many years to complete, but little is known about how students' activities during this period affect their future outcomes.

Our analysis has shown that working while studying is negatively related to migration. University and polytechnic graduates are observed to be more geographically mobile than similar vocational school graduates, but work experience accumulated during the studies decreases the migration probability after graduation. We find that the negative relationship between work and migration propensity is larger outside the Helsinki capital region and that the intensity of work matters, as full-time work hinders migration more than part-time work. Results are also heterogeneous to prior mobility.

Our results are consistent with the theoretical view that working while studying expands local labour-market opportunities such as local personal networks (and thus stability in the region), which is likely to reduce the propensity to move after graduation. The observed negative relationship between working while studying and graduate migration can also provide one explanation why Häkkinen (2006) found no earnings gains from work during university studies in Finland. Geographical mobility is often required to obtain the full benefits from investments in university education (cf. di Cintio and Grassi, 2013). Mobility has been shown to decrease the probability of over-education, because it improves education–job matches after graduation (Iammarino and Marinelli, 2015; see also Jauhiainen, 2011). In future investigations, it may be possible to quantify the magnitude to which geographical mobility mediates the effect of student employment on labour-market outcomes after graduation from higher education.

Further research should be undertaken to investigate the causal effects of student employment on graduate migration, for example by utilising institutional changes. Many countries have made changes to their education system during recent decades. These changes – exogenous to individuals' education decisions – can provide opportunities for robust results. The identification of the causal effects is also enhanced by the increased availability of micro-level register data that hold information on all individuals (that is, population) in a specific country (see for example Koster and Venhorst, 2014, for the Netherlands). Furthermore, student registers from educational institutions should be linked with employee–employer data. When these data become available for research, they will allow researchers to more finely control for observed heterogeneity.

Moreover, research is needed on the quality of job matches in which students work. Industrial or occupational mobility related to the field of studies might significantly improve future employment opportunities. However, low-skilled jobs (that is, 'McJobs') might place a negative stigma on the students. Hence, the quality of jobs may also have an effect on the future mobility. Finally, it would be interesting to study how working while studying relates to firm-level outcomes. Do firms have incentives to hire and invest in the students' human capital because they are particularly prone to move away from the study region after graduation?

6.7 CONCLUDING REMARKS

In this chapter, we have documented a negative relationship between working while studying and graduate migration. Our results for Finland also show that the negative relationship between working while studying and graduate migration is stronger for higher levels of education and outside the Helsinki capital region. Increases in student employment can thus provide one possible explanation for why geographic mobility among Finnish graduates from higher education has decreased recently over time and why some prior studies have found little effect of working while studying on labour-market success. In future investigations, it is important to investigate whether or not the decline in geographical mobility has worsened the match between jobs and graduates.

ACKNOWLEDGEMENTS

We would like to thank Kari Hämäläinen, Kristian Koerselman, Jani-Petri Laamanen and seminar participants at the RSAI – British and Irish Section Annual Conference (Cambridge, 2013), the Allecon meeting (Jyväskylä, 2013), the XXX Summer Meeting of Finnish Economists (Jyväskylä, 2013) and the Government Institute for Economic Research, VATT (Helsinki, 2013) for helpful comments. This project is supported by the Strategic Research Council at the Academy of Finland (no 293120 and no 303552). Hannu Karhunen would also like to thank the Alfred Kordelin Foundation and the Finnish Work Environment Fund (no 114440) for their financial support.

NOTES

*   Email: mika.p.haapanen@jyu.fi.
**   Email: hannu.a.karhunen@jyu.fi.
1.   In the United States, population-level migration rates have also declined dramatically since the end of the 1990s (Kaplan and Schulhofer-Wohl, 2012; Partridge et al., 2012).
2.   Molloy et al. (2014) show that labour-market transitions (switching employers or occupations) and geographical mobility are strongly positively correlated in the US. Hence, the stability in human capital accumulation might explain at least partly why migration has declined.
3.   The decision to move is often made simultaneously with job acceptance. For example, Détang-Dessendre and Molho (1999) find that unemployed individuals are more likely to undertake contracted migration as opposed to speculative long-distance migration.
4.   According to a survey by the Ministry of Education and Culture, one in five students had taken a student loan in the academic year 2005–06, and the major reason why students do not take student loans is their unwillingness to live in debt (Viuhko, 2006).
5.   From 1995 to 1997, students were allowed to earn €303 per subsidy month. Allowances were cut by 10 per cent on every €50 above the limit. Students who earned more than €1,180 per month on average were not entitled to student benefits. In 2008, earnings limits were raised by 30 per cent.
6.   Bachelor's degrees are not relevant here, because it was very uncommon to graduate with a bachelor's degree from universities before the Bologna process was adopted in Finland in 2005.
7.   Nomenclature des Unités Territoriales Statistiques.
8.   Months of employment are also available in our data, but we believe that earnings are a more accurate measurement of work, particularly for students. Students can work irregularly for a few hours per day. In the administrative files one hour of work per day is counted as a work-day, and fourteen work-days is registered as a work-month. This might distort the measurement of work particularly for students who are relatively distinct from the remainder of the labour force.
9.   Probit estimates are available on request from the authors.

REFERENCES

Abreu, M., A. Faggian and P. McCann (2015), 'Migration and inter-industry mobility of UK graduates', *Journal of Economic Geography*, 15(2), 353–385.

Ahlin, L., M. Andersson and P. Thulin (2014), 'Market thickness and the early labour market career of university graduates: an urban advantage?', *Spatial Economic Analysis*, 9(4), 396–419.

Avdic, D. and M. Gartell (2015), 'Working while studying? Student aid design and socioeconomic achievement disparities in higher education', *Labour Economics*, 33, 26–40.

Bell, M. and E. Charles-Edwards (2013), 'Cross-national comparisons of internal migration: an update on global patterns and trends', *Population Division Technical Paper*, No 2013/1, New York: United Nations Department of Economic and Social Affairs.

Blanchard, O.J., L.F. Katz, R.E. Hall and B. Eichengreen (1992), 'Regional evolutions', *Brookings Papers on Economic Activity*, 1, 1–75.

Böckerman, P. and M. Haapanen (2013), 'The effect of polytechnic reform on migration', *Journal of Population Economics*, 26(2), 593–617.

Böckerman, P., U. Hämäläinen and R. Uusitalo (2009), 'Labour market effects of the polytechnic education reform: the Finnish experience', *Economics of Education Review*, 28(6), 672–681.

Body, K.M.D., L. Bonnal and J.F. Giret (2014), 'Does student employment really impact academic achievement? The case of France', *Applied Economics*, 46(25), 3061–3073.

Borjas, G. (1999), 'The economic analysis of immigration', in O. Ashenfelter and D. Card (eds), *Handbook of Labor Economics*, Amsterdam and New York: North Holland, pp. 1697–1760.

Bowles, S. (1970), 'Migration as investment: empirical tests of the human investment approach to geographical mobility', *The Review of Economics and Statistics*, 52(4), 356–362.

Champion, T. and I. Shuttleworth (2015), 'Are people moving home less? An analysis of address changing in England and Wales, 1971–2011, using the ONS longitudinal study', SERC discussion papers, 0177, London: Spatial Economics Research Centre.

Cintio, M. di and E. Grassi (2013), 'Internal migration and wages of Italian university graduates', *Papers in Regional Science*, 92(1), 119–140.

Cockx, B. and M. Picchio (2012), 'Are short-lived jobs stepping stones to long-lasting jobs?', *Oxford Bulletin of Economics and Statistics*, 74(5), 646–675.

Darolia, R. (2014), 'Working (and studying) day and night: heterogeneous effects of working on the academic performance of full-time and part-time students', *Economics of Education Review*, 38, 38–50.

DaVanzo, J. (1983), 'Repeat migration in the United States: who moves back and who moves on?', *The Review of Economics and Statistics*, 65(4), 552–559.

Davis, J. (2012), 'School enrollment and work status: 2011', *American Community Briefs*, 11–14, U.S. Census Bureau.

Détang-Dessendre, C. and I. Molho (1999), 'Migration and changing employment status: a hazard function analysis', *Journal of Regional Science*, 39(1), 103–123.

Diem, A. (2015), 'Overeducation among graduates from universities of applied sciences: determinants and consequences', *Journal of Economic & Financial Studies*, 3, 63–77.

Doiron, D. and T. Gørgens (2008), 'State dependence in youth labor market experiences and the evaluation of policy interventions', *Journal of Econometrics*, 145(1–2), 81–97.

Faggian, A., P. McCann and S. Sheppard (2006), 'An analysis of ethnic differences in UK graduate migration behaviour', *The Annals of Regional Science*, 40(2), 461–471.

Faggian, A., P. McCann and S. Sheppard (2007), 'Some evidence that women are more mobile than men: gender differences in UK graduate migration behavior', *Journal of Regional Science*, 47(3), 517–539.

Faggian, A., J. Corcoran and P. McCann (2013), 'Modelling geographical graduate job search using circular statistics', *Papers in Regional Science*, 9(2), 329–343.

Geel, R. and U. Backes-Gellner (2012), 'Earning while learning: when and how student employment is beneficial', *Labour*, 26(3), 313–340.

Glocker, D. (2011), 'The effect of student aid on the duration of study', *Economics of Education Review*, 30(1), 177–190.

Gordon, I.R. and I. Molho (1995), 'Duration dependence in migration behaviour: cumulative inertia versus stochastic change', *Environment and Planning A*, 27(12), 1961–1975.

Groen, J.A. (2010), 'The effect of college location on migration of college-educated labor', *Journal of Econometrics*, 121(1–2), 125–142.

Greenwood, M.J. (1997), 'Internal migration in developed countries', in M.R. Rosenzweig and O. Stark (eds), *Handbook of Population and Family Economics*, Vol. 1, Part B, Amsterdam: Elsevier, pp. 647–720.

Gunnes, T., L.J. Kirkebøen and M. Rønning (2013), 'Financial incentives and study duration in higher education', *Labour Economics*, 25, 1–11.

Haapanen, M. and H. Tervo (2012), 'Migration of the highly educated: evidence from residence spells of university graduates', *Journal of Regional Science*, 52(4), 587–605.

Häkkinen, I. (2006), 'Working while enrolled in a university: does it pay?', *Labour Economics*, 13(2), 167–189.

Häkkinen, I. and R. Uusitalo (2003), 'The effect of a student aid reform on graduation: a duration analysis', Working Paper 8, Department of Economics, Uppsala University.

Hotz, V.J., L. Xu, M. Tienda and A. Ahituv (2002), 'Are there returns to the wages of young men from working while in school?', *The Review of Economics and Statistics*, 84(2), 221–236.

Huff, J.O. and W.A.V. Clark (1978), 'Cumulative stress and cumulative inertia: a behavioral model of the decision to move', *Environment and Planning A*, 10(10), 1101–1119.

Iammarino, S. and E. Marinelli (2015), 'Education–job (mis) match and inter-regional migration: Italian university graduates' transition to work', *Regional Studies*, 49(5), 866–882.

Jauhiainen, S. (2011), 'Overeducation in the Finnish regional labour markets', *Papers in Regional Science*, 90(3), 573–588.

Jewell, S. (2014), 'The impact of working while studying on educational and labour market outcomes', *Business and Economics Journal*, 5(3), doi: 10.4172/2151-6219.1000110.

Kaplan, G. and S. Schulhofer-Wohl (2012), 'Understanding the long-run decline in interstate migration', NBER Working Paper, 18507.

Koster, S. and V.A. Venhorst (2014), 'Moving shop: residential and business relocation by the highly educated self-employed', *Spatial Economic Analysis*, 9(4), 436–464.

Light, A. (2001), 'In-school work experience and the returns to schooling', *Journal of Labor Economics*, 19(1), 65–93.

Malamud, O. and A. Wozniak (2012), 'The impact of college on migration: evidence from the Vietnam generation', *Journal of Human Resources*, 47(4), 913–950.

Marinelli, E. (2013), 'Sub-national graduate mobility and knowledge flows: an exploratory analysis of onward- and return-migrants in Italy', *Regional Studies*, 47(10), 1618–1633.

Ministry of Education and Culture (2012), 'Opintotuen rakenteen kehittäminen 2012', Opetus- ja kulttuuriministeriön työryhmämuistioita ja selvityksiä 2012, 29, Helsinki. (Text only in Finnish.)

Molho, I. (1995), 'Migrant inertia, accessibility and local unemployment', *Economica*, 62(245), 123–132.

Molitor, C.J. and D.E. Leigh (2005), 'In-school work experience and the returns to two-year and four-year colleges', *Economics of Education Review*, 24(4), 459–468.

Molloy, R., C.L. Smith and A. Wozniak (2011), 'Internal migration in the United States', *The Journal of Economic Perspectives*, 25(3), 173–196.

Molloy, R., C.L. Smith and A. Wozniak (2014), 'Declining migration within the US: the role of the labor market', NBER Working Paper, 20065.

Mroz, T.A. and T.H. Savage (2006), 'The long-term effects of youth unemployment', *Journal of Human Resources*, 41(2), 259–293.

Nakosteen, R.A., O. Westerlund and M. Zimmer (2008), 'Migration and self-selection: measured earnings and latent characteristics', *Journal of Regional Science*, 48(4), 769–788.

Neumark, D. (2002), 'Youth labor markets in the United States: shopping around vs. staying put', *The Review of Economics and Statistics*, 84(3), 462–482.

Neumark, D. and M. Joyce (2001), 'Evaluating school-to-work programs using the new NLSY', *The Journal of Human Resources*, 36(4), 666–702.

Newbold, K.B. (2001), 'Counting migrants and migrations: comparing lifetime and fixed-interval return and onward migration', *Economic Geography*, 77(1), 23–40.

Nivalainen, S. (2004), 'Determinants of family migration: short moves vs. long moves', *Journal of Population Economics*, 17(1), 157–175.

Nonis, S.A. and G.I. Hudson (2006), 'Academic performance of college students: influence of time spent studying and working', *Journal of Education for Business*, 81(3), 151–159.

Oreopoulos, P., T. Von Wachter and A. Heisz (2012), 'The short- and long-term career effects of graduating in a recession', *American Economic Journal: Applied Economics*, 4(1), 1–29.

OSF (2012), 'Entrance to education [e-publication]', *Applicants to Education by Educational Sector and Prior Education in 2012*, Helsinki: Statistics Finland, available at: http://tilastokeskus.fi/til/khak/2012/02/khak_2012_02_2014-04-29_tau_002_en.html (accessed 14 December 2014).

OSF (2016), 'Employment of students [e-publication]', Helsinki: Statistics Finland, available at: http://www.stat.fi/til/opty/index_en.html (accessed 21 March 2016).

Partridge, M.D., D.S. Rickman, M.R. Olfert and K. Ali (2012), 'Dwindling US internal migration: evidence of spatial equilibrium or structural shifts in local labor markets?', *Regional Science and Urban Economics*, 42(1), 375–388.

Ruhm, C.J. (1997), 'Is high school employment consumption or investment?', *Journal of Labor Economics*, 15(4), 735–776.

Ryan, P. (2001), 'The school-to-work transition: a cross-national perspective', *Journal of Economic Literature*, 39(1), 34–92.

Saks, R.E. and A. Wozniak (2011), 'Labor reallocation over the business cycle: new evidence from internal migration', *Journal of Labor Economics*, 29, 697–739.

Saniter, N. and T. Siedler (2014), 'Door opener or waste of time? The effects of student internships on labor market outcomes', IZA Discussion Paper, No 8141.

Sjaastad, L.A. (1962), 'The costs and returns of human migration', *Journal of Political Economy*, 70(5), 80–93.

Statistics Finland (2000), *Income Distribution Statistics*, Helsinki: Official Statistics of Finland.

Statistics Finland (2013), 'Oppilaitostilastot 2012', Helsinki: Official Statistics of Finland. (Summary in English.)

Sullivan, P. (2010), 'Empirical evidence on occupation and industry specific human capital', *Labour Economics*, 17(3), 567–580.

Triventi, M. (2014), 'Does working during higher education affect students' academic progression?', *Economics of Education Review*, 41, 1–13.

Venhorst, V., J. Van Dijk and L. Van Wissen (2010), 'Do the best graduates leave the peripheral areas of the Netherlands?', *Tijdschrift voor economische en sociale geografie*, 101(5), 521–537.
Venhorst, V., J. Van Dijk and L. Van Wissen (2011), 'An analysis of trends in spatial mobility of Dutch graduates', *Spatial Economic Analysis*, 6(1), 57–82.
Viuhko, M. (2006),'Opiskelijatutkimus 2006: Korkeakouluopiskelijoiden toimeentulo ja työssäkäynti', *Opetusministeriön julkaisuja*, 51. (Text only in Finnish.)
Wachter, T. von and S. Bender (2006), 'In the right place at the wrong time: the role of firms and luck in young workers' careers', *The American Economic Review*, 96(5), 1679–1705.
Wozniak, A. (2010), 'Are college graduates more responsive to distant labor market opportunities?', *Journal of Human Resources*, 45(4), 944–970.
Yamaguchi, S. (2012), 'Tasks and heterogeneous human capital', *Journal of Labor Economics*, 30(1), 1–53.

7. Graduates and migration in France: between urban labour-market attraction and interest in amenities

Cécile Détang-Dessendre* and Virginie Piguet**

7.1 INTRODUCTION

France is one of the OECD (Organisation for Economic Co-operation and Development) countries in which the level of education increased dramatically between two generations: in 2009, the proportion of 25–34-year-olds with at least upper secondary education was 43 per cent, more than twice the proportion of 55–64-year-olds (OECD, 2011). In contrast, the average increase across the OECD countries was around 65 per cent. This increase affects all areas from large urban centres to the most remote rural areas. However, as in other OECD countries, there is still a positive relationship between the size of the metropolitan area and the share of the population with a university degree. Paris shows an extreme configuration, with a very strong over-representation of graduates, especially those with a master's or doctoral degree, and very few residents with lower qualifications or with short vocational training. At the same time, the share of the population with a university degree is higher in the south and west of France than in other regions.

As noted by Faggian and Franklin (2014), human capital is important both for individuals and for society. There are two ways for a region to increase its human capital stock: to increase the level of its population (and retain educated people) and to attract educated people from other regions. Beyond the stock effect that we will characterise, this chapter focuses on migration flows by age and educational level. Starting from the determinants of individual migration choices (Greenwood, 1997), we build some hypotheses on the main pull and push factors that affect migration flows of educated people, depending on age, between local labour markets. In particular, we distinguish factors that play a role in the professional and residential dimensions of migration choices. We introduce the idea that as well as the characteristics of origin and destination areas, the differences *between* the two are also very important.

We estimate extended gravity models to explain origin–destination flows of people between 288 local labour markets. The aim is to delineate the major mechanisms of the recent migration waves in France. Because of an excess of zeros, we estimate a zero-inflated negative binomial (ZINB) model. Beyond the classical results of gravity models (impacts of distance and population), we show that migration flows of young educated people are essentially linked with the characteristics of local labour markets, rather than with climates and amenities. The characteristics of the destination area impact flows of educated people more than flows of less-educated people.

Our chapter is organised as follows. In Section 7.2, based on the economic literature, we outline our major hypothesis. Section 7.3 presents the data and our empirical strategy. Section 7.4 draws a picture of the spatial distribution of educated people in France, as well as of migration flows between different types of areas on a rural–urban gradient. Section 7.5 provides and discusses the empirical results of the gravity model and Section 7.6 concludes.

7.2   THEORETICAL BACKGROUND AND MAIN HYPOTHESIS

In a microeconomic framework, migration results from the comparison of utilities provided by different locations net of any migration costs. Individuals obtain a certain utility level from each location, depending on their preferences and endowments, and on the characteristics of the location in terms of the labour market, housing and amenities (Greenwood, 1997). Many studies have analysed the impact of educational level on migration decisions and show that young educated people move the most (see, for example, Détang-Dessendre et al., 2008 for France; Faggian et al., 2007 for the UK; Haapanen and Tervo, 2012 for Finland; or Brown and Scott, 2012 for Canada). Individual characteristics such as age, educational level and marital status influence individual migration decisions, as do expected wages, housing prices and amenities (Plantinga et al., 2013). The position in the life cycle also explains the heterogeneity of migration behaviour (Détang-Dessendre et al., 2008), as younger people give priority to employment motivations before taking residential motivations into account when they get older.

The factors that attract, repel or retain people in a region constitute another way to analyse migration flows, especially from a regional policy viewpoint. To that end, gravity models became very popular in the migration literature in the mid twentieth century (Zipf, 1946; Lowry, 1966). The basic model hypothesises that migration flows are directly related to the size of the origin and destination zones and inversely related to distance. The modified versions of the gravity model introduce variables to give behavioural content. As Etzo (2011) argues, they offer a framework to capture local economic, labour-market, environmental and policy conditions driving migration flows. Greenwood and Hunt (2003) point out that gravity models and the migration decision process have not always been tight. Nevertheless, Guimarães et al. (2003) show that by taking advantage of an equivalence relation between the likelihood function of the conditional logit and the Poisson regression it is possible, under certain circumstances, to model the number of flows between different areas instead of the individual choice.

The number of migrants from region i to region j, M_{ij} depends on the population size in each region P_i and P_j, on the distance between the two regions D_{ij} and on s exogenous variables $X_{s,i}$ characterising the origin i and $X_{s,j}$ characterising the destination j.

$$M_{ij} = k^{\gamma_0} \frac{P_i^{\gamma_1} P_j^{\gamma_2}}{D_{ij}^{\gamma_3}} \prod_{s=1}^{n} \frac{X_{s,j}^{\alpha_s}}{X_{s,i}^{\beta_s}}$$

After log-transformation, the regression equation is specified as

$$\log M_{ij} = \gamma_0 \log k + \gamma_1 \log P_i + \gamma_2 \log P_j - \gamma_3 \log D_{ij}$$
$$+ \sum_{s=1}^{n} (\alpha_s \log X_{s,j} - \beta_s \log X_{s,i}) \qquad (7.1)$$

The negative impact of the distance on migration has been attributed to several factors, which include direct costs of moving, opportunity costs, information costs and psychic costs of moving (Greenwood, 1997, p. 648). For all these reasons, distance is introduced into the migration model as a proxy for all these costs (Plantinga et al., 2013).

Thisse and Zenou (1995) show that greater density of labour supply and demand leads to easier matches in urban labour markets. Conversely, employment turnover is lower in low-density (rural) labour markets and jobs are thus steadier (Jayet, 2000). Zenou (2009) argues that not only are employment turnover and nominal wages higher in urban than in rural labour markets, but also that technological job opportunities are more prevalent than those for more basic jobs. Furthermore, due to urbanised economies, high skills are better remunerated in urban areas. Therefore, the attraction of urban labour-market areas (LMAs) in terms of employment probability and wages rises with education. The spatial differential in expected income in favour of urban areas thus increases with the worker's skill level, so that migration toward urban areas (big labour markets) can be particularly profitable for educated workers, while low-skilled workers have fewer incentives to leave smaller LMAs to find a job.

Size will not capture the entire impact of labour market characteristics in structure and in dynamic. In a disequilibrium approach, people will choose areas with higher economic perspectives. Educated people will be attracted to a local labour market with a high share of executive jobs and a low unemployment rate. Considering that highly educated people are more likely to find information of good quality, the impact of characteristics of areas should be higher for them, especially characteristics of destination areas as information is more difficult to obtain.

In addition to the disparities in earnings, local tax plays a role in differentiating total income. However, the impact is difficult to measure: local residential taxes on households are determined by characteristics of the housing (for example, location, size, comfort, etc.) and on income level. If we only consider an income effect, people should leave areas with a higher local residential tax level and move to areas with a lower level. However, the impact may depend on income and the link may not be linear, as people with a very low income may be exempted from taxation. Moreover, the local tax level can also capture the local level of the public services offered as taxation is the major source of local jurisdiction revenues. It could be posited that local residential tax will be of secondary interest to young people as they are less concerned by public services (in particular healthcare) and especially to low-qualified people, as they may not pay it.

We now consider residential motivations. Assuming that it is reasonable to treat households as price-takers in housing markets, the effects of housing prices on migration decisions can be measured in studies using household data. Nevertheless, housing prices are endogenous to area-level migration (Mueser and Graves, 1995), so this variable is typically excluded from analyses with aggregate data. Since the development of the equilibrium assumption in migration analysis (Graves, 1979), moving decisions are significantly related to local amenities, namely climate (Mueser and Graves, 1995; Hunt and Mueller, 2004; Cheshire and Magrini, 2006), recreational opportunities (Lewis et al., 2002) or cultural amenities (Clark and Hunter, 1992). The impact of amenities should increase with age, and, following Faggian and Franklin (2014), we assume that for the youngest-qualified, amenities might not act as a strong 'retention' factor but might act as 'attractive local characteristics' (p. 384).

The debate on the impact of regional differences, including income and local amenities, and on migration choice is the fulcrum of the equilibrium–disequilibrium controversy. Hicks in 1932, quoted by Greenwood (1997), pointed out that regional differences in wages would cause a 'gradual flow of labour' (p. 73). He also believed that regional differences would persist because of the 'indirect attractions of living in certain localities' (ibid., p. 74). Very little research based on the gravity model has tested the impact of destination–origin differences for the exogenous variables to explain the origin–destination flows. Lewer and Van den Berg (2008) is an exception in an international context. We test both specifications, first considering origin and destination characteristics and, second, the differences between the two.

7.3   DATA AND ECONOMETRIC METHOD

Data on population, migration and employment came from the French National Censuses (1999 and 2008) collected by the French National Institute of Statistics and Economic Studies (INSEE). Information is available by *commune*, which is the smallest administrative area in France (there were 36,570 communes in 2008). We aggregate them by *zone d'emploi* (ZE). This spatial classification, built and revised by the INSEE in 2010, divides French territory into 297 areas (excluding Corsica). The goal is to define areas where workers live and work, that is, local labour markets. The definition of employment areas is based on the observation of workers' commuting, maximising the number of within-area migrations between work and home. The lowest values of the ratio of the number of workers living and working in the employment area to the number of workers in the area concern employment areas in the Ile-de-France region (the region of the capital city, Paris) and may range up to less than 40 per cent. So, following Détang-Dessendre et al. (2016), we aggregated nineteen greater Paris region zones into ten zones to form more independent zones in order to obtain a ratio of over two-thirds for all areas. Then we worked on 288 employment areas (see Figure 7.1). On average, the areas cover 1,860 km² with around 215,000 inhabitants. As a comparison, US counties are spread over 2,900 km² on average with 100,000 inhabitants (US Census Bureau, 2015).

Next, migration flows between ZEs are built using the declarations in the census on the previous residential location (five years before) of people aged over 5 in 2008. We focus on two populations: 20–64-year-olds to analyse the core of the French active population, and 20–29-year-olds to capture youth specifics. The question 'where did you live on 1–01–2003?'

Table 7.1   Description of the variables

Variables	Source	Mean[a] (standard deviation)
Distance between the 288 ZEs	Own calculation based on Odomatrix, in minutes	373.84 (164.53)
Characteristics of the population		
Population	INSEE, National	202,285 (397,858)
Share 20–29 in educated population	Census in 1999	23.71 (4.58)
Share 20–29 in low-educated population		11.85 (1.59)
Share educated in population aged 20–64		16.26 (4.46)
Characteristics of local labour market		
Share high-qualified employment (HQE)	INSEE, National census in 1999	16.51 (4.19)
Unemployment rate		12.56 (3.44)
Characteristics of residential area		
Local tax rate	DGFIP, 1999	12.61 (3.30)
January cold days	Météo	3.40 (2.37)
July hot days	France, 1971–2000	5.80 (3.82)
January rainy days		10.83 (2.31)
Coastline	Own construction	0.19 (0.39)
High share of natural area	French Ministry of Environment, 2007	0.32 (0.47)

Note: a. The statistics are calculated on 288*287 (82,656) origin–destination ZEs for distance and on 288 zones for all other variables.

and the current location serve to measure the residential change between two periods. It thus undervalues the migrations, as neither multiple migrations nor return migrations are taken into account. In this research, we analyse internal migrations.[1] We then compute the 82,656 flows between the 288 ZEs.

Table 7.1 lists the sources and gives descriptive statistics on the variables introduced in the model. Distances between areas are calculated using the Odomatrix 2013 software (Hilal, 2010). It measures time–distance by road[2] between poles (city halls of largest cities) in the ZEs. To avoid an endogeneity problem, population sizes and characteristics of areas are considered in 1999. Following Greenwood (1997), the population composition of the origin is controlled (share of the 20–29 bracket and share of the educated population, that is, having a university diploma) to capture the impact of population at risk. The share of executive jobs tied to intellectual services, design/research, business-to-business trade, management, culture and leisure (share HQE in Table 1) and unemployment rate are introduced to capture the local labour-market conditions. The local residential tax rate (*'taxe d'habitation'*) has to be paid as soon as people use the dwelling (as permanent housing or not) and is based on housing characteristics. Climate variables are built using municipal data produced by Joly et al. (2010) using the records from Météo France in the years 1971 to 2000. We retain the number of days colder than –5°C (23°F) in January, the number of days higher than 30°C (86°F) in July and the number of rainy days in January. Coastline is a dummy variable for proximity to ocean or sea. Finally, the high share of natural area is a dummy variable which means that the proportion of the surface area included in at least one protected area or area of natural interest is over 30 per cent.

The starting point for the econometric strategy is Guimarães et al. (2003). The basic idea is to estimate a Poisson model explaining the number of flows between each pair of origin–destination areas (equation (7.1)). Nevertheless, this count data model is valid only if the conditional variance and the mean of the dependent variable are equal. This is far from what can be observed in our case: the variances of the flows are more than ten times the means (Table 7.2) and more than half the couples in ZEs have zero flows. The negative binomial (NB) model, by introducing an individual unobserved effect in the conventional Poisson model can solve the problem of overdispersion of the data (Greene, 2012). There is a debate about the excess of zeros and the need to implement a zero-inflated negative binomial (ZINB) model (Allison, 2012). In that case, zero and non-zero flows are treated differently by combining a binary process with a count process and zero flows can arise either from the logit specification or from the negative binomial specification. Equation (7.2) gives $f(y)$ the

Table 7.2   Characteristics of the flows

	20–64		20–29	
	University diploma	Below university	University diploma	Below university
Number of non-zero flows:	39,758	47,555	27,885	32,873
N (share)	(48.1)	(57.5)	(33.7)	(39.8)
Number of flows: mean	26.1	32.5	12.2	12
(standard deviation)	(312.2)	(341.1)	(135.8)	(111.6)

probability function of the outcome y in the ZINB model with p the probability that the outcome is zero and $g(y)$ the negative binomial probability function (Winkelmann, 2008).

$$f(y) = p(1 - \min(y, 1)) + (1 - p)g(y) \qquad y = 0, 1, 2, \ldots \qquad (7.2)$$

There is no economic reason to suspect two types of zero for flows or to justify the need for a two-regime model such as ZINB. Nevertheless, the Vuong test, comparing ZINB and NB models, suggests that in our case the ZINB model fits the data better and is a significant improvement over a standard negative binomial model (see Table 7.4).

7.4   STATISTICAL EVIDENCE ON POPULATION STOCKS AND FLOWS

Before estimating our empirical model, we describe the stocks of population of employment areas, given the size of the largest urban centre of the zone. Then we discuss migration flows by education level. We distinguish five categories of zones (Figure 7.1): (i) ZEs whose largest pole has more than 100,000 inhabitants in the Ile-de-France administrative region; (ii) other ZEs whose largest pole has more than 100,000 inhabitants; (iii) ZEs whose largest pole has between 50,000 and 99,999 inhabitants; (iv) ZEs whose largest pole has between 25,000 and 49,999 inhabitants; and (v) ZEs organised around the smallest cities, of less than 25,000 inhabitants.

7.4.1   The French Population Aged 20–64 Years in a Few Figures

In line with the historic trend, the average educational level continued to rise between 1999 and 2008: at the end of the period, almost 30 per cent of the population aged 20–64 had completed a university diploma (level 1–3 in Table 7.3). This share increased by 34 per cent over the decade. The spatial differentiation of education level is a well-known fact, with the urban population being on average more educated than the rural one (Détang-Dessendre and Piguet, 2016). A hierarchy appears within urban areas depending on the size of the major city centre of the area: in the 'Paris employment area', more than 42 per cent of the population of interest had completed a university diploma, with this figure rising to more than 59 per cent in Paris city centre. The share then decreases with the size of the urban centre, and is very similar in the three smallest types of areas, between 20 and 23 per cent (urban centres smaller than 100,000 inhabitants). In other words, concerning university diplomas, three main groups appear: ZEs

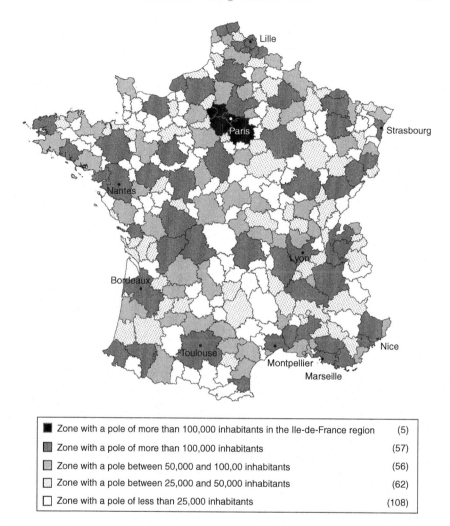

Figure 7.1   French zones d'emploi (ZEs)

under the direct influence of Paris, 'urban ZEs' (under the influence of large cities, more than 100,000 inhabitants) and areas under the influence of medium and small city centres. The reverse hierarchy emerges at the other end of the educational scale.

Nevertheless, a spatial catching-up process emerges (essentially at the baccalauréat and undergraduate levels) which is driven by a stronger increase in education level in smaller areas: +32 per cent (+15 per cent)

Table 7.3 *Highest year of school or degree completed in 1999 and 2008 for French residents aged 20–64 (as a percentage)*

Years	ZE with Paris as city centre		Other ZE with city centre >100,000 inh.		ZE with city centre 50,000–99,999 inh.		ZE with city centre 25,000–49,999 inh.		ZE with city centre <25,000 inh.		France	
	1999	2008	1999	2008	1999	2008	1999	2008	1999	2008	1999	2008
Level 6[a]	28.6	22.9	32.6	25.1	36.9	28.0	38.5	29.6	39.8	30.2	33.8	26.1
Level 5	20.5	16.0	28.3	25.5	32.0	30.5	32.0	30.8	32.6	32.1	28.3	25.8
Level 4	16.9	18.4	16.5	19.1	14.9	18.5	14.3	18.0	13.7	17.7	15.8	18.6
Level 3	13.1	15.1	11.5	15.1	9.4	13.3	9.0	12.7	8.3	12.1	10.9	14.3
Level 2 and 1	20.9	27.6	11.2	15.2	6.8	9.7	6.3	8.8	5.6	7.9	11.1	15.2

Note: a. Correspondence between French levels and US categories: Level 6, 9th and below; Level 5, short vocational training generally two years after junior high school; Level 4, 'baccalauréat', 12th grade; Level 3, undergraduate; Level 1 and 2, pool postgraduate (MA, MS and PhD).

Sources: INSEE RP 1999 and EAR 2008.

between 1999 and 2008 in the Paris ZE for postgraduates (undergraduates) and +42 per cent (+44 per cent) in the smallest ZEs. The distribution of qualifications reflects the spatial distribution of the education level, with a strong concentration of executives in areas under the influence of Paris or big cities (Aubert and Détang-Dessendre, 2014). In fact, more than 40 per cent of the active population in the Paris city centre work as executives (28 per cent in the zone with Paris as pole). This share drops to 8 per cent in the smallest ZEs. The same profile, although smaller in magnitude, appears for technicians and the associated professional group. Blue-collar workers are only the third group in volume in France in 2009, but comprise the first in the smallest ZEs, with more than 30 per cent of the active population. In the ZE of the biggest cities their share is 23 per cent (14 per cent in the Paris area).

7.4.2 Migration Flows of Educated People

9.6 million French residents aged 20–64 in 2008 moved between munici-palities during the 2003–2008 period (27 per cent of the whole population of interest). Among them, about half changed employment area (around 14 per cent). If we consider the population who completed a university diploma, more than 20 per cent changed ZE during the same period, providing a first illustration of the higher residential mobility of educated people.

The volume of cross flows between different types of ZE foreshadows the intricacy of the motivation for migration between residential and pro-fessional (Figure 7.2). With 1.2 million out- and in-flows from and to the ZEs of the big city centres (excluding the Paris ZE), the balance is close to zero. The ZEs organised around medium and small poles gain popula-tions in their exchanges with the ZEs of big cities, including the Paris ZE. Conversely, these areas lose residents in all their exchanges. Focusing on educated people (level 3, 2 and 1), the deficit of the Paris area is smaller and its attractiveness is highlighted for the youngest group (20–29). Regarding the latter, the balance is in favour of Paris areas in all cases. The ZEs organised around the other big cities also attract the youngest group, but to a lesser extent.

7.5 GRAVITY MODEL ESTIMATION

We estimate the extended gravity model on the active 20–64 population and on the 20–29 population, distinguishing people with high and low levels of education. We focus the discussion on the educated population,

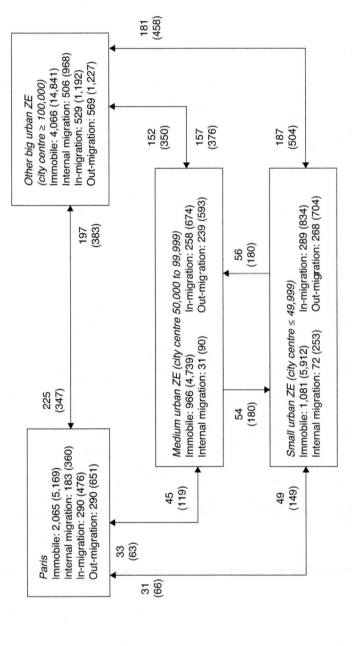

Figure 7.2   Migration flows 2003–2008 of educated people between different types of local labour markets in thousands, all 20–64 years in brackets

using the other results to emphasise the specificity of the former. We only produce the count model results. Keep in mind that the estimates of the first regime are coherent with the parameters of the second regime.[3]

The discussion of the results in Table 7.4 starts from the gravity variables which, as in previous analysis, have all the expected signs and statistically significant coefficients (Greenwood and Hunt, 2003; LeSage and Pace, 2008; Etzo, 2011). The share of young qualified people in the population is introduced to take into account the impact of the structure of the population. Indeed, as Greenwood (1997) suggested, an area with a young, educated population may register more departures as its population is more likely to migrate. The coefficient estimated for travel time indicates that migration flows between two zones decrease when travel time increases. Regarding the cost of migration, we expected a smaller impact of distance on the flows of the youngest, highly educated people. In fact, results show a similar impact of distance across all estimations; the difference between qualified and less-qualified people is weak and null for the youngest age group. Population size positively affects migration flows: a positive sign for both origin and destination zones suggests that bigger local labour markets lead to more in- and out-migrations. The bigger the area, the higher the flows of educated people toward the area. This is also true when we focus on the youngest.

As expected, labour-market characteristics act to explain migration flows. Labour markets with a high share of executive jobs firstly retain educated people (negative and significant coefficient of the share at the origin) and secondly attract them (positive and significant coefficient of the share at the destination). The first effect seems to be higher than the second. The unemployment rate also acts as a push factor when the rate is high in a local labour market (increases out-migration and decreases in-migration). The push factor at the destination seems to be higher than at the origin: for educated people, it is the only significant effect while both act for less educated young people. For the educated, it is not so much that a depressive local labour market leads people to migrate, but that a depressive labour market definitely does not attract people.

Concerning residential motivations, the impact of the local tax rate is ambiguous. Across all active flows, a high level of local tax has a negative impact on in-migration flows, especially for the less educated. However, the out-flows including the youngest, active, educated people seem to be positively correlated with the local tax, while the out-flows of the less educated are negatively correlated.

Climate characteristics act as expected: more cold days in January in an area (hot days in July) decreases (increases) the in-flows. The number of rainy days also has a negative impact on the volume of in-flows. The

Table 7.4   ZINB models: estimation of the 288*287 migration flows

	20–64		20–29	
	University diploma	Below university	University diploma	Below university
Log(Distance)	-1.405***	-1.460***	-1.435***	-1.429***
	(0.015)	(0.015)	(0.015)	(0.015)
Log(Population of OZE[a])	0.710***	0.704***	0.637***	0.619***
	(0.023)	(0.040)	(0.027)	(0.026)
Log(Population of DZE[b])	0.764***	0.687***	0.763***	0.666***
	(0.016)	(0.013)	(0.020)	(0.016)
Log(Share 20–29 in educated population in OZE)	0.061	–	0.367***	–
	(0.107)		(0.126)	
Log(Share 20–29 in less-educated population in OZE)	–	0.552***	–	-0.044
		(0.168)		(0.131)
Log(Share educated in population aged 20–64 in OZE)	1.167***	0.452***	1.692***	0.546***
	(0.089)	(0.129)	(0.121)	(0.102)
Log(Share HQE in OZE)	-0.298***	-0.151	-0.934***	-0.470***
	(0.101)	(0.163)	(0.127)	(0.134)
Log(Share HQE in DZE)	0.272***	-0.342***	0.601***	0.004
	(0.042)	(0.039)	(0.055)	(0.049)
Log(Unemployment rate in OZE)	0.064	0.114	0.076	0.105*
	(0.065)	(0.078)	(0.073)	(0.060)
Log(Unemployment rate in DZE)	-0.471***	-0.346***	-0.450***	-0.356***
	(0.031)	(0.034)	(0.036)	(0.040)
Log(January cold days in OZE)	0.001	-0.040	-0.026	-0.036
	(0.026)	(0.039)	(0.026)	(0.033)
Log(January cold days in DZE)	-0.172***	-0.225***	-0.077***	-0.110***
	(0.012)	(0.013)	(0.014)	(0.014)
Log(July hot days in OZE)	-0.059***	-0.051**	-0.001	-0.045**
	(0.023)	(0.026)	(0.028)	(0.021)

Log(July hot days in DZE)	0.073***	0.054***	0.148***	0.112***
	(0.016)	(0.014)	(0.013)	(0.012)
Log(January rainy days in OZE)	-0.033	0.147*	-0.253**	0.015
	(0.083)	(0.082)	(0.104)	(0.075)
Log(January rainy days in DZE)	-0.222***	-0.102**	-0.252***	-0.178***
	(0.046)	(0.047)	(0.036)	(0.039)
Log(Local tax rate in OZE)	-0.049	0.150**	-0.172**	0.061
	(0.073)	(0.066)	(0.086)	(0.089)
Log(Local tax rate in DZE)	-0.178***	-0.137***	-0.382***	-0.270***
	(0.038)	(0.033)	(0.032)	(0.028)
Coastline in OZE	0.081	0.169***	0.054	0.046
	(0.051)	(0.043)	(0.062)	(0.040)
Coastline in DZE	0.250***	0.219***	0.384***	0.301***
	(0.023)	(0.023)	(0.019)	(0.019)
High share of natural area in OZE	0.015	0.007	0.030	0.014
	(0.031)	(0.032)	(0.037)	(0.027)
High share of natural area in DZE	-0.000	0.068***	0.039***	0.077***
	(0.016)	(0.015)	(0.011)	(0.012)
Intercept	-3.374***	-10.994***	-3.485***	-8.616***
	(0.427)	(0.652)	(0.505)	(0.603)
$Log(\alpha)$	-0.215***	-0.262***	-0.262***	-0.375***
	(0.018)	(0.020)	(0.015)	(0.016)
N	82,656	82,656	82,656	82,656
LL	-150,377	-126,964	-224,561	-183,129
Vuong test	170.64***	217.33***	207.88***	260.67***

Notes: a. Origin ZE. b. Destination ZE.
*** Significant at the 1% level; ** significant at the 5% level; * significant at the 10% level.
Standard errors are robust to heteroscedasticity and clustered within 288 areas of origin.

153

impact in the sending zone is not so clear: while out-flows decrease with the number of hot days in July, the impact of the winter climate is not univocal. As emphasised by Faggian and Franklin (2014), climate characteristics act more as pull than push factors for the active population, and younger people are less sensitive to climate than older people. Finally, dummies are introduced to control natural amenities: coastal zones and a high share of natural area. The results express the high level of activity in coastal areas, with a higher pull impact: in-flows are more impacted than out-flows for young people with a university diploma and in-flows have the only significant effect for other groups. A high share of natural area has a very weak impact on migration flows, especially for the youngest, less qualified people, for whom the impact is insignificant.

Complementary information on migration flow structure is provided by taking into account differences between locations instead of characteristics of origin and destination. The models being stable, Table 7.5 only reports parameters concerning the variables measuring differences between areas. All in all, the flows are positively linked with the relative dynamic of the labour market: migration flows, whatever the life-cycle position and educational level, are bigger when the unemployment rate at the destination is lower than at the origin. Flows of educated people and especially the youngest are driven by job offers: the larger the share of skilled jobs at the destination compared to the origin, the larger the migration flows. This is also the case, to a lesser extent, for young, less qualified people; this criterion also captures the degree of urbanisation of the ZEs. Additionally, older, less qualified people tend to leave these areas. The results demonstrate the smaller impact of residential drivers on the migration of the youngest. Regardless of the age and the educational level, people seem to be attracted to a milder climate than that of their location of origin.

7.6   CONCLUSION

As in all developed countries, educated French people are concentrated in dense local labour markets. The descriptive analysis of the matrix of flows between types of ZEs tends to show a slight net out-migration of educated people from the ZEs organised around big cities and net in-migration in smaller ZEs. Nevertheless, gravity models offer a complementary picture: the size of the origin and destination zones positively affects migration flows and the composition of the population in the origin zones at least partly explains the out-migration from high-populated zones. As expected, variables controlling the local labour-market structure explain flows: educated people choose ZEs with a high level of executive jobs and with a low

Table 7.5 ZINB models with variables in difference

	20–64		20–29	
	University diploma	Below university	University diploma	Below university
DZE–OZE difference in log(HQE share)	0.330***	-0.174**	0.772***	0.192***
	(0.053)	(0.075)	(0.062)	(0.063)
DZE–OZE difference in log(Unemployment rate)	-0.245***	-0.214***	-0.255***	-0.221***
	(0.038)	(0.049)	(0.039)	(0.041)
DZE–OZE difference in log(January cold days)	-0.091***	-0.102***	-0.025	-0.044**
	(0.016)	(0.031)	(0.016)	(0.022)
DZE–OZE difference in log(July hot days)	0.090***	0.117***	0.027*	0.064***
	(0.014)	(0.017)	(0.015)	(0.014)
DZE–OZE difference in log(January rainy days)	-0.108**	0.008	-0.112**	-0.088*
	(0.043)	(0.064)	(0.046)	(0.053)
DZE–OZE difference in log(Local tax rate)	-0.185***	-0.129**	-0.141***	-0.084*
	(0.047)	(0.052)	(0.035)	(0.043)

Notes: *** Significant at the 1% level; ** significant at the 5% level; * significant at the 10% level. Standard errors are robust to heteroscedasticity and clustered within 288 areas of origin.

155

unemployment rate. Amenity variables, in particular climate conditions, also affect migration flows, especially flows of older people. The local residential tax rate also acts as a repellent factor.

Extended gravity models explaining flows between local labour markets underestimate residential drivers as a large part of migrations; short-distance migrations within a local labour market are not taken into account. Moreover, they do not produce a causal analysis of migration flows. Nevertheless, they provide a picture of the main links between middle- and long-distance flows and local characteristics influencing professional and residential motivations.

NOTES

*   Email: cecile.detang-dessendre@inra.fr.
** Email: virginie.piguet@inra.fr.
1. Nevertheless, we have to keep in mind that around 1 million people living in France (mainland delimitation) in 2008 lived outside it five years previously. Seventy-five per cent of these immigrants chose to live in big urban centres.
2. We also tested physical distance. Results are available upon request.
3. This concordance between the two regimes raises questions about the choice of the ZINB form. Nevertheless, while there is no great difference, it seems that the magnitude of some parameters varies. The decrease in the estimated value of α (over-dispersion parameter) in ZINB models, compared to the ones obtained in the NB models, also pleads for the former. Results of the first regime as well as the NB models are available on request.

REFERENCES

Allison, P.D. (2012), *Logistic Regression using SAS: Theory and Application* (2nd edn), Cary, NC: SAS Publishing.

Aubert, F. and C. Détang-Dessendre (2014), 'L'emploi rural, des bassins de production agricoles aux zones d'emploi urbaines', in P. Jeanneaux and Ph. Perrier-Cornet (eds), *Repenser L'économie Rurale*, Versailles: Quae, pp. 123–141.

Brown, W.M. and D.M. Scott (2012), 'Human capital location choice: accounting for amenities and thick labor markets', *Journal of Regional Science*, 52(5), 787–808.

Cheshire, P.C. and S. Magrini (2006), 'Population growth in European cities: weather matters – but only nationally', *Regional Studies*, 40, 23–37.

Clark, D.E. and W.J. Hunter (1992), 'The impact of economic opportunity, amenities and fiscal factors on age-specific migration rates', *Journal of Regional Science*, 32, 349–365.

Détang-Dessendre, C. and V. Piguet (2016), 'La population des villes et des campagnes: des mobilités qui comblent les disparités historiques?', in S. Blancard, C. Détang-Dessendre and N. Renahy (eds), *Enjeux économiques et sociaux des espaces ruraux contemporains*, Versailles: Quae, pp. 9–22.

Détang-Dessendre, C., F. Goffette-Nagot and V. Piguet (2008), 'Life cycle and migration to urban and rural areas: estimation of a mixed logit model on French data', *Journal of Regional Science*, 48, 789–824.
Détang-Dessendre, C., M. Partridge and V. Piguet (2016), 'Local labor market flexibility in a perceived low migration country: the case of French labor markets', *Regional Science and Urban Economics*, 58, 89–103.
Etzo, I. (2011), 'The determinants of recent interregional migration flows in Italy: a panel data analysis', *Journal of Regional Science*, 51, 948–966.
Faggian, A. and R.S. Franklin (2014), 'Human capital redistribution in the USA: the migration of the college-bound', *Spatial Economic Analysis*, 9(4), 376–395.
Faggian, A., P. McCann and S. Sheppard (2007), 'Some evidence that women are more mobile than men: gender differences in U.K. graduate migration behavior', *Journal of Regional Science*, 47(3), 517–539.
Graves, P. (1979), 'A life-cycle empirical analysis of migration and climate, by race', *Journal of Urban Economics*, 6, 135–147.
Greene, W.H. (2012), *Econometric Analysis* (7th edn), Boston: Prentice Hall.
Greenwood, M. (1997), 'Internal migration in developed countries', in M. Rosenzweig and O. Stark (eds), *Handbook of Population and Family Economics*, Amsterdam: Elsevier, pp. 647–720.
Greenwood, M.J. and G.L. Hunt (2003), 'The early history of migration research', *International Regional Science Review*, 26, 3–37.
Guimarães, P., O. Figueirdo and D. Woodward (2003), 'A tractable approach to the firm location decision problem', *Review of Economics and Statistics*, 85(1), 201–204.
Haapanen, M. and H. Tervo (2012), 'Migration of the highly educated: evidence from residence spells of university graduates', *Journal of Regional Science*, 52(4), 587–605.
Hicks, J. (1932), *The Theory of Wages*, London: Macmillan.
Hilal, M. (2010), ODOMATRIX, 'Calcul de distances routières intercommunales', Cahier des Techniques de l'INRA, 69, *Numéro spécial: Méthodes et outils de traitement des données en sciences sociales, Retours d'expériences*, pp. 41–63.
Hunt, G.L. and R.E. Mueller (2004), 'North American migration: returns to skill, border effects, and mobility costs', *The Review of Economics and Statistics*, 86, 988–1007.
Jayet, H. (2000), 'Rural versus urban location: the spatial division of labor', in J.M. Huriot and J.F. Thisse (eds), *Economics of Cities: Theoretical Perspectives*, Cambridge, UK: Cambridge University Press, pp. 390–414.
Joly, D., T. Brossard, H. Cardot, J. Cavailhes, M. Hilal and P. Wavresky (2010), 'Les types de climats en France, une construction spatiale', *Cybergeo*, article 501, available at: http://cybergeo.revues.org/23155.
LeSage, J.P. and R.K. Pace (2008), 'Spatial econometric modelling of origin–destination flows', *Journal of Regional Science*, 48, 941–967.
Lewer, J.J. and H. van den Berg (2008), 'A gravity model of immigration', *Economics Letters*, 99(1), 164–167.
Lewis, D.J., G.L. Hunt and A.J. Plantinga (2002), 'Public conservation land and employment growth in the northern forest region', *Land Economics*, 78, 245–259.
Lowry, I. (1966), *Migration and Metropolitan Growth: Two Analytical Models*, San Franscisco: Chandler.

Mueser, P. and P. Graves (1995), 'Examining the role of economic opportunity and amenities in explaining population redistribution', *Journal of Urban Economics*, 37, 176–200.

OECD (Organisation for Economic Co-operation and Development) (2011), 'Education at a glance', in *2011 OECD Indicators*, Paris: OECD.

Plantinga, A.J., C. Détang-Dessendre, G.L. Hunt and V. Piguet (2013), 'Housing prices and inter-urban migration', *Regional Science and Urban Economics*, 43, 296–306.

Thisse, J.-F. and Y. Zenou (1995), 'Appariement et concurrence spatiale sur le marché du travail', *Revue Économique*, 46, 615–624.

US Census Bureau (2015), 'Annual estimates of the resident population: April 1, 2010 to July 1, 2015', available at: http://factfinder.census.gov/faces/tableservices/jsf/pages/productview.xhtml?pid=PEP_2015_PEPANNRES&prodType=table.

Winkelmann, R. (2008), *Econometric Analysis of Count Data* (5th edn), Berlin and Heidelberg: Springer.

Zenou, Y. (2009), *Urban Labor Economics*, New York: Cambridge University Press.

Zipf, G. (1946), 'The P1P2/D hypothesis: on the intercity movement of persons', *American Sociological Review*, 11, 677–686.

8. Graduate migration in Spain: the impact of the Great Recession on a low-mobility country

Raul Ramos and Vicente Royuela*

8.1 INTRODUCTION

Between 1995 and 2007, the proportion of foreign residents in Spain increased from 2 per cent to 12 per cent. Between the 1960s and the 2000s, Spain went from being a sender to a receiver country. The Great Recession, however, was a new turning point in the migration dynamics from and to Spain. The flow of immigrants reduced in a significant way, and, according to the Statistics of Residential Variations, the net external balance in 2012, 2013 and 2014 has been negative. From 2008, the emigration of Spaniards showed a clear upward trend, although this was still compensated by net inflows of foreigners until 2012. This changing trend is explained by two factors: first, the return migration of a proportion of the immigrants that had arrived in Spain during the economic boom back to their countries of origin or to another European country; and second, by a new migratory wave of Spaniards who sought new opportunities in labour markets with better prospects than those of Spain. The latter phenomenon has generated a situation of alarm and worry in Spanish society due to the negative social and economic effects of the massive emigration of a generation of highly qualified youngsters, particularly from those regions with worse labour prospects.

It must be acknowledged that available datasets have some limitations in providing an accurate picture of recent migratory flows of young people. The *Estadística de Migraciones* (Migration Statistics) analyses migration dynamics in Spain by providing annual information from 2008 onwards.[1] Data from this source are based on the residence variations of individuals according to municipal registers. In this sense, their main drawback is that, while immigrants arriving in Spain have benefits to register such as access to public education and public health systems, emigrants do not have any incentive to delist from the register because there are potential benefits of remaining a registered resident. In fact, although Spaniards living abroad can communicate their change of residence to the Spanish consulate in the country of destination, it is not mandatory. Despite this limitation, statistics indicate that the number of emigrating Spaniards (Spanish who were born in Spain) increased from 34,427 in 2008 to 71,068 in 2013. In 2013, Spanish emigrants represented a 13.4 per cent of total outflows and less than 0.2 per cent of the total Spanish population. The emigration rate in Spain was over 1.1 per cent in 2013 – a rate which overtook the previous highest record of 0.72 per cent in 1964 (Izquierdo et al., 2014). Most emigration is due to foreign-born individuals returning to their country of origin. In 2013, 43 per cent of total emigrants were aged between 15 and 34 years old. Izquierdo et al. (ibid.) extensively analysed these data and found that emigration is still not an option for most Spaniards as the costs of migration are high due to the non-existence of networks that facilitate the job search in foreign countries. However, they also found that Spaniards with higher educational levels show a greater propensity to emigrate than those with lower qualifications.

In this chapter, we extend the analysis by Izquierdo et al. (ibid.) by concentrating on the impact of the Great Recession in Spain on the international migration of graduates. To this end, we analyse two datasets with available information for university graduates. First, in Section 8.2, we take advantage of the recent publication of the Institut für Arbeitsmarkt- und Berufsforschung (IAB) brain-drain data. We examine aggregate trends of the stock of Spanish migrants at twenty OECD (Organisation for Economic Co-operation and Development) destination countries by gender, country of origin and educational level, for the period 1980–2010. Second, in Section 8.3, we use individual data from surveys addressed to Catalan universities: one for graduates and another one for recent PhD holders carried out by the Catalan University Quality Assurance Agency (AQU) in order to analyse the drivers in their migration behaviour. The chapter concludes in Section 8.4 by summarising this empirical evidence.

8.2   ANALYSIS OF THE STOCK OF SPANISH MIGRANTS IN OECD COUNTRIES BY LEVELS OF EDUCATION

In this section, we briefly review the aggregate trends of the Spanish migration by means of an analysis of the IAB brain-drain dataset developed by Brücker et al. (2013).[2] This database on international migration includes information for twenty OECD destination countries for the years 1980–2010 (at five-year intervals), for people aged 25 years and older, by gender, country of origin and educational level. This database is built by merging national censuses and population registers from the twenty OECD receiving countries. The database considers migration according to country of birth rather than foreign citizenship as a significant number of people acquire citizenship particularly in countries such as the United States (US), Canada, France, the United Kingdom (UK), Germany and Australia. The IAB brain-drain dataset reports data on the stock of immigrants in twenty OECD receiving countries who have come from 195 countries.

As we mentioned above, Spain has had very high emigration rates in recent years. Data from the World Bank Bilateral Migration Database[3] demonstrates that around 3 per cent of the world's population live outside their country of birth. In Spain, this figure has been much higher. In 1970, 2.4 million Spaniards lived abroad, representing 6.7 per cent of the Spanish population. In the period from 1960 to 1985, about 80 per cent of emigrants went to other European countries. For example, in 1980, the top two destination countries were France, with over 420,000 Spaniards, and Germany, with over 185,000 residents. In 1986, Spain joined the European Union, which initiated a long path of economic growth and prosperity that positioned the country as a new immigration destination rather than an emigration source. In contrast to previous years, foreign-living Spanish in 2001 were just 1.1 million (2.6 per cent of the Spanish population), with 59 per cent of Spaniards living abroad residing in one of the countries considered in the IAB database. According to the IAB database, the stock of Spanish emigrants in 2001 in the other nineteen OECD countries included in this database was 25 per cent lower than in 1980. For example, in 2010, about 240,000 Spaniards lived in France and 90,000 in Germany, figures substantially lower than those from 1980.

Despite the advantages the database brings, the global figures mask diverging trends for different groups of people. Yet, as the data includes individuals aged 25 years and older, it allows for comparisons of educational attainment figures between countries and in a number of other international migration databases. It considers three educational categories: low-, medium- and high-skilled.[4] Figure 8.1 displays the stock of Spanish migrants in nineteen OECD countries by gender and educational categories and the total stocks by top destination country.

As the country has converged towards the European Union averages with respect to social and economic terms, the total number of migrants has decreased. Nevertheless, this result has had more effect on the number of migrants with lower educational levels. The stock of medium-skilled migrants has evolved cyclically, while rates of migration of high-skilled

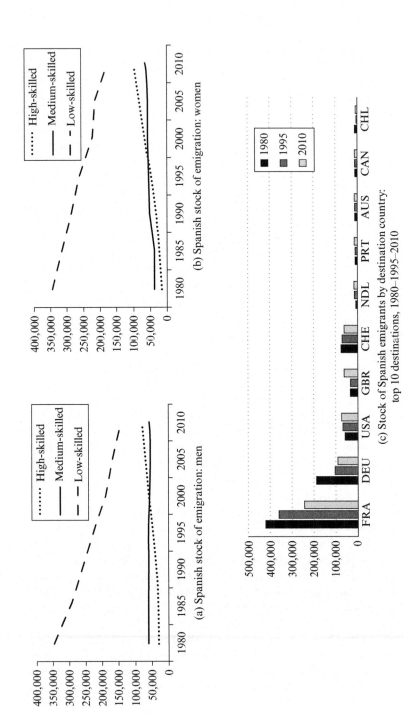

Source: Own elaboration from the IAB database.

Figure 8.1 Stock of Spanish migrants in OECD countries by gender and educational levels

workers have soared, with annual increases over 3 per cent for men and 6 per cent for women. While in 1980 only 5 per cent of the total stock of migrants could be labelled as high-skilled, in 2010 that proportion rose to 29 per cent. This increase has been particularly important in the UK, where in 1980 only 1,000 out of 33,000 Spaniards living in the UK (a mere 3.1 per cent) were high-skilled, while in 2010 35,000 out of 61,000 (57 per cent) were high-skilled. In fact, the UK is now the second destination for high-skilled Spaniards, while in 1980 this position was held by Germany. In contrast, the US has had a consistently higher number of Spanish high-skilled migrants over the 1980–2010 period. In 1980 there were 12,500 high-skilled Spaniards, while in 2010 this number sat at 43,000. In fact, during the whole considered period, the US has been the preferred destination for high-skilled Spaniards.

What are the factors that have driven the change in international migration and what are the relative impacts of these factors? And in particular, are these factors different for low-, medium- and high-skilled? According to migration theory, migrants estimate the costs and benefits of moving to alternative locations and migrate to where the expected discounted net returns are greatest over some time horizon. This estimation includes not only the net expected earning but also the probability of finding a job. The empirical model is grounded on the random utility maximisation theoretical model, based on differences in economic expectations between the origin and destination.[5] With this model, as applied in a vast empirical literature such as Beine et al. (2013), Bertoli et al. (2013), Izquierdo et al. (2014) and Royuela (2015), we seek to explain the log of emigrants as a function of the differential between origin (Spain) and destination (nineteen OECD countries) in terms of income and/or unemployment. In particular, we estimate the following model:

$$ln(m_{jt}) = \beta_1[ln(GDPpc_{jt-1}) - ln(GDPpc_{ESPt-1})] + \beta_2[Unemp_{jt-1} - Unemp_{ESPt-1}] + \delta_t + \theta_j + \varepsilon_{jt}, \qquad (8.1)$$

where the log of the stock of Spanish migrants in destination country j at time t depends on differentials between the origin (Spain) and destination countries, in terms of the income measured by means of the GDP per capita purchasing-power-parity (PPP)-adjusted (constant 2011 international dollars) and on unemployment. We also include a list of dummy variables for every destination (θ_j), which account for fixed country-specific characteristics such as distance from Spain, and year dummies (δ_t) that control for global cycles. These time dummies account for global shocks, including aspects in countries other than OECD destinations.[6,7]

In order to avoid endogeneity problems associated with simultaneity bias, the explanatory variables are referred to the previous available period. For data availability, the estimation is referred only to three time points: 2000, 2005 and 2010 – three periods that cover the most recent cycle of the Spanish economy.

Table 8.1 displays the results. Two comments can be made from the estimates of these parsimonious models. First, we can see that Spanish migrants are sensitive to differentials in terms of income. The regressions for high- and medium-skilled migrants report significant parameters for income differentials. And second, the number of Spanish migrants is not sensitive to differentials in terms of unemployment rates. This result is only partially true, as the effect of the increase in unemployment in Spain as a result of the Great Recession is captured by the time dummy corresponding to 2010, which is highly significant. Yet this dummy is significant only for medium- and high-skilled levels, with rates being higher for the highly skilled and for women. We can also see that the adjustment of the models is far higher in the estimates for high-skilled migrants, which might suggest that the responses of this group are more elastic to economic conditions in foreign destinations.

8.3   WHAT AFFECTS THE MIGRATION DECISIONS OF RECENT CATALAN UNIVERSITY GRADUATES AND PhD HOLDERS?

The previous analyses highlight that high-skilled people have a differentiated migration pattern compared to the rest of the population, and that the push factors are most relevant in the most recent periods. In this section, we analyse the migration behaviour of highly educated individuals in one Spanish region, Catalonia, by means of a sample of graduates. The Catalan University Quality Assurance Agency (AQU) and the Catalan universities jointly carried out surveys on early labour-market outcomes of recent university graduates and PhD holders. Specifically, we use information from the surveys, which were carried out in three waves in 2008, 2011 and 2014, and which collated responses from students who graduated four years before the survey year. Both surveys use a very similar questionnaire. Although there is no other similar survey for the rest of Spain, the conclusions from our analysis contribute further evidence to the findings shown in the previous section. According the 2011 Population Census, Catalonia represented 16 per cent of the total Spanish population, and according to the Migration Statistics, in that year 29 per cent of total Spanish emigrants to other countries

Table 8.1 *Migration estimates: Spanish stock of emigrants, 2000–2005–2010*

	Low-skilled		Medium-skilled		High-skilled	
	Men	Women	Men	Women	Men	Women
ln GDP pc	0.375	0.423	1.482***	1.535***	1.406*	1.187*
	(0.704)	(0.595)	(0.525)	(0.561)	(0.764)	(0.603)
Unemployment	−0.0228	−0.0262	0.0121	0.0202	−0.0141	0.00589
	(0.0237)	(0.0201)	(0.0177)	(0.0189)	(0.0257)	(0.0203)
δ_{2005}	0.161	0.255*	−0.000351	−0.0160	0.388**	0.283*
	(0.170)	(0.143)	(0.127)	(0.135)	(0.184)	(0.145)
δ_{2010}	0.325	0.432*	0.0994	0.0552	0.640*	0.497*
	(0.296)	(0.250)	(0.221)	(0.236)	(0.321)	(0.253)
Constant	6.268***	6.653***	6.120***	6.669***	5.916***	6.829***
	(0.305)	(0.258)	(0.227)	(0.243)	(0.330)	(0.261)
Country dummies	Yes	Yes	Yes	Yes	Yes	Yes
Observations	57	57	57	57	57	57
R-squared	0.094	0.218	0.530	0.567	0.615	0.776
Countries	19	19	19	19	19	19

Notes: Standard errors in parentheses. *** $p < 0.001$, ** $p < 0.01$, * $p < 0.05$.

were Catalan residents. Consequently, even though these surveys are not representative of the whole country, we can infer that important trends of emigrants from this region can be extrapolated to Spanish emigrants more broadly.

The sampling frame consisted of students born in Spain who completed a university degree or a PhD in the Catalan public universities in the academic years 2004/2005, 2006/2007 and 2010/2011. Graduates were contacted four years after completing their studies and those who agreed to participate in the survey were interviewed using a computer-assisted telephone interview (CATI) system. Response rates demonstrated some variation, with around 50 per cent of university graduates completing the survey, and 60–70 per cent of PhD holders returning the survey. As these rates are relatively high, the non-response bias was not deemed to be a problem.

The sample size of the three cross-sections for the graduate sample is 43,530 observations and for the PhD holders is 3,585.

The two upper panels of Figure 8.2 show the employment rate of the three considered cohorts. They illustrate that nearly the 95 per cent of graduates in the academic year 2004/2005 were employed in 2008, though this share has fallen by almost 10 points when we look at the employment situation of the cohort graduated in 2010/2011 in 2014. This trend is observed both for men and women and is in line with the general evolution of unemployment in Catalonia (and Spain) between 2008 and 2014. The situation for PhD holders is similar, although employment rates are higher and have not been so severely affected by the crisis.

The two lower panels of Figure 8.2 show the evolution of the emigration rate for the three cohorts of recent graduates and PhD holders distinguished by gender. They demonstrate that emigration rates are clearly higher for PhD holders than for graduates, but the patterns of evolution have been similar between categories. Between 2008 and 2014, emigration rates have doubled. It should, however, be noted that due to potential non-response biases, these figures should be understood as conservative thresholds as the number of graduates and PhD holders who have migrated to other countries could be even higher.

The three waves of the survey provide detailed information on some individual characteristics that could help to identify the main factors behind international migration decisions. The literature on the topic proposes that migration choices are driven by individual expectations about the labour market in the destination country compared to the origin, but also to some extent by the personal characteristics that make individuals more prone to migrate (see Faggian et al., 2006). Workers with higher levels of human capital (which can be proxied as better academic performance

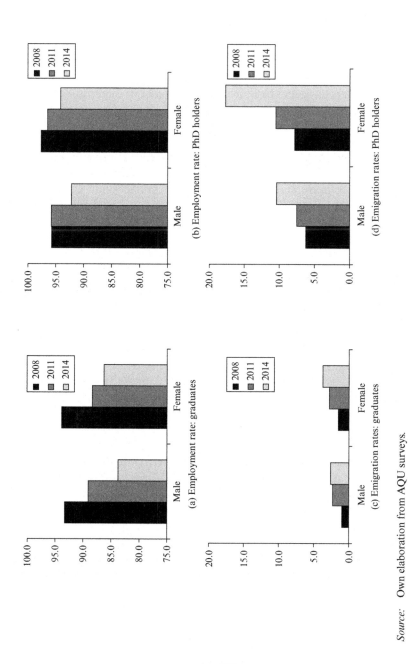

Source: Own elaboration from AQU surveys.

Figure 8.2 *Employment rates and emigration rates of recent graduates and PhD holders*

as per the work of Venhorst et al., 2010) are more likely to migrate as their potential gains are usually higher than for less qualified workers. Moreover, they do not only value pecuniary factors but other variables such as a better match between their education and their job. After all, labour mobility is the human side of the agglomeration story: as stressed in the 2009 World Development Report, 'an important insight of the agglomeration literature – that human capital earns higher returns where it is plentiful – has been ignored by the literature of labour migration' (World Bank, 2009, p. 158).

Some other individual characteristics could also exert an influence on the migration decisions as they reduce the associated costs. Previous works, such as Parey and Waldinger (2011) and di Pietro (2012), have found that previous migration experiences, like stays abroad during studies, have a positive influence in migration decisions as they provide individuals with language skills and further exposure to new cultures, both of which make a future migration experience more viable. Graduates in technical studies could also be more likely to migrate than graduates in other disciplines (de Grip et al., 2010) as the international transferability of their knowledge and skills is usually larger, given the fact that the kind of skills usually required in the workplace are less dependent on specific human capital (that is, language knowledge).

To evaluate the relative contribution of these factors to explain migration decisions of recent graduates and PhD holders in Catalonia, we have estimated a logit model on migration for the current job, four years after migration. Following Faggian et al. (2007), we estimated separate models for men and women. The list of explanatory variables for graduate decisions include age, field of studies (with health studies as the base category), average academic grade, plus two dummies capturing work experience while studying and mobility experience previous to graduation. For PhD holders, information on work experience during studies and average grade are not included in the model as both variables do not vary between individuals. However, we include two additional variables of interest: first, we add a dummy variable that captures whether the PhD dissertation was written in Catalan or Spanish instead of English and, second, we include a dummy variable related to the European PhD distinction that allows an easier international recognition of the PhD credentials. It is essential to note that in order to get a distinction, it is compulsory to carry out a research stay abroad. As a consequence, this variable is highly correlated with previous mobility experience. Finally, in both specifications we also engage dummy variables related to the period of analysis, taking as a reference the survey carried out in 2008.

Table 8.2 shows the results of estimating the logit models by maximum likelihood. As reflected in Netz and Jaksztat (2014), age has a negative

Table 8.2 Logit estimates of the choice to migrate of recent graduates and PhD holders

Variables	Graduates		PhD holders	
	Males	Females	Males	Females
Age	−0.0581***	−0.0825***	−0.136***	−0.116***
	(0.0152)	(0.0157)	(0.0367)	(0.0235)
Humanities	0.754***	0.0512	0.661*	−0.471
	(0.174)	(0.263)	(0.400)	(0.344)
Social sciences	−0.293*	−0.462**	−0.240	−1.619***
	(0.161)	(0.222)	(0.481)	(0.484)
Experimental	0.346*	−0.450	0.835***	0.113
	(0.202)	(0.288)	(0.312)	(0.258)
Technical	0.577***	0.151	0.904**	−0.577**
	(0.189)	(0.210)	(0.372)	(0.288)
Average grade	0.224***	0.209**		
	(0.0840)	(0.0918)		
Work experience	−0.162	0.00459		
during studies	(0.103)	(0.111)		
Mobility experience	1.385***	1.239***	0.688***	0.617***
during studies	(0.106)	(0.106)	(0.232)	(0.190)
Dissertation in			−0.536**	−0.394**
Catalan/Spanish			(0.218)	(0.180)
European distinction			0.257	0.268
PhD			(0.236)	(0.188)
2011 wave	0.700***	0.565***	0.572*	0.637***
	(0.146)	(0.154)	(0.302)	(0.233)
2014 wave	0.917***	0.904***	0.976***	1.282***
	(0.143)	(0.147)	(0.310)	(0.232)
Constant	−3.819***	−2.409***	0.955	1.454*
	(0.480)	(0.533)	(1.232)	(0.844)
Observations	21,504	14,746	1,658	1,751
Pseudo-R^2	0.0961	0.0762	0.1389	0.1676
Log-likelihood	−1898.373	−1703.99	−411.224	−546.079

Notes: Standard errors in parentheses. *** $p < 0.01$, ** $p < 0.05$, * $p < 0.1$.

Source: Own elaboration from AQU surveys.

effect on migration decisions. Graduates in experimental and technical sciences have a higher propensity to migrate when compared to health graduates (particularly for men), while the opposite result is observed for graduates in social sciences. Regarding the effect of human capital as reflected in the average grade at graduation, the estimation results show that individuals with high grades in their studies more often migrate after graduation. As expected, the probability to migrate is also higher for those with previous mobility experiences. Language knowledge seems also to be relevant for the case of PhD holders while the European distinction does not seem to affect migration decisions as coefficients are not statistically significant. Finally, year dummies are positive and significant, a result that can be interpreted as evidence that the changing trend in migration decisions is not due to compositional changes of new cohorts, but to other economic underlying factors related to push and pull factors as seen in the previous section. In summary, the higher the educational level, the larger the impact of the Great Recession in the probability of migration.

8.4   FINAL REMARKS

Although the emigration rate from Spain is one of the highest on record, most Spanish emigrants are foreign-born and are returning to their country of origin. Still, the number of emigrating Spaniards more than doubled between 2008 and 2013. Previous works have shown that people with higher educational levels show a greater propensity to emigrate than those with lower qualifications.

In this chapter, we analysed recent migration trends of university graduates in Spain. By means of a macro-approach using the IAB brain-drain database we identified that Spanish migrants are responsive to income differentials with other countries. In contrast, unemployment differentials between countries do not appear to be important factors, but, rather, the Great Recession in Spain acts as a push factor and may be a contributing factor for the number of high-skilled Spanish emigrants.

As a smaller case study, we followed a micro perspective analysing the migration decisions of three waves of a survey of Spanish graduates and PhD holders in Catalan universities. Results show that people with higher grades in their studies are more prone to migrate after graduation. Previous mobility experiences and foreign-language knowledge also impact positively upon migration decisions. Again, we have found that the higher the educational level, the larger the impact of the Great Recession in the probability of migration.

NOTES

* The authors gratefully acknowledge financial support from the Spanish Ministry of Economy and Competitiveness through the project ECO2016-75805-R. Microdata from the Graduate and PhD holders surveys have been provided by the Catalan University Quality Assurance Agency (AQU) (www.aqu.cat).
1. Migration Statistics from the Spanish Institute of Statistics reports migration flows broken down by a list of characteristics (sex, year of birth, country of origin and destination, etc.). They maintain consistency with the population figures and the vital statistics of the country. This information is disseminated on an international level as official migration data for Spain. More details can be found at: http://www.ine.es/jaxi/menu.do?t ype5pcaxis&path5%2Ft20%2Fp277&file5inebase&L51.
2. http://www.iab.de/en/daten/iab-brain-drain-data.aspx.
3. http://data.worldbank.org/data-catalog/global-bilateral-migration-database. Here we used the version gathered and revised by Ramos (2013).
4. Low-skilled includes primary education: lower secondary, primary and no schooling. Medium-skilled includes secondary education: high-school leaving certificate or equivalent. High-skilled includes tertiary education: higher than high-school leaving certificate or equivalent. No information on age cohorts is present in the database.
5. For further details on the derivation of the empirical model from a theoretical framework, we recommend Beine et al. (2016).
6. Even though most theoretical models use migration flows rather than stocks, Ortega and Peri (2009) and Grogger and Hanson (2011) use stocks by admitting that this 'creates a tension with the underlying micro-foundations of the gravity model' (Beine et al., 2016, p. 16). By including country fixed effects included in the model we interpret the changes in the stock of migrants as within variation in a panel model, which can be interpreted as net flows.
7. All variables are extracted from World Bank database – see http://data.worldbank.org/.

REFERENCES

Beine, M., P. Bourgeon and J.C. Bricongne (2013), 'Aggregate fluctuations and international migration', CESifo Working Paper Series 4379, CESifo Group Munich.

Beine, M., S. Bertoli and J. Fernández-Huertas Moraga (2016), 'A practitioners' guide to gravity models of international migration', *The World Economy*, 39(4), 596–612.

Bertoli, S., J. Fernández-Huertas Moragas and F. Ortega (2013), 'Crossing the border: self-selection, earnings, and individual migration decisions', *Journal of Development Economics*, 101, 75–91.

Brücker H., S. Capuano and A. Marfouk (2013), 'Education, gender and international migration: insights from a panel-dataset 1980–2010', Norface Research Programme on Migration, Migration: New Developments, Spring 2013, London: Norface Migration, pp. 31–32, available at: http://www.norface-migration.org/files/NORFACE_2013_single.pdf.

Faggian, A., P. McCann and S. Sheppard (2006), 'An analysis of ethnic differences in UK graduate migration behaviour', *Annals of Regional Science*, 40(2), 461–471.

Faggian, A., P. McCann and S. Sheppard (2007), 'Some evidence that women are more mobile than men: gender differences in U.K. graduate migration behavior', *Journal of Regional Science*, 47(3), 517–539.

Grip, A. de, D. Fouarge and J. Sauermann (2010), 'What affects international migration of European science and engineering graduates?', *Economics of Innovation and New Technology*, 19(5), 407–421.

Grogger, J. and G.H. Hanson (2011), 'Income maximization and the selection and sorting of international migrants', *Journal of Development Economics*, 95(1), 42–57.

Izquierdo, M., J.F. Jimeno and A. Lacuesta (2014), 'La emigración de españoles durante la Gran Recesión (2008–2013)', *Cuadernos Económicos ICE*, 87, 57–84.

Netz, N. and S. Jaksztat (2014), 'Mobilised by mobility? Determinants of international mobility plans among doctoral candidates in Germany', *International Perspectives on Higher Education Research*, 11, 35–49.

Ortega, F. and G. Peri (2009), 'The causes and effects of international migrations: evidence from OECD countries 1980–2005', Working Paper No 14883, National Bureau of Economic Research, Cambridge, MA: NBER.

Parey, M. and F. Waldinger (2011), 'Studying abroad and the effect on international labour market mobility: evidence from the introduction of ERASMUS', *Economic Journal*, 121(551), 194–222.

Pietro, G. di (2012), 'Does studying abroad cause international labor mobility? Evidence from Italy', *Economics Letters*, 117(3), 632–635.

Ramos, R. (2013), 'Analysing migration flows from and to ENC through the MIG-SEARCH databases', WP3/01 SEARCH working paper, Barcelona: SEARCH.

Royuela, V. (2015), 'The role of urbanisation on international migrations: a case study of the EU and ENP countries', *International Journal of Manpower*, 36(4), 469–490.

Venhorst, V., J. Van Dijk and L. Van Wissen (2010), 'Do the best graduates leave the peripheral areas of the Netherlands?', *Tijdschrift voor Economische en Sociale Geografie*, 101(5), 521–537.

World Bank (2009), *World Development Report 2009: Reshaping Economic Geography*, Washington, DC: World Bank.

9. Migration of graduates in Mexico

Norman Maldonado*

9.1 INTRODUCTION

Accumulation of human capital is one of the main sources of economic growth and development. At the aggregate level, human capital increases productivity and has a positive external effect on the economy (Lucas, 1988).[1] However, the regional level presents a different picture. Regions with relatively high wages attract highly qualified workers and experience subsequent increases in productivity and growth, while outflows of human capital are observed in regions with low wages (Faggian and McCann, 2009b). Thus, earnings play a central role in explaining regional growth and divergence by determining the in- and outflows of highly trained workers.

It has been widely recognized that earnings are mainly determined by schooling and experience (Mincer, 1974). However, recent evidence from developed economies has shown that migration of highly qualified workers after graduation from college might also play an important role in determining earnings (Jewell and Faggian, 2014), either because better-educated people have higher returns and lower costs of migration, or because migration is a search mechanism that allow them to find a job that meets their higher reservation wage.

This chapter analyses migration of graduates in Mexico. Specifically, it explores how migration affects the chances of graduating from college, and once a person graduates, what is the wage premium for moving to a different location. Mexico is a remarkable case for several reasons. First of all, most of the literature on migration in Mexico has focused attention on low-skilled workers migrating to the United States (US) (Chiquiar and Hanson, 2005; Fomby, 2005; Massey and Espinosa, 1997) and the role that remittances have on growth and development (Conway and Cohen, 1998; Massey and Parrado, 1994), leaving aside the role of human capital and location decisions as the main drivers of regional economic growth. A second reason is that most studies on the migration of graduates have been done for developed countries, usually the US or Europe, and the work on developing countries, in particular on Latin America, has rather been scarce. This is due, in part, to the development stage of the region where many countries cannot be defined as knowledge-based economies (OECD, 1996) but instead are still setting up the institutions and/or infrastructure (physical capital) to catch up in the development transition, which gives human capital a secondary role in growth policies. Although this still holds for many countries in the region, Mexico has started structural reforms in education to overcome constraints for growth at the national and regional level (Brunner et al., 2008; World Bank, 2015), making it a developing country whose growth strategy relies on the accumulation of human capital.

The chapter is organized as follows. Section 9.2 provides a framework for the analysis, while Section 9.3 describes the data and the methodology. Results of the analysis are presented in Section 9.4 and conclusions in Section 9.5.

9.2   BACKGROUND

From a theoretical perspective, location decisions of graduates can be explained by the human-capital or the job-search theories (Faggian and McCann, 2009b). Under the former, graduates are more likely to move because they have higher returns, lower costs and lower risk of moving to a different location, and so the expected returns of investing in migration are higher than those for non-graduates. In contrast, under the job-search theory, the investment in college education increases the reservation wage and, in order to find a job that compensates for a higher reservation wage, the individual has to move further across space in the search process.

Empirical attention has concentrated on how the migration of highly educated people occurs in developed countries. For example, Faggian and McCann (2009a) estimate the relationship between flows of highly qualified human capital and innovative behaviour of firms in British regions, and Faggian et al. (2007) study how employment–migration decisions differ between men and women. Also, for the US, Kodrzycki (2001) characterizes the decision of migrating from the location where graduates attended school or college by looking at the role played by individual and local characteristics on such decisions.

There is little empirical work on migration in developing countries, especially for Latin America (Lucas, 1993). This is due, in part, to the development stage of the region where many countries cannot be defined as knowledge-based economies (OECD, 1996). Some of the few studies on the region have used cross-sections of developing countries to analyse the role of brain-drain on growth (Beine et al. 2001; 2008). Rosenzweig (2008) studies international migration of graduates in Asia by combining data on developed and developing countries in the region. He analyses the determinants of both the location choices for migrant students and the stay rates in the US for foreign students, using estimates of skill prices at the country level. However, focusing on international migration ignores the role of internal migration in studying relocation of highly skilled workers.

In Latin America, Brazil is one of the countries that has received attention because of its size and the number of migrants flowing across regions. Sahota (1968) studies the determinants of the flows of inter-regional migration of adult males in Brazil by comparing the state of birth and state of residence on the day of enumeration of data recorded on the census. However, education and human capital is included in the model aggregated at the regional level to represent the stock of human capital in the origin and destination regions, but not at the individual level as individuals' choices. Yap (1976) analyses rural-to-urban migration in Brazil by using a general equilibrium framework, whereby human capital is a factor of production represented by skilled labour. Nevertheless, simulations emphasize economic growth driven by relocation of workers and do not differentiate between the flows of graduates and non-graduates across regions.

There are also a few studies for Colombia, which focus on internal migration and human capital. These studies find that internal migration for low-skilled workers leads to lower wages (Silva, Guataqu'r, and Gonzalez 2007), and that there are significant differences in migration patterns for high-skilled workers (Gomez 2014).

Mexico has also received attention due to the important flows of migrants to the US. Most studies have analysed international migration of low-skilled workers to these countries (Borjas, 2005; Fomby, 2005; Massey and Espinosa, 1997), exploring self-selection of migrants (Chiquiar and Hanson, 2005; McKenzie and Rapoport, 2010; Orrenius and Zavodny, 2005), the role of remittances on growth and development (Conway and Cohen, 1998; Massey and Parrado, 1994; Taylor, 1992), the way networks of migrants help in reducing the costs of migration, adaptation and job search (Dolfin and Genicot, 2010; McKenzie and Rapoport, 2007) and the relationship between wages and migration (Hanson and Spilimbergo, 1999; Mishra, 2007) .[2]

Studies on inter-regional migration in Mexico have been scarce, despite Mexico being the second-largest country in Latin America in terms of population (following Brazil) and the third-largest in terms of land area. Greenwood (1978) conducted one of the few studies on internal migration for this country. He estimates a system of two simultaneous equations representing in- and out-migration in states as functions of local conditions such as employment, wages, economic inequality and population, but does not focus on human capital. Another study by Deb and Seck (2009) analyses selection bias in migration for Indonesia and Mexico, but does not study the relationship between human capital and migration. Caudillo-Cos and Tapia-McClung (2014) use network analysis on data from the census to characterize migration patterns of graduates, and Sobrino (2013) discuss methods and sources of information for internal migration in Mexico and describes pathways of internal migration in Mexico using data on sample surveys taken for the 2000 and 2010 Population and Housing Census. However, the analysis of these studies is purely descriptive and economic behaviour behind those patterns is beyond their scope.

In this chapter, the migration patterns of graduates in Mexico are examined. Mexico is an interesting case study for several reasons. First, Mexico is one of the biggest countries in the region, and having a polycentric system of cities and universities scattered across the country provides an environment that favours migration of human capital. Also, patterns of migration of graduates in developing countries might be different from the ones in developed countries. Thus, as a developing country with an economic growth strategy based on accumulation of human capital (Brunner et al., 2008; World Bank, 2015), Mexico makes a good setting for the study of this phenomenon in less-developed countries.

In addition to working in a different setting, the dataset used in these analyses is unique in that a self-report household survey permits a more refined analysis of the migration of graduates. First, having a full history of each migration episode provides information to explain the probability of graduating from college and wage gaps for graduates. This contrasts with most studies on the migration of graduates that can only identify whether the current location of the individual is different from the location where they were born or where they attended college. Another advantage is that working with a household survey allows for a comparison of graduates and non-graduates, and to identify the variation of the wage gap that comes from finishing college, and from migration. In addition, it makes it possible to compare people from different cohorts to analyse the heterogeneity of migration behaviour across cohorts.

9.3 DATA AND METHODOLOGY

9.3.1 Modelling Framework

To describe the migration path over time for graduates, I estimate three models corresponding to three sequential stages of such a path. The first represents migration choices before attending college, the second represents the chances a person has to graduate from college, and the last is an earnings equation representing returns to human capital. Formally, the set of equations to be estimated is:

$$Migrate12B = \alpha X_M + E_M \tag{9.1}$$
$$Graduate = \beta Migration_G + \gamma X_G + E_G \tag{9.2}$$
$$LWage = \delta Migration_W + \eta Graduate + \theta X_W + E_W. \tag{9.3}$$

In equation (9.1), *Migrate12B* is a dummy variable equal to 1 if the individual had any episode of migration before graduating from college, that is, between being twelve years old (as measured in the survey) and the date the person graduated college. For those who did not attend college or attended but did not graduate, the cut-off value to classify migration episodes as happening before or after college is the age of 25, which is the 50th percentile value for age of graduation from college in the survey. Thus, 25 is an upper bound for the age of potential graduation from college. X_M is a vector of covariates for this decision, and includes migration during childhood, individual characteristics, socio-economic conditions and type of location when the person was twelve years old.

With respect to equation (9.2), the endogenous variable is *Graduate*, a dummy variable equal to 1 for those who graduated from college and 0 otherwise. X_G is a vector of covariates for the decision of graduation, and is a subset of the variables in X_M.[3] *Migration_G* is a set of variables describing migration episodes occurring before the person graduated from college, or, for those who did not attend college, before the age of 25. *Migration_G* includes *Migrate12B* which, by the time of graduating from college, is a past event and therefore is considered an exogenous variable in equation (9.2). Other variables included in *Migration_G* are the number of episodes of permanent migration, and the median and standard deviation of the type of location for the sequence of events.

As for the earnings equation (9.3), *LWage* is the log of the current nominal wage rate per hour.[4] The nominal wage rate per hour is the total (across jobs) nominal labour income received by the individual in the last month divided by the total number of hours worked in the same period.[5]

Migration$_W$ contains the number of episodes of migration before and after graduation and the median and standard deviation of the type of location for the sequence of events. *Graduate* captures the increase in wage as a result of graduating from college. These three variables are past events in this equation and can be considered exogenous variables. X_W contains a set of contemporary covariates for wages, including schooling, experience, migration after graduating from college (*MigrateA*) and local conditions represented by a dummy variable for each state (location–year fixed effects).

The vector $\varphi = (\alpha, \beta, \gamma, \delta, \eta, \theta)$ represents the parameters of the model, and $E = (E_M, E_G, E_W)$ is the error term of the set of equations.[6]

Identification of φ relies on variation across individuals and on the recursive structure of the set of equations, which guarantees exogeneity of the right-hand-side variables for each equation. In order to get consistent estimates, a binary-dependent variable model has to be used for equations (9.1) and (9.2), while OLS estimation is appropriate for equation (9.3). A potential source of bias is self-selection of migrants in equation (9.3). Other authors have addressed the migrant selectivity problem by using Propensity Score matching (Jewell and Faggian, 2014), the Heckman correction (Nakosteen and Zimmer, 1982) and sub-groups of population (Yankow, 2003). Here, I use the maximum likelihood estimator for binary treatment effects when the dichotomous variable *Migrate12* is included in the model (Maddala, 1983) and instrumental variables for continuous treatment effects such as the number of migration episodes.

9.3.2 Data

The source of data is the Mexican Family Life Survey (MXFLS), a longitudinal dataset that collected information for a nationally representative sample of Mexican households in 2002, with follow-ups in 2005 and 2009.[7] For the baseline wave (2002) the MXFLS had 8,440 households with 35,677 individuals. The survey has data at the individual, household and community level. At the individual and household level, it resembles a typical household survey, collecting data on household members' age, gender, literacy, education, health and employment status, as well as households' consumption, assets, investments and dwelling. At the community level, it has data on population, infrastructure, educational and medical services, local industry, prices and natural disasters.

The element that differentiates this dataset from other household surveys is the information for migration decisions of individuals. The MXFLS has two sub-sets of data for migration. The first takes the 2002 wave as the baseline to identify and interview individuals who had migrated to the US or other locations in Mexico by the time of the 2005 follow-up. This corresponds to the classic 'snapshot' structure found in most migration studies, where data is collected at two different moments and identification of parameters therefore relies on individuals who moved to a different location between those two moments. Unfortunately, due to restrictions on the data, there is no access to information from the interviews to migrants. Thus, migrants in 2005 can be identified but there is no additional information about them. Although this data can be used to carry out other types of analysis, such as the selection of migrants and effects on the household's members left behind (Ambrosini and Peri, 2011; Antman, 2011; Farfan et al., 2012), it does not provide the necessary information to characterize the migration of graduates.

The second sub-set of information, and the one used in this chapter, is the history of temporary and permanent migration. The survey defines temporary migration as episodes of being away for more than one month and less than twelve months, and permanent as episodes of more than twelve months. For the purpose of this chapter, only permanent migration – internal and international – is taken into account because relocation due to school or work will usually be for a period that is longer than twelve months.[8]

The information is collected for all adults[9] in the first wave and for non-migrant adults in the follow-ups. In order to minimize self-selection bias and to focus on the history of migration, only the baseline wave in 2002 is used in this analysis.

To assess migration records, the survey starts by asking for the type of location where the individual was born (communal land [*ejido*], village, small town or city) and the type of location and characteristics of the dwelling that they were living at when they were twelve. The survey then asks about the date and length of each migration episode that has happened since the individual was twelve years old, and characteristics of the location to which the person moved.[10] In addition, records on education in the MXFLS distinguish whether the individual graduated from college or not (*Graduate* in equation (9.2)). By combining the date when the person finished college and the cut-off value of age 25 for non-graduates, migration episodes were classified as happening before or after actual or potential graduation from college. Once migration episodes were classified, the variable *Migrate12B* in equation (9.1), the total number of migration episodes before and after finishing college, and the median and average of type of place in the migration path were calculated for each individual. The wage rate per hour in equation (9.3)) was calculated using data for labour income (earnings) and number of hours worked.

The sample of interest consists of working-age individuals, defined as individuals aged twenty years or older[11] in the first wave of the survey (2002). Thus, the sample has a total of 20,037 individuals and 8,411 households. Estimations of parameters in equations (9.1) and (9.2) are carried out with the full sample.[12] Once equation (9.3) is included, estimations only take into account individuals who are currently working and report labour income and hours of work. Sampling weights were used in descriptive statistics and estimations to take advantage of the fact that the data are nationally representative and allow for inferences about the behaviour of all the households in the country. For the sake of providing context before getting into estimates, the next section presents a description of the behaviour of the main variables in the model.

9.3.3 Descriptives

Two variables are at the core of the analysis: the one describing human capital (*Graduate*) and the ones describing migration behaviour before and after accumulation of human capital (*MigrateB* and *MigrateA*).[13] Recall that *Graduate* is a dummy variable equal to one for those who graduated from college, and zero otherwise.

In the migration behaviour variable, *MigrateB* equals 1 if the person relocated between the age of twelve and the year when they graduated from college; and for people who did not attend college, the variable is equal to 1 if there was any migration episode between the age of 12 and 25. *MigrateA* follows the same coding but identifies any episode after graduating from college or after turning 25 years old. To account for heterogeneity by age, a description of the variables and econometric estimates are presented by cohorts – that is, sub-groups of individuals aged 20 to 39, 40 to 59, 60 to 79 and 80 to 99, with 10,331, 6,358, 2,796, and 464 individuals, respectively.

The MXFLS has 15,493 non-graduates and 896 graduates. Figure 9.1 shows the proportion of individuals in each cohort who migrated before graduating from college (9.1a), after graduating from college (9.1b) and both (9.1c). It can be seen that graduates have a higher propensity to migrate than non-graduates in all cohorts, regardless of whether they moved before or after college. There is an increasing trend across cohorts, capturing the fact that as individuals age, they have more time and opportunities to migrate. Figure 9.1c shows that graduates are more likely to migrate before and after attending college, suggesting that repeated migration plays an important role for graduates.

With regard to episodes before college, 24 per cent of graduates aged 20–39 had migration episodes, which is higher than the proportion for

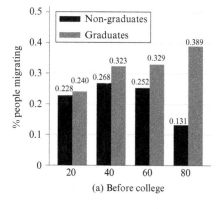

(a) Before college

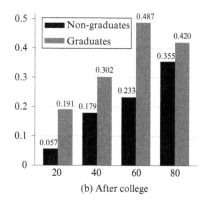

(b) After college

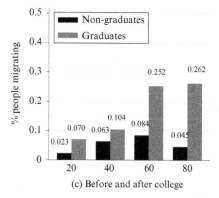

(c) Before and after college

Source:　MXFLS 2002.

Figure 9.1　*Proportion of people with migration episodes before and after attending college, by cohort*

non-graduates (22.8 per cent). For the 40–59 cohort, 32.3 per cent of graduates had migration episodes, 6 points higher than the 26.8 per cent of non-graduates, and very similar to the difference between graduates and non-graduates in the cohort 60–79.

Comparing Figures 9.1a and 9.1b, it can be seen that the propensity to migrate for graduates in the cohort 20–39 is 24 per cent before college, and reduces to 19.1 per cent after attending college. For the cohort 40–59 the difference between both categories is smaller, with 32.3 per cent before college and 30.2 per cent after college. For the cohort 60–79 the trend moves in the opposite direction, with a higher propensity to migrate after college (48.7 per cent) than before college (32.9 per cent). The differences

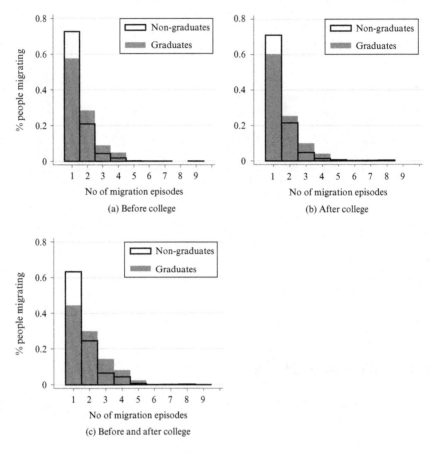

(a) Before college

(b) After college

(c) Before and after college

Source: MXFLS 2002.

Figure 9.2   Distribution of the number of migration episodes before and after attending college

in propensity to migrate before and after college for non-graduates are higher, with 22.8 per cent vs 5.7 per cent for the cohort 20–39, 26.8 per cent vs 17.9 per cent for the 40–59 cohort and 25.2 per cent vs 23.3 per cent for the cohort 60–79.

Figure 9.1 describes the migration choices at the extensive margin, that is, the proportion of people who migrated. Figure 9.2 shows the migration behaviour at the intensive margin, in this case represented by the number of migration episodes each person had before or after graduating from college. For the majority of people, the number of episodes of permanent migration before or after college totals one. Comparing graduates vs non-graduates, the proportion of people with one migration episode is higher for non-graduates in all cases (9.2a, 9.2b and 9.2c). In other words, graduates are relatively concentrated at the right of the distribution while non-graduates are relatively concentrated at the left of the distribution. This means that graduates not only have a higher propensity to migrate (extensive margin), but they also have more episodes of permanent migration than non-graduates (intensive margin).

The box plots in Figure 9.3 (p. 185) show the distribution of wages for graduates (9.3a) and non-graduates (9.3b), and compare this distribution for those who did and did not migrate after college. The figure shows that, as expected, wages for graduates are higher than wages for non-graduates, regardless of migration decisions. The median wage of graduates is about three times that of non-graduates, and wages for graduates have a larger deviation around the median.

Comparing migration choices for graduates (Figure 9.3a), the median wage for the individuals who migrated after graduating from college is slightly higher than those who did not migrate. The difference is also very small for the non-graduates. This suggests that there is not a wage premium associated with migration episodes after graduating from college – a result that contrasts with findings for developed countries.

Each of these results still holds when the cut-off value for non-graduates increases to 30 years (the 75th percentile). Nevertheless, these results are purely descriptive, and cannot be conclusive. The next section uses econometric models to analyse the migration behaviour of graduates, based on equations (9.1)–(9.3).

9.4 RESULTS

9.4.1 Migration after Twelve Years of Age

Table 9.1 (pp. 186–187) shows the estimated probability of having migration episodes after the age of twelve and before graduating from college. Column (a) represents the benchmark, with consistent and unbiased maximum likelihood estimates for a probit model, with heteroscedasticity-consistent standard errors. Column (b) shows estimates of the marginal effects, and columns (c)–(e) display the estimates of marginal effects for individuals aged 20–39, 40–59 and 60–89 years old, respectively, in order to check heterogeneous migration behaviour across cohorts.[14]

Column (a) shows that there is an inverted U-shaped cohort effect. On the one hand, the linear term for Age with a positive and significant coefficient shows that younger cohorts have lower chances of having migration episodes than older cohorts. This is expected, as older people have had, by definition, more time and therefore opportunities to migrate. On the other hand, the negative and significant coefficient of the non-linear effect (Age^2) shows that the oldest cohorts were less likely to have migration episodes, capturing the fact that mobility has increased over time, making it easier for younger individuals to relocate. Both effects compensate each other, leading the marginal effect of age to be close to zero and non-significant (column (b)), and this holds for all cohorts (columns (c)–(e)).

With respect to gender differences, the non-significant coefficient for Men in column (a) suggests that being male does not affect the likelihood of having episodes of migration before college. When looking at heterogeneity across cohorts, gender does not play a significant role on the probability of migration in any cohort.

The type of place where the individual was born plays an important role on subsequent migration decisions. The negative sign of the coefficients for the type of place where the individual was born (village, small town or city, village being the base level) suggests that, the bigger the place of birth, the less likely it is for the individual to migrate. Estimates in column (b) suggest that being born in a small town makes it less likely to migrate compared to being born in a village, although the marginal effect is not significant. Regarding heterogeneity, the coefficient is only significant for the youngest cohort, suggesting that over time migration from rural areas like villages to urban areas has become more likely. There is a significant negative effect of being born in a city relative to being born in a village, and the effect is higher than that of small towns, suggesting that people born in rural areas have higher incentives to migrate than people born in cities. With respect to heterogeneity, people born in a city are less likely to migrate than people born in a village regardless of the cohort, although the effect is only significant for the working-age cohorts (20–39 and 40–59).

Migrating during childhood has a positive effect on migration later in life. The marginal effect of the variable *Migrate child* is positive and significant, suggesting that people who had moved before the age of twelve had an increased probability (around 7 per cent) of moving again between the ages of 12 and 25. Across cohorts, the effect is stronger for the youngest cohort than it is for the 40–59 and the 60–79 cohorts.

Two variables represent socio-economic conditions when individuals were twelve years of age: access to water and sanitation. For access to water, the variable has two categories: (i) getting water from a bottle or from a tap inside the house, and (ii) getting water from a tap outside the house or from a truck. The first category represents better socio-economic

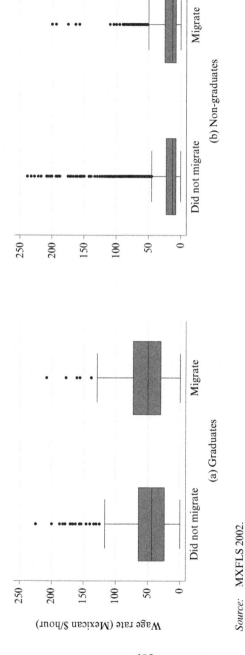

Source: MXFLS 2002.

Figure 9.3 Distribution of wages by migration after college

Table 9.1 Probability of having migration episodes after 12 and before 25 years old

Variable	Probit (a)	Marginal (b)	Marginal 20–39 (c)	Marginal 40–59 (d)	Marginal 60–79 (e)
Age	0.02380*** (0.006)	0.00010 (0)	0.00140 (0.001)	0.00250 (0.002)	−0.00370 (0.003)
Age²	−0.00030*** (0)				
Man	−0.02300 (0.034)	−0.00690 (0.01)	−0.00350 (0.014)	−0.02460 (0.018)	0.02370 (0.026)
Small town (born)	−0.11120* (0.067)	−0.03490 (0.021)	−0.07860** (0.031)	0.01290 (0.037)	−0.02230 (0.051)
City (born)	−0.19260*** (0.071)	−0.05890*** (0.022)	−0.07760** (0.031)	−0.08370** (0.037)	−0.01910 (0.066)
Migrate child	0.22840*** (0.039)	0.07120*** (0.013)	0.08850*** (0.017)	0.03160 (0.022)	0.06610* (0.035)
Outside/truck (12)	0.18630*** (0.045)	0.05670*** (0.014)	0.05590*** (0.019)	0.04970** (0.025)	0.06110 (0.04)
Latrine (12)	0.00170 (0.047)	0.00050 (0.014)	0.00840 (0.018)	−0.01200 (0.028)	−0.00710 (0.045)
No sanitary (12)	−0.04920 (0.057)	−0.01460 (0.017)	0.00050 (0.024)	−0.04610 (0.03)	0.00310 (0.049)

Small town (12)	−0.04530	−0.01520	0.00870	−0.05420	−0.00370
	(0.069)	(0.023)	(0.033)	(0.04)	(0.057)
City (12)	−0.38820***	−0.11680***	−0.10160***	−0.12690***	−0.11660*
	(0.075)	(0.023)	(0.031)	(0.043)	(0.061)
Constant	−0.97810***				
	(0.133)				
N	15,898	15,898	8,289	5,107	2,228
Pseudo R^2	0.04030				
Chi^2	299.2				
P-value	0.00000				

Notes: White-consistent standard errors are shown in parentheses below the estimates. (*) denotes significance at 10 per cent, 5 per cent (**) and 1 per cent (***).

Source: MXFLS 2002.

187

conditions, and it is used as the base level in the estimations. The positive and significant coefficient on Outside/truck implies that individuals with access to water outside the house were more likely to migrate than those with access to bottled water or tap water inside the house. This means that people in lower living conditions when they were twelve years old were more likely to migrate after twelve, and the result holds across cohorts.

The second variable is whether the house where the person was living when twelve had a toilet (base level), a latrine or has no sanitary services, with the toilet representing better living conditions. The results suggest that sanitation services at age twelve do not affect the probability of migrating after twelve. Having a higher probability of migration when the person was facing lower living conditions or when the person was born in a village reinforce each other, as living conditions are usually lower in rural areas.

With respect to the type of place where the person was living when twelve years old, living in a small town does not affect the probability of having migration episodes after twelve, relative to living in a village. However, living in a city at twelve years old reduces the chances of moving somewhere else between the ages of 12 and 25 by approximately 11 per cent, and the result is significant across cohorts. Although cities provide more opportunities, information and skills to migrate, the better living conditions in cities seem to play a different role, providing incentives for people to stay once they get there.

The estimation of a probit model for a dichotomous variable with past events as explanatory variables guarantees consistency and ensures that the estimates shown in Table 9.1 are unbiased. However, estimates might be sensitive to the choice of the critical value of 25 as an age to classify migration episodes as either before or after potential graduation from college. To check the robustness of the results, additional estimations (not shown here) were carried out, changing the critical value from 25 to 30 as the upper bound for the age of potential graduation from college. Although some parameters changed the magnitude slightly, most of them kept the direction and significance shown in Table 9.1, making the results robust to changes in the cut-off value.

Another way to look at the migration behaviour between the ages of 12 and 25 is the number of migration episodes that the person had during that period. Since the number of episodes can take only non-negative integer values (count data), the model was also estimated by Poisson regression, with heteroscedasticity-robust errors. Estimates of the parameters for this variable (not shown here) tell the same story. Age has linear and non-linear cohort effects and gender does not play a role on migration. People being born in small town and in cities are less likely to migrate compared to those born in villages, although the effect is stronger for those born in cities. Migrating when the person was a child increases the chances of migrating after twelve years old, and the same holds for low living conditions as measured by access to water and sanitation services. Also, living in a city when aged twelve significantly reduces the chances of migrating afterwards. The next section looks at how migration might have affected the probability of graduating from college.

9.4.2 Graduating from College

The next equation estimates the probability of an individual graduating from college. Table 9.2 shows the estimation of equation (9.2) using a probit model. In addition to the variables included in the model for migrating after age twelve, this estimation adds the variable *Move12B* to check if migration after age twelve and before actually or potentially finishing college affects the chances of graduating from college. It also models the number of migration episodes between 12 and 25 in a linear (*NEpisodesB*) and squared (*NEpisodesB²*) specification. Column (a) shows the estimates of the model, while column (b) presents the marginal effects for each variable. Columns (c)–(e) estimate the model for sub-samples based on age.

As expected, estimates for the linear term for age show that the older the person the more likely it is that they graduated from college, and the squared term suggests that there is an age after which graduating from college becomes more and more difficult over time. The marginal effect for this variable indicates that the first effect prevails. By cohorts, the first effect is stronger for the youngest cohort, and both effects cancel each other out for the oldest cohorts.

Regarding gender, the positive and significant coefficient suggests that men are more likely to graduate from college than women. According to the marginal effect in column (b), men are 2.4 per cent more likely to graduate. However, this appears to be a generational difference, with the marginal effects on cohorts suggesting that these differences have decreased over time, with the youngest generation having no significant differences between men and women. The significance in column (b) shows that, overall, the difference by gender was high enough in older generations to overwhelm the lack of gender differences in the 20–39 cohort.

When looking at the type of place where the person was born, a small town does not seem to provide an advantage over villages in graduating from college. However, being born in a city significantly increases the chances of graduating from college compared to being born in a village. This effect is not homogeneous across cohorts. For the youngest cohort, being born in a city does not increase the chances of graduating from college. However, the effect becomes significant for older cohorts,

Table 9.2 Probability of graduating from college

Variable	Probit (a)	Marginal (b)	Marginal 20–39 (c)	Marginal 40–59 (d)	Marginal 60–79 (e)
Age	0.11180***	0.00240***	0.00470***	-0.00130	-0.00190
	(0.012)	(0)	(0.001)	(0.001)	(0.001)
Age^2	-0.00110***				
	(0)				
Male	0.19760***	0.02420***	0.01290	0.04580***	0.02660**
	(0.051)	(0.006)	(0.008)	(0.013)	(0.012)
Small town (born)	0.16190	0.01510	0.00540	0.02450	0.02210*
	(0.128)	(0.011)	(0.017)	(0.02)	(0.013)
City (born)	0.43180***	0.04930***	0.02520	0.07730***	0.09350**
	(0.135)	(0.014)	(0.018)	(0.024)	(0.039)
Migrate child	-0.02910	-0.00350	-0.00740	-0.00330	0.01200
	(0.062)	(0.007)	(0.009)	(0.015)	(0.015)
Outside/truck (12)	-0.35230***	-0.03940***	-0.03520***	-0.05840***	-0.02500**
	(0.069)	(0.007)	(0.009)	(0.015)	(0.012)
Latrine (12)	-0.31520***	-0.03880***	-0.02690***	-0.06870***	-0.02600*
	(0.07)	(0.008)	(0.01)	(0.017)	(0.015)
No sanitary (12)	-0.59540***	-0.06100***	-0.03190**	-0.10070***	-0.04690***
	(0.095)	(0.008)	(0.013)	(0.016)	(0.014)

	(1)	(2)	(3)	(4)	(5)
Small town	0.20500	0.02380	0.02300	0.04950*	-0.05560
(12)	(0.143)	(0.015)	(0.016)	(0.029)	(0.039)
City	0.13070	0.01440	0.03890**	-0.00190	-0.07220*
(12)	(0.149)	(0.016)	(0.015)	(0.028)	(0.042)
Move 12B	-0.10860	-0.01270	-0.00710	-0.05070*	-0.00490
	(0.17)	(0.019)	(0.046)	(0.028)	(0.04)
NEpisodesB	0.32360**	0.03580**	0.02740	0.07980***	0.03220
	(0.151)	(0.016)	(0.046)	(0.023)	(0.038)
NEpisodesB^2	-0.03260				
	(0.026)				
Constant	-4.17690***				
	(0.265)				
N	15,730	15,730	8,251	5,050	2,169
Pseudo R^2	0.12670				
Chi2	338.1				
P-value	0.00000				

Notes: White-consistent standard errors are shown in parenthesis below the estimates. (*) denotes significance at 10 per cent, 5 per cent (**) and 1 per cent (***).

Source: MXFLS 2002.

191

capturing the fact that as time passes, there is more access to education services as well as infrastructure that make it easier to get access to tertiary education in smaller locations.

Migrating as a child does not seem to have a direct effect on graduating from college: neither the coefficient nor the marginal effects are significant. This suggests that migration as a child only has an indirect effect on graduating from college through the effect it has on migration between age 12 and age 25. Socio-economic conditions at age twelve directly affect the chances of graduating from college, and in the opposite direction as they did for migrating between 12 and 25 years of age. This suggests that facing tougher economic conditions at twelve years of age (such as not having access to water in the house or not having sanitary services) creates an incentive to migrate in order to find better living conditions, although this is dependent on an individual successfully completing elementary, middle and high school and gaining entrance to college. By adding the estimates of marginal effects for both variables, the results show that living in low economic conditions at age twelve reduces the chances of graduating from college by 8–13 per cent. Across cohorts, the effect is non-linear, with the 40–59 cohort having the highest impact of economic conditions at age twelve on the probability of graduating from college.

Living in a small town or a city at age twelve does not increase the chances of graduating from college relative to living in a village. For the youngest cohort, living in a city at age twelve significantly increases the probability of graduating from college relative to people living in a village. A similar trend was identified for the people in the 40–59 cohort.

There is no direct effect of migration between ages 12 and 25 (*Move12B*) on graduating from college, but there is an indirect effect through the number of migration episodes. That might be explained by people migrating to cities to get access to better living conditions, and once they get to a city, there are no additional incentives to find opportunities in other places for access to tertiary education. The sign and significance on the coefficient for the number of migration episodes confirms that. Estimates for the linear term (*NEpisodesB*) suggest that a higher number of migration episodes between the ages of 12 and 25 significantly increases the probability of graduating from college by 23.5 per cent. This result implies that migration between 12 and 25 years old (*Move12B*) is not sufficient for graduating from college. One migration episode might help to overcome tough economic conditions in rural areas, but is not enough for increasing the chances of graduating from college. For that to happen, more episodes of permanent migration are necessary. The sign of the coefficient for number of episodes is consistent across cohorts, although the 40–59 cohort has the highest impact. The non-linear term (*NEpisodesB^2*) captures the fact that too many migration episodes do not contribute to graduate from college, as they might eventually become a reason to drop out.

An important limitation of these results is that they do not control for parental level of education, which is expected to significantly influence the chances of attending and graduating from college. Unfortunately, the MXFLS only collects parental level of education for individuals whose parents are alive and live with them, which is very unlikely for individuals who graduated from college. One indirect way to control for differences in parental level of education is through the age variable that captures cohort-level effects, such as the increasing importance of education as recognized by newer generations.

9.4.3 Earnings

The third series of models considers the wage rate across different conditions. The endogenous variable for the earnings equation (9.3) is the log of the wage rate. For the current (2002) wage rate, schooling and experience, the main determinants of earnings are past events and can be assumed as exogenous. Variables related to local conditions might also explain differences in wage rate. However, some variables have missing values for some locations, and this significantly reduces the number of individual-level observations to be included in the model. This further contributes to the loss caused by estimating the equation only with people who are currently working. In order to minimize the number of observations excluded from the estimation and avoid the attrition bias coming from this omitted data, the model is estimated using location fixed effects to control for unobservable local conditions. Table 9.3 shows the estimates of equation (9.3), for the whole sample (column (a)) and by cohorts (columns (b)–(d)).

The estimates for control variables have the expected sign. More experience, represented by age, is associated with increased wages. The negative coefficient for the non-linear term (age^2) suggests that the effect of experience goes in the opposite direction for the oldest workers, and the effect is significant only for the 40–59 cohort. Male workers earn a wage 15 per cent higher than women. Examining education, having elementary school as the education level increases the wage by 38.2 per cent relative to the wage for people with no education (base level), while having high school has a wage 68.1 per cent higher and college a wage 123.1 per cent higher.

With regard to graduates, the estimates show that graduating from college significantly increases the wage by 37 per cent, with heterogeneous effects across cohorts. In particular, the younger the cohort, the lower the reward of graduating from college, perhaps an artefact of college degrees becoming more common. Socio-economic conditions at age twelve matter

Table 9.3   Log of wage rate

Variable	OLS (a)	OLS 20–39 (b)	OLS 40–59 (c)	OLS 60–79 (d)
Age	0.05310 ***	0.06210	0.21420 **	0.23950
	(0.008)	(0.042)	(0.1)	(0.369)
Age²	−0.00060 ***	−0.00070	−0.00220 **	−0.00190
	(0)	(0.001)	(0.001)	(0.003)
Man	0.15440 ***	0.14830 ***	0.14090 **	0.15140
	(0.035)	(0.04)	(0.066)	(0.151)
Elementary school	0.38250 ***	0.47580 **	0.36950 **	0.33070 **
	(0.096)	(0.191)	(0.157)	(0.162)
High school	0.68160 ***	0.70010 ***	0.76340 ***	0.62250 **
	(0.103)	(0.188)	(0.171)	(0.244)
College	1.23130 ***	1.28180 ***	1.20410 ***	0.47530
	(0.119)	(0.199)	(0.21)	(0.335)
Graduate	0.37010 ***	0.25840 ***	0.58500 ***	1.14640 ***
	(0.077)	(0.089)	(0.149)	(0.331)
Outside/truck (12)	−0.21020 ***	−0.25290 ***	−0.11880	−0.24550
	(0.045)	(0.053)	(0.081)	(0.333)
Small town (12)	0.02480	−0.08800	−0.02900	0.61390 ***
	(0.055)	(0.078)	(0.092)	(0.146)
City (12)	0.19060 ***	0.11280	0.16390	0.69850 ***
	(0.056)	(0.075)	(0.102)	(0.262)
# Episodes before	−0.10650	−0.21870	−0.08040	−0.19110
	(0.083)	(0.164)	(0.149)	(0.274)
# Episodes² before	0.01370	0.04520	0.00460	0.02720
	(0.019)	(0.039)	(0.025)	(0.05)
Median before	0.05160	0.10110 *	0.02290	−0.02960
	(0.038)	(0.055)	(0.074)	(0.138)
SDeviation before	0.24320 ***	0.16890 *	0.30400 ***	0.68330 ***
	(0.068)	(0.102)	(0.111)	(0.247)
# Episodes after	0.00140	0.11860	0.17120	0.08420
	(0.119)	(0.218)	(0.233)	(0.302)
# Episodes² after	0.00260	−0.02040	−0.05050	−0.00070
	(0.016)	(0.048)	(0.044)	(0.032)
Median after	0.02530	−0.00860	−0.03330	0.01600
	(0.05)	(0.073)	(0.094)	(0.13)
SDeviation after	0.01260	−0.27070	0.19850	−0.03100
	(0.204)	(0.401)	(0.215)	(0.487)
Constant	1.02950 ***	0.86960	−2.90430	−5.53390
	(0.182)	(0.628)	(2.39)	(12.547)
N	6,809	3,893	2,321	567
R² Adjusted	0.2860	0.2598	0.2956	0.2613
F	43.2667	23.4847	18.9303	9.0276

Notes: White-consistent standard errors are shown in parentheses below the estimates. (*) denotes significance at 10 per cent, 5 per cent (**) and 1 per cent (***). The model includes location fixed-effects.

Source: MXFLS 2002.

for subsequent wage. As in previous models, these conditions are represented by having access to water outside the house, relative to having access inside the house (base level). The estimates show that, as expected, people with lower initial socio-economic conditions have a lower wage than those with better living conditions. Also, the type of place where the person was living at age twelve seems to make a difference to wage; in particular, living in a city at age twelve increases the current wage relative to those who were living in villages.

The next block of estimates has to do with the characteristics of the migration episodes: the first four variables describe the migration path before graduating from college, while the next four do so for episodes after college. The first variable is the number of episodes of permanent migration, represented by '# *Episodes*' for the linear term and '# *Episodes*^{2}' for the quadratic term. The estimates suggest that the number of times the person migrated before or after attending college does not have any impact on current wages.

The second variable is Median, defined as the median type of place of a person's migration sequence. Recall that the type of place is 1 for village, 2 for small town and 3 for city. Thus, a person with 4 migration episodes with the sequence 1233 means that the person was living in a village (1) when twelve, then migrated to a small town (2), then moved to a city (3) and finally moved to another city (3). The median of the sequence is 3, showing that most migration episodes occurred moving to a city. Also the standard deviation of the sequence indicates how heterogeneous the migration path was. A standard deviation of zero represents no heterogeneity, and is obtained for migration paths such as 111 or 33, while a high standard deviation describes migration paths such as 321 or 13213. Thus, the median measures the most common type of place to which the individual migrated, and the standard deviation (*SDeviation*) captures how heterogeneous the path was.

The estimates show that the median of the migration path before graduating from college affects wages for the 20–39 cohort The positive coefficient suggests that people who move to a higher type of place before graduating – that is, to a more populated place – obtained better remuneration for their work. The type of place to which the individual migrates after attending college does not matter when it comes to getting better remuneration.

The only significant effect of migration on wages for all cohorts comes from the standard deviation of the migration path before graduating from college. The estimates show that a higher standard deviation before graduating from college increases wages by 24.3 per cent, with heterogeneous effects across cohorts. This means that the key for success in migration is to change places, that is, to migrate from villages to small towns, or from small towns to cities, and do so before graduating from college. Combined with the results on previous sections, this suggests that migrating to a different type of place matters for graduating from college. Since universities are mostly located in the main cities of the country, moving there to get a degree has an additional effect of getting the person to a place with a larger labour market with more and better job opportunities. Once the person graduates, there is no reward in moving to a different place, because the person is already in one of the biggest markets in the country, and as there are not many of those, changing between them does not make a difference in terms of earnings.

All variables related to migration are strongly correlated. Thus, the results suggest that studying migration of graduates by using 'snapshots' of them to identify the location where they were born, the place they graduated from and the place where they are currently working might be misleading, as it captures whether the individual moved or not, but it does not capture where they moved to, and how heterogenous their migration path was. In other words, the results found here show that what matters for wages is where the individual moved to and when, not just whether the individual migrated or not.

9.5   CONCLUSION

This chapter described migration paths of graduates in Mexico using the MXFLS, a unique dataset that collects information on the history of migration from twelve years of age. Results in Mexico suggest that migration during childhood increases the opportunities for migration after twelve, although living in a city at twelve has the opposite effect. This implies that migration decisions are not homogeneous across space. Another result is that graduating from college is positively influenced by the number of migration episodes before attending college. This means that just having migration episodes might help to overcome tough economic conditions in rural areas, but is not enough for increasing the chances of graduating from college. For that to happen, more episodes of permanent migration are necessary.

Regarding returns to human capital, migration creates a wage gap through the type of location to which the person moved before college, but not through migration episodes after college. This differs from results for developed countries where there is empirical evidence supporting a wage gap caused by migration after graduating from college. The results for the decision to migrate before college, and for the probability of graduating from college, suggest that individuals migrate in order to overcome hard living conditions, and once they make it to a city and graduate, they have no additional incentives to move somewhere else. In other words, in a developing country like Mexico, what matters is the rural-to-urban migration looking for better living conditions, but not the urban–urban or the urban–rural migration found in developed countries where individuals look for a return to the human capital they accumulated in college.

One important result is regarding the relevance of heterogeneity in the migration path before graduating from college. Findings show that the higher this heterogeneity is, the higher is the wage premium, which means that moving across different types of places before graduating from college matters in getting returns for accumulated human capital. In addition, the result suggests that the analysis based on 'snapshots' of graduates to describe their migration behaviour might be misleading as it confounds the effect of migrating with the effect of the number of episodes and the heterogeneity of the migration path – that is, they might lead to estimates with omitted variable bias. From a policy perspective, the result suggests that the focus should change towards providing not just one but multiple opportunities for permanent migration across heterogeneous locations, especially for potential college students living in small cities or villages.

For further research, episodes of migration can be disaggregated into moves before and after eighteen years of age This is relevant because, before this threshold, the episodes are more likely to be family decisions, while after this age, the episodes are more likely to be personal decisions. Thus, the model used in this chapter can be extended to model the individual decision of migrating before finishing college. Furthermore, by using the categories for type of place defined for each migration episode in discrete choice models (Train, 2009), it is possible to model the individual choice of type of place for each episode and how the time distance between graduating and the episode affects that choice and the subsequent earnings. Another extension consists of exploiting the panel structure of the survey to get rid of time-invariant unobserved variables that might affect migration, graduation from college and wages.

NOTES

*   Email: norman.maldonado@usa.edu.co.
1.   Lucas (1988) defines human capital either as schooling or learning-by-doing. This chapter uses the first definition.
2.   In addition to these studies, the Office of Population Research at Princeton University, USA, and the Departamento de Estudios Sobre Movimientos Sociales at the Universidad de Guadalajara, Mexico, started the Mexican Migration Project in 1982,

   with the purpose of understanding the complexity of the migration process from Mexico to the US.

3. This is one of the limitations of working with the history of migration. Since migrations are past events, the information for each event is limited.

4. Migration episodes include both internal and international migration, which suggests wages should be adjusted by purchasing power parity (PPP). However, only a small fraction (3.72 per cent) of migration episodes in the survey correspond to international migration. For this reason, the effect of differences in prices across countries can be dismissed.

5. Using the wage rate instead of total income allows us to account for differences in earnings due to differences in decisions about the number of hours worked (intensive margin).

6. Econometrics can be used to estimate the system (equations (9.1, 9.2, 9.3)) as a recursive dynamic system. However, there is no economic theory supporting a dynamic structure linking migration decisions before attending college, finishing college and labour-market outcomes. For this reason, I do not estimate a system but instead I estimate each equation separately.

7. A detailed description of the survey can be found in Farfan et al. (2012).

8. second reason is that shorter (temporary) episodes of migration are harder to remember than longer (permanent) ones. Hence, data on temporary migration has more noise and becomes noisier for older cohorts.

9. Individuals aged fifteen and over.

10. One of the questions collects data on the specific location where the individual moved to, which might be used to construct distance variables and work with geo-coded data on the model. However, the data are not publicly available and so they were not used in the analysis.

11. Twenty years is a lower bound for the age of graduating from college, and I use it to make graduates and non-graduates comparable in age. With respect to the upper bound, according to the Statistics on average effective age and official age of retirement in OECD countries in 2007–2012, Mexico had the highest effective age of retirement for men (72.3) and the third-highest for women (68.7). Since the effective age is so high and also above the official age (65 for men and 60 for women), I do not impose any upper bound in defining working-age individuals.

12. There are 3,498 missing values due to individuals who were not at home at the time of the interview. In these cases, another household member provided information for a sub-set of questions for the missing person. When these proxy data are added, the sample is left with 1,868 missing observations for most variables.

13. For a description of general patterns of international migration from Mexico, see OECD (2006). Information on internal migration is harder to collect and monitor, and for this reason there is no systematic collection on data and generation of reports. Thus, the only source to get some perspective on internal migration in Mexico is specific studies like the ones cited above. Due to the focus on human capital, a description of general patterns of internal migration in Mexico based on the MXFLS is beyond the scope of this chapter.

14. Older individuals were excluded from the sub-samples because the size of the group comes down to about 300 observations for people between 80 and 100 and it is even smaller for older individuals, which makes the standard errors of the coefficients higher than the ones for other cohorts and takes away precision from the estimates.

REFERENCES

Ambrosini, William and Giovanni Peri (2011), 'The Determinants and the Selection of Mexico–US Migrants', Working paper, University of California–Davis.

Antman, Francisca M. (2011), 'International Migration and Gender Discrimination among Children Left Behind', *The American Economic Review*, 3, 645–649.

Beine, Michel, Fréderic Docquier and Hillel Rapoport (2001), 'Brain Drain and Economic Growth: Theory and Evidence', *Journal of Development Economics*, 64(1), 275–289.

Beine, Michel, Fréderic Docquier and Hillel Rapoport (2008), 'Brain Drain and Human Capital Formation in Developing Countries: Winners and Losers', *The Economic Journal*, 118(528), 631–652.

Borjas, George (ed.) (2005), *Mexican Immigration to the United States*, Chicago: National Bureau of Economic Research/University of Chicago Press.

Brunner, José Joaquín, Paulo Santiago, Carmen García Guadilla, Johann Gerlach and Léa Velho (2008), *Mexico*, Paris: OECD Reviews of Tertiary Education.

Caudillo-Cos, Camilo and Rodrigo Tapia-McClung (2014), 'Patterns of Internal Migration of Mexican Highly Qualified Population through Network Analysis', in Beniamino Murgante, Sanjay Misra, Ana Maria Rocha, Carmelo Torre, Jorge Gustavo Rocha, Maria Irene Falcao, David Taniar, Bernady O. Apduhan and Osvaldo Gervasi (eds), *Computational Science and its Applications: ICCSA 2014*, Volume 8582 of *Lecture Notes in Computer Science*, pp. 169–184.

Chiquiar, Daniel and Gordon H. Hanson (2005), 'International Migration, Self-Selection, and the Distribution of Wages: Evidence from Mexico and the United States', *Journal of Political Economy*, 113(2), 239–281.

Conway, Dennis and Jeffrey H. Cohen (1998), 'Consequences of Migration and Remittances for Mexican Transnational Communities', *Economic Geography*, 74(1), 26–44.

Deb, Partha and Papa Seck (2009), 'Internal Migration, Selection Bias and Human Development: Evidence from Indonesia and Mexico', Human Development Research Paper (HDRP) Series 31, no 2009.

Dolfin, Sarah and Garance Genicot (2010), 'What Do Networks Do? The Role of Networks on Migration and "Coyote" Use', *Review of Development Economics*, 14(2), 343–359.

Faggian, Alessandra and Philip McCann (2009a), 'Human Capital, Graduate Migration and Innovation in British Regions', *Cambridge Journal of Economics*, 33(2), 317–333.

Faggian, Alessandra and Phillip McCann (2009b), 'Human Capital and Regional Development', in Roberta Capello and Peter Nijkamp (eds), *Handbook of Regional Growth and Development Theories*, Cheltenham, UK and Northampton, MA: Edward Elgar, pp. 133–151.

Faggian, Alessandra, Philip McCann and Stephen Sheppard (2007), 'Some Evidence that Women are More Mobile than Men: Gender Differences in U.K. Graduate Migration Behavior', *Journal of Regional Science*, 47(3), 517–539.

Farfan, Maria Gabriela, María Genoni, Luis Rubalcava, Graciela Teruel, Duncan Thomas and Andrea Velasquez (2012), 'Mexicans in America', Working paper, Carolina Population Center, University of North Carolina.

Fomby, Paula (2005), *Mexican Migrants and their Parental Households in Mexico: The New Americans*, New York: LFB Scholarly Publishing.

Gomez, Norma (2014), 'Human Capital Migration: The Case of Colombia', Working paper, AED Economics, The Ohio State University.

Greenwood, Michael J. (1978), 'An Econometric Model of Internal Migration and Regional Economic Growth in Mexico', *Journal of Regional Science*, 18(1), 17–30.

Hanson, Gordon H. and Antonio Spilimbergo (1999), 'Illegal Immigration, Border Enforcement, and Relative Wages: Evidence from Apprehensions at the U.S.–Mexico Border', *American Economic Review*, 89(5), 1337–1357.

Jewell, Sarah and Alessandra Faggian (2014), 'Interregional Migration "Wage Premia": The Case of Creative and Science and Technology Graduates in the UK', in Karima Kourtit, Peter Nijkamp and Robert Stimson (eds), *Applied Modeling of Regional Growth and Innovation Systems: Advances in Spatial Science*, Berlin: Springer, pp. 197–214.

Kodrzycki, Yolanda (2001), 'Migration of Recent College Graduates', *New England Economic Review*, Jan/Feb, 13–34.

Lucas, Robert Jr. (1988), 'On the Mechanics of Economic Development', *Journal of Monetary Economics*, 22(1), 3–42.

Lucas, Robert E.B. (1993), 'Internal Migration in Developing Countries', in M.R. Rosenzweig and O. Stark (eds), *Handbook of Population and Family Economics*, Vol. 1 of Handbook of Population and Family Economics, Amsterdam: Elsevier, pp. 721–798.

Maddala, G.S. (1983), *Limited–Dependent and Qualitative Variables in Econometrics*, New York: Cambridge University Press (Cambridge Books Online).

Massey, Douglas S. and Kristin E. Espinosa (1997), 'What's Driving Mexico–U.S. Migration? A Theoretical, Empirical, and Policy Analysis', *American Journal of Sociology*, 102(4), 939–999.

Massey, Douglas S. and Emilio Parrado (1994), 'Migradollars: The Remittances and Savings of Mexican Migrants to the USA', *Population Research and Policy Review*, 13(1), 3–30.

McKenzie, David and Hillel Rapoport (2007), 'Network Effects and the Dynamics of Migration and Inequality: Theory and Evidence from Mexico', *Journal of Development Economics*, 84(1), 1–24.

McKenzie, David and Hillel Rapoport (2010), 'Self-Selection Patterns in Mexico–U.S. Migration: The Role of Migration Networks', *The Review of Economics and Statistics*, 92(4), 811–821.

Mincer, Jacob (1974), *Schooling, Experience and Earnings*, New York: Columbia University Press.

Mishra, Prachi (2007), 'Emigration and Wages in Source Countries: Evidence from Mexico', *Journal of Development Economics*, 82(1), 180–199.

Nakosteen, Robert A. and Michael A. Zimmer (1982), 'The Effects on Earnings of Interregional and Interindustry Migration', *Journal of Regional Science*, 22(3), 325–341.

OECD (Organisation for Economic Co-operation and Development) (1996), 'The Knowledge-Based Economy', Technical Report OCDE/GD(96)102, Organisation for Economic Co-operation and Development.

OECD (Organisation for Economic Co-operation and Development) (2006), 'Policy Note: Mexico and International Migration', Technical Report, Organisation for Economic Co-operation and Development (OECD), Directorate for Employment, Labour and Social Affairs.

Orrenius, Pia M. and Madeline Zavodny (2005), 'Self-Selection Among Undocumented Immigrants from Mexico', *Journal of Development Economics*, 78(1), 215–240.

Rosenzweig, Mark (2008), 'Higher Education and International Migration in Asia: Brain Circulation', in Justin Yifu Lin and Boris Pleskovic (eds), *Higher Education and Development*, Washington, DC: The World Bank.

Sahota, Gian S. (1968), 'An Economic Analysis of Internal Migration in Brazil', *Journal of Political Economy*, 76, 218–245.

Silva, Carolina, Juan Carlos Guataquí and Patricia Gonzalez (2007), 'The Effect of Internal Migration on the Colombian Labor Market', *Global Journal of Business Research*, 1(1), 70–82.

Sobrino, Jaime (2013), 'Analysing Internal Migration Pathways in Mexico', in Peter Kresl and Jaime Sobrino (eds), *Handbook of Research Methods and Applications in Urban Economies*, Cheltenham, UK and Northampton, MA: Edward Elgar, pp. 396–422.

Taylor, J. Edward (1992), 'Remittances and Inequality Reconsidered: Direct, Indirect, and Intertemporal Effects', *Journal of Policy Modeling*, 14(2), 187–208.

Train, Kenneth (2009), *Discrete Choice Methods with Simulation*, 2nd edn, New York: Cambridge University Press.

World Bank (ed.) (2015), *Global Economic Prospects: Having Fiscal Space and Using It*, Washington, DC: The World Bank.

Yankow, Jeffrey J. (2003), 'Migration, Job Change, and Wage Growth: A New Perspective on the Pecuniary Return to Geographic Mobility', *Journal of Regional Science*, 43(3), 483–516.

Yap, Lorene (1976), 'Internal Migration and Economic Development in Brazil', *The Quarterly Journal of Economics*, 90(1), 119–137.

10. Human-capital migration and salaries: an examination of US college graduates

Alessandra Faggian, Jonathan Corcoran and Rachel S. Franklin

10.1 INTRODUCTION

With in excess of 4,000 degree-awarding post-secondary institutions and 20.6 million students enrolled in 2012 (NCES, 2015), the United States is the world's single largest higher-education provider. Not only is the absolute number of enrolled students enormous, but its rate of growth has also been substantial in recent decades. Between 1992 and 2002, the number of students enrolled grew by about 15 per cent, followed by a further 24 per cent in the decade to 2012 (ibid.), placing the United States in an enviable position in the global education market.

Behind these striking numbers is the basic idea that 'human capital' (Becker, 1962) is the key to *success*, both for the overall economy and for individuals. To this end, if a country, a state or a region is to grow, the first ingredient in the 'recipe for success' is a highly educated workforce. Human capital has been linked to innovation, entrepreneurship and creativity, all factors that, in turn, at some point or another, have been labelled as 'engines of growth'.

Given their contribution to economic growth, highly educated individuals are also rewarded with higher salaries. A large number of contributions in the literature have focused on the topic of returns to education, revealing that investing in human capital is the single best investment individuals can make, with returns higher than any other form of financial investment. The returns to schooling vary greatly by country, individual characteristics (including gender, ethnicity and socio-economic background) and period analysed. However, in the case of the United States, a recent report prepared by the Department of the Treasury (with the Department of Education) estimates that 'the median weekly earnings of a full-time, bachelor's degree holder in 2011 were 64 percent higher than those of a high school graduate

($1,053 compared to $638)' (Department of the Treasury, 2012, p. 3). The report also specifies that these returns are likely to be an underestimation of the real economic benefits, as jobs held by college graduates also have higher fringe benefits and other forms of non-wage compensation such as paid vacation and employer-provided health insurance.

Most of the scholarly contributions studying human capital, growth and returns to education fall under the domain of labour and education economics. However, there is one aspect that is often overlooked by labour and education economists, and that is 'space'. This is where regional economics comes to lend a hand. Space can be entered into the analysis either in a 'comparative static' fashion through examining performance of different areas in terms of, say, producing or rewarding human capital (for example, higher-education provision or graduate salaries) or in a more dynamic way through looking at the interconnections between different areas. The latter perspective implies the study of student and graduate migration.

It is surprising that the study of student and graduate migration is still lagging in the United States. While there have been substantial advancements in recent years in other countries (such as the United Kingdom, the Netherlands, Australia and Finland), this phenomenon seems to be still rather unexplored in the United States. Underpinning this deficit are data limitations, as large-scale national individual micro-data on student and graduate mobility patterns have become available in some European countries and Australia but are not yet available in the United States.

Our study aims to close this gap in the literature by providing the first analysis of graduate mobility patterns in the United States using restricted longitudinal individual data collected by the National Science Foundation (NSF). We are particularly interested in the effect that migration might have on graduate salaries. While a wide array of studies exists on the determinants of migration (both international and inter-regional) and on the salary effects of international migration (both on the resident population and immigrants), surprisingly few contributions focus specifically on the effects of inter-regional migration on salaries or individual income. Jewell and Faggian (2014) found that there is a wage premium associated with inter-regional migration in the United Kingdom. Individuals who migrated away from their parental domicile to study, and then moved again to enter the labour market, receive a salary about 15 per cent higher than individuals who never moved. This premium varies with the subject studied (qualification) as well as by the various characteristics of the individual. No such study yet exists for the United States.

The chapter starts with a brief review of the relevant literature (Section 10.2) followed by a description of our data and modelling strategy

(Section 10.3). The results are presented and discussed in Section 10.4 before some concluding remarks and avenues for further studies in Section 10.5.

10.2　THEORETICAL BACKGROUND

The transition of individuals first into education and then from education to work has important implications for both individual career pathways and, equally importantly, for regional economic development, as population ageing elevates pressures on social support, pension and health systems, and imposes potentially severe labour-market shortages. Understanding the geographical reallocation of these high human-capital individuals is therefore crucial.

Several studies have exploited the recent availability of data on students and graduates to shed light on their migration behaviour and its determinants (Faggian et al., 2007 and 2013 and Faggian and McCann, 2009 for the UK; Venhorst et al., 2010 and 2011 for the Netherlands; Corcoran et al., 2010 for Australia; Iammarino and Marinelli, 2011, Dotti et al., 2012 and Marinelli, 2012 for Italy; Haapanen and Tervo, 2012 for Finland). Franklin (2003) shows that, in the case of the United States in the period covered by the 2000 census, younger individuals (aged 25–39) with a college degree were much more mobile than their peers without a degree. This analysis, though, was at the aggregate – not individual – level and focused on macro-level patterns of movement rather than explanations for, and effects of, that migration. Despite the heterogeneity of results,[1] all the contributions point at a positive relationship between the level of education and the likelihood to migrate.

The reason is intuitive and consistent with the human-capital migration theory *à la* Sjaastad (1962) that sees migration as an investment activity, which has costs and renders returns. The basic idea is that highly educated individuals reap the highest net returns from the migration process (Sabot, 1987) because of a combination of higher benefits and lower costs.

On the cost side, the migration process is assumed to be less costly for the highly educated for a variety of reasons. DaVanzo (1983) claims that highly educated individuals are better in finding and processing information. DaVanzo and Morrison (1981) also show that they are less reliant on family and friends, while Levy and Wadycki (1974) point out that they are, in general, more 'adaptable' to new living conditions. Faggian et al. (2007) show that moving away from the parental domicile to study increases substantially the probability of migrating again to enter the labour market after graduating (repeat migration). This is consistent with the idea of migration as an investment in human capital and with the idea of *mobility capital* (Murphy-Lejeune, 2002). Although applying it to international rather than inter-regional migration (and to the European Erasmus program in particular), Murphy-Lejeune uses the idea of *mobility capital* to describe how students with mobility experience develop a taste for it. As a result, higher proportions of such individuals live and work in a different location following the mobility experience.

Most importantly, highly educated individuals are assumed to attain greater benefits from migration. For working-age individuals, one key element of the 'future benefit' is labour income, so finding a good job is a crucial element in the decision to migrate. As Faggian et al. (2013) point out, higher-skilled jobs are likely to be more sparsely distributed across space – and sometimes clustered in particular locations such as larger cities – implying a bigger search radius and a higher migration probability. Migration increases the chances of high human-capital individuals to find the best job match for their abilities. This has been confirmed also by empirical studies. Kodrzycki (2001) used data from the National Longitudinal Survey of Youth from 1979 to 1996 to examine cross-state migration in the five-year period after completion of schooling. The author finds that education beyond high school is associated with substantially greater mobility and that college graduates who attended college out of state continued to be quite mobile after graduation (when entering the labour market). As for migration benefits, Yankow (2003) finds that highly educated migrants in the United States have an average salary benefit associated with migration of about 11.3 per cent compared to 8.1 per cent for those with lower levels of education.

Although migration of highly skilled individuals is supposed to be more common than migration of the general population and might have serious implications for both local regional growth and individual returns, only a handful of contributions in the United States have focused on the topic (Tornatzky et al., 2001; Gottlieb and Joseph, 2006). Moreover, these contributions focus on the determinants of migration in order to inform brain-drain policies, as opposed to examining the issue from the perspective of the individual.

Our chapter builds on previous contributions by focusing on individual migration benefits as measured by increased salaries. Our contribution differs from previous studies as it looks not just at migration from college to work but also from the state of domicile to college. The aim is to study the sequential migration of United States graduates using a unique micro-individual longitudinal dataset detailing both migration to study and employment-mobility behaviours of university graduates across the country. Capturing the interaction of individual, university and locational characteristics, findings highlight their relative importance in shaping graduate labour-market outcomes.

10.3   DATA AND EMPIRICAL MODELLING

The main source of data in our study is SESTAT (Scientists and Engineers Statistical Data System), provided by the National Science Foundation (NSF) under a restricted license agreement. SESTAT is a combination of three surveys (the National Survey of College Graduates, the National Survey of Recent College Graduates and the Survey of Doctorate Recipients) conducted biennially since the 1970s, which include data on United States residents who hold a doctorate, master's or bachelor's degree in science or engineering, or who worked in science or engineering occupations during the survey week. The social sciences are included within the NSF's definition of science and engineering, but professional degrees/occupations like business, law and clinical medicine are not. Despite the limitation associated with the field, SESTAT is a unique source of information for examining various characteristics of college-educated individuals, including occupation, work activities, salary, the relationship of degree field and occupation, and demographic information. This chapter draws on the 2010 survey, the most recently available, which includes 108,337 observations.

In our empirical analysis we employ a bipartite methodology integrating a spatial descriptive analysis to capture the migration behaviour of individuals along with a salary-modelling component in which the sequential migration behaviour is explicitly taken into account.

Following Faggian et al. (2007), 'sequential migration behaviour' is defined by looking at whether individuals migrated from the initial state to a different state to attend university and then – later on – migrated again to a third state when entering the labour market. The combination of these two migration decisions gives rise to five possible outcomes, depicted in Figure 10.1. 'Repeat migrants' are the most mobile group as they have migrated twice, first to attend college and second to enter the labour market. The least mobile are those captured in the 'non-migrant' group which includes individuals who have not moved from their initial state. In our analysis the non-migrant group will serve as the reference group.

We use the five migration categories described above as regressors in an earning equation, *à la* Mincer,[2] where we also include controls for individual, higher-education and job characteristics. Formally:

$$log\ w_i = \alpha_i + \beta IND_i + \gamma HEI_i + \delta JOB_i +$$
$$+ \theta_1 REPEAT + \theta_2 RETURN + \theta_3 UNISTAY + \theta_4 LATEMIG + \varepsilon_i. \qquad (10.1)$$

The vector of individual characteristics *(IND)* in equation (10.1) includes: age, gender, marital status, ethnicity, parental education and residency

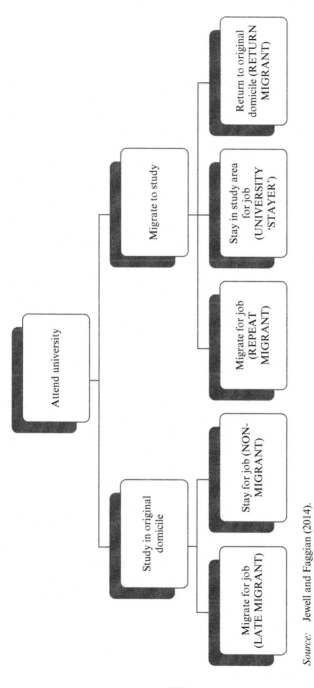

Source: Jewell and Faggian (2014).

Figure 10.1 Migration categories

status (naturalized, permanent resident, temporary resident with US citizen as base reference category). Higher-education characteristics *(HEI)* include a series of dummy variables for the different types of institutions attended based on the Carnegie classification and the number of years since graduation. Job characteristics *(JOB)* include the occupation types as classified by SESTAT itself (self-employed, business for profit, business non-profit, government with academia as base reference category). Our variables of interest are the four sequential migration dummies (*REPEAT, RETURN, UNISTAY* and *LATEMIG*) with their related parameters (θ_1, θ_2, θ_3, θ_4). Significant coefficients of the migration variables would be evidence that a traditional Mincerian earning equation – without accounting for migration – suffers from omitted variable bias. Different versions of equation (10.1) are estimated. First, to make sure that our results are robust we estimate equation (10.1) with two different dependent variables. We use both average salaries, traditionally employed in this type of analysis, and median salaries. The latter equation is estimated using a quantile regression approach rather than the more traditional OLS. Heteroscedasticity is also taken into account by means of robust standard errors. Second, we estimate equation (10.1) for the whole sample of graduates and separately for individuals holding bachelor's (undergraduates) versus post-graduate degrees.

10.4   RESULTS AND DISCUSSION

In this section we present and discuss our results starting with some descriptive statistics (Section 10.4.1) and then move to the estimation of our earning equations augmented with the migration variables (Section 10.4.2).

10.4.1   Descriptive Statistics on Sequential Migration Patterns

Before looking at how migration influences salaries, we perform some preliminary analysis on the migration behaviours of the individuals in our sample. As Table 10.1 shows, a substantial number of individuals are return migrants (44.29 per cent). However, this is mainly due to the very large proportion of international students who go back home after graduation (77.49 per cent). If we focus on domestic students, the picture is rather different. About one-third of students (32.24 per cent) belong to the 'repeat migrants' category, the most mobile group, followed by 'late migrants' and 'non-migrants'. Only a small percentage of graduates (5.35 per cent) end up back in their original state to work. Looking at the

Table 10.1   *Distribution of individuals by migration category*

Migration category	All	US	Inter-national	PhDs	Other graduates
Repeat migrants	14,718	11,963	2,755	10,286	4,432
	(15.26)	(32.24)	(4.64)	(33.47)	(6.74)
Return migrants	47,987	1,986	46,001	1,260	46,727
	(49.74)	(5.35)	(77.49)	(4.10)	(71.08)
University stayers	6,120	3,865	2,255	2,255	3,865
	(6.34)	(10.42)	(3.80)	(7.34)	(5.88)
Late migrants	19,436	11,087	8,349	13,941	5.495
	(20.15)	(29.88)	(14.07)	(45.37)	(8.36)
Non-migrants	8,206	8,206	–	2,986	5,220
	(8.51)	(22.11)		(9.72)	(7.94)

last two columns, it is remarkable how the distribution of the migration categories of PhD students more closely resembles the distribution of domestic students, while that for other graduates looks more similar to the distribution of international students, due to the very high number of return migrants in this group.

As graduates represent an important source of knowledge or human capital, retention is a big issue for policy-makers. Figure 10.2 shows the percentage of graduates staying in their initial state to both study and work (non-migrants). California is the best state in terms of graduate retention with a percentage of non-migrants of about 41 per cent. Texas, Kentucky and North Carolina also do well with percentages of about 37 per cent, 31 per cent and 30 per cent respectively. The high percentage in California is no surprise given the amenities the state possesses, but keeping in mind that the graduates in our sample are mainly in STEM (science, technology, engineering and mathematics) subjects.

The lowest values of retention rates are associated either with small states in the northeast (New Hampshire, Vermont, Maine, Delaware) or large states in the west (Montana, Idaho, Nevada). These states have fewer higher-education institutions, forcing students to leave who might otherwise have remained in their state of residence. In the case of the smaller east-coast states, small size also means that shorter moves (whether for study or work) are captured as inter-state migration. A common factor for each of these states is relatively few education and work opportunities and a location fairly close to large economic hubs (for example, Boston, Philadelphia, San Francisco, or Los Angeles). Recent research (Faggian and Franklin, 2014; Franklin and Faggian, 2014) on college-bound student migration has shown size of state and number of higher-education

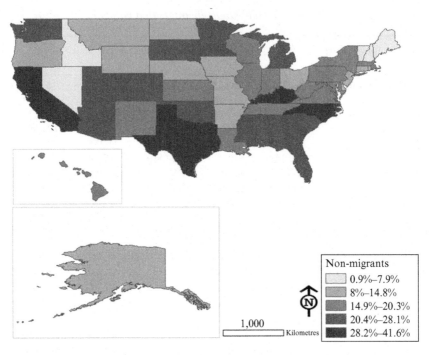

Figure 10.2   Proportion of non-migrants by state

institutions may matter for retaining students, but spatial context (that is, what is going on in neighbouring states) is also an important factor.

Figure 10.3 shows the percentage of graduates who went back to their original state after graduation. This is more informative of quality of life and labour-market conditions for graduates rather than tertiary-education supply. Certain states, despite not having large higher-education institutions, fare well in attracting individuals back home after graduation.

It is interesting that the two states topping the ranking in terms of percentage of return migrants are the two most remote: Hawaii (10.6 per cent) and Alaska (10.53 per cent). This may reflect the attractiveness of a unique quality of life, but may also be an indication of the 'specialness' of these remote locations: those who leave Hawaii or Alaska to study will likely be unable to replicate their surroundings elsewhere. They are also likely to be further from family and networks than those from the contiguous 48 states.

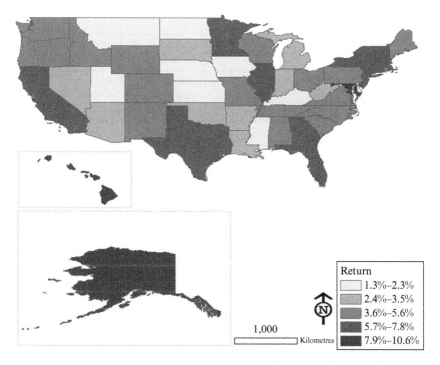

Figure 10.3   Proportion of return migrants by state

10.4.2   Sequential Migration and Salaries

This section presents the results on the Mincer earning estimations as in equation (10.1). We present two sets of three models. The models complement each other by giving us slightly different information. The first set of OLS regression models (Table 10.2) captures the effect of sequential migration behaviour on the mean salary, after controlling for individual, higher-education and job characteristics. The second set of models (Table 10.3) looks at the effect of sequential migration on median salaries using quantile regression. Quantile regression is a useful complement to OLS, because median salaries are unaffected by extreme values at the tails. This is especially important when looking at salaries, where outliers are common.

Model 1 in Table 10.2 estimates the Mincer equation for all the graduates in our sample, including international students and doctorate holders. The results are very similar to the results reported by Jewell and Faggian (2014) for the United Kingdom. Sequential migration does affect the

Table 10.2   OLS regression results (dependent variable: log mean salary)

	Variable	Model 1: all graduates	Model 2: only domestic	Model 3: below PhD
Personal characteristics	Age	0.118***	0.136***	0.115***
	Age^2	−0.001***	−0.002***	−0.001***
	Female	−0.355***	−0.246***	−0.354***
	Married or co-habiting	0.108***	0.186***	0.107***
	Ethnicity (ref group: other)			
	Asian	0.043	0.128**	0.046
	Black	−0.038	0.025	−0.041
	White	0.022	0.035	0.019
	Education mother: less than high school	−0.030	−0.021	−0.032*
	Education father: less than high school	−0.039	−0.024	−0.039**
	Citizenship (ref group: born US citizen)			
	Naturalized	0.121***	−0.128	0.118***
	Permanent resident	−0.025	0.284**	−0.024
	Temporary resident	−0.119***	0.299	−0.086
	Number of children	0.003	−0.012	0.002
	Years since graduation	0.014***	0.032***	0.013***
University-related characteristics	*Carnegie University Classification (ref group: research university)*			
	Doctorate awarding	−0.089***	−0.029	−0.088***
	Comprehensive	−0.158***	−0.101***	−0.155***
	Liberal art colleges	−0.101***	−0.095***	−0.099***
	Two-year colleges	−0.217***	−0.064***	−0.215**
	Specialized schools	−0.037*	0.200***	−0.036
Job character.	*Occupation type (ref group: academia)*			
	Self-employed	−0.233***	−0.331***	−0.216***
	Business for profit	0.331***	0.366***	0.346***
	Business not for profit	0.219***	0.284***	0.236***
	Government	0.327***	0.342***	0.345***
	State fixed effects (work)	Yes	Yes	Yes
Migration history	*Migration category (ref group: non-migrant)*			
	Repeat migrant	0.163***	0.105***	0.099***
	Return migrant	0.108***	0.113***	0.086*
	University 'stayer'	0.018	0.053*	0.013
	Late migrant	0.146***	0.074**	0.076**
Constant		8.066***	7.467***	8.096***
R-squared		0.1818	0.2591	0.1801

Note: * significant at 10 per cent, ** significant at 5 per cent, *** significant at 1 per cent.

Table 10.3   Quantile regression results (dependent: median salary)

	Variable	Model 4: all graduates	Model 5: only domestic	Model 6: below PhD
Personal characteristics	Age	0.092***	0.103***	0.092***
	Age^2	−0.001***	−0.001***	−0.001***
	Female	−0.225***	−0.157***	−0.227***
	Married or co-habiting	0.107***	0.128***	0.105***
	Ethnicity (ref group: other)			
	Asian	0.055**	0.176***	0.072**
	Black	−0.010	0.026**	−0.008
	White	0.016	0.064***	0.013
	Education mother: less than high school	−0.019	−0.010	−0.013
	Education father: less than high school	−0.046***	−0.008	−0.051***
	Citizenship (ref group: born US citizen)			
	Naturalized	0.087***	−0.382***	0.084***
	Permanent resident	−0.054**	0.268***	−0.062*
	Temporary resident	−0.117***	−0.199**	−0.105**
	Years since graduation	0.015***	0.023***	0.015***
University-related characteristics	*Carnegie University Classification (ref group: research university)*			
	Doctorate awarding	−0.082***	−0.032***	−0.082***
	Comprehensive	−0.114***	−0.075***	−0.110***
	Liberal art colleges	−0.102***	−0.072***	−0.100***
	Two-year colleges	−0.381***	−0.148***	−0.382***
	Specialized schools	−0.009	0.135***	−0.020***
Job character.	*Occupation type (ref group: academia)*			
	Self-employed	−0.172***	−0.179***	−0.166***
	Business for profit	0.332***	0.359***	0.337***
	Business not for profit	0.144***	0.196***	0.157***
	Government	0.265***	0.269***	0.268***
	State Fixed Effects (Work)	Yes	Yes	Yes
Migration history	*Migration category (ref group: non-migrant)*			
	Repeat migrant	0.132***	0.101***	0.082***
	Return migrant	0.195***	0.099***	0.194***
	University 'stayer'	0.001	0.020***	−0.002
	Late migrant	0.098***	0.101***	0.038*
Constant		8.552***	8.355***	8.590***
Pseudo *R*-squared		0.1370	0.1998	0.1335

Note: * significant at 10 per cent, ** significant at 5 per cent, *** significant at 1 per cent.

final salary received by graduates even after accounting for differences in their individual characteristics. Moreover, the most mobile group (repeat migrants) has the highest benefits, which amounts to about 16.3 per cent of all graduates. The second-most advantageous migration strategy is late migration, which is associated with a salary benefit of about 14.6 per cent. Return migration is also positively associated with salaries (a gain of about 10.8 per cent), while staying to work in the state where the last degree was obtained is not significantly different from non-migrating. When restricting the estimates to the sample of US-born graduates (Model 2), most of the results hold, with the exception of return migration becoming the option associated with highest returns (11.3 per cent), just slightly higher than the returns linked to repeat migration (10.5 per cent).

There are also differences between doctorate holders and the rest of the sample. Migration benefits seem to be higher, the higher the level of the degree obtained. Model 3 shows the results for the sub-sample of graduates with a degree below a PhD. Although the benefits of migration are still significant and positive, the magnitude is lower. The salary gains of repeat migration are just slightly below 10 per cent (around 9.9 per cent), followed by return migration (8.6 per cent but only significant at the 10 per cent confidence level) and late migration (7.6 per cent).

Most of the results for the other control variables are consistent with the majority of the labour and regional economics literature. The salary penalty for female workers is well documented and also applies to the graduates in our sample. It is significant in all models, although it seems to be lower in magnitude for domestic graduates (about 24.6 per cent versus 35.5 per cent for the whole sample). Experience, measured both by age and years since graduation, is associated with higher salaries, although the effect of age is stronger. As for the type of occupation, jobs in the government and in for-profit business are the most remunerative, followed by non-profit business. Self-employment is the only one less remunerative than academia (the base category). Lower returns for self-employment are well documented in the economics literature. Hamilton (2000), in his highly cited contribution in the *Journal of Political Economy*, finds that most entrepreneurs have both lower initial earnings and lower earning growth, implying a median-earning differential of 35 per cent for individuals in business for ten years. He also points out that these earning differentials are not explained by lower abilities of the self-employed. Although we do not have a direct measure of individual abilities, we do have data on parental education and on the type of higher-education institution attended. The coefficients on paternal and maternal education are significant only in Model 3 where PhD holders have been excluded.

As for the type of institution attended, all institutions types (as per the Carnegie classification), except 'specialized schools', are doing worse than 'research universities' (the reference category). This could be because of a combination of the fact that research universities provide graduates with the best education (higher human-capital argument *à la* Becker, 1962) and the fact that employers perceive these institutions to be more prestigious (signalling argument *à la* Spence, 1973). Similar results have been found for the UK (Jewell and Faggian, 2014). An interesting, and unexpected, result is that 'specialized schools' do better than research universities when restricting the sample to US-born-only graduates. Specialized schools may have the benefit of selecting for the most talented in their subject area and, in their narrow niche, may do better than the more general research university at producing highly qualified graduates in that area.

State fixed effects are included in all models to control for inter-state differences not explicitly modelled.

Table 10.3 presents the second set of models where median salaries have been modelled using quantile regressions. This is a useful complement to the models presented in Table 10.1, as the distribution of salaries tend to be positively skewed due to extreme values on the upper-right tail. This also applies to our salary distribution with a mean value (US$83,807) higher than the median (US$72,000).

Most of the results in Table 10.3 mirror those in Table 10.2. However, some important differences are worth noting. Starting with the effect of sequential migration on median salaries, repeat migration is still the best migration strategy for domestic graduates (together with late migration), but return migration is now the best for the overall sample and for non-doctorate graduates (19.5 per cent and 19.4 per cent salary increase respectively). The fact that repeat migration is not the best category overall for median salaries, but it is for mean salaries, points to the fact that the distribution of salaries of repeat migrants might be more positively skewed (higher values in the upper tail). By looking at Table 10.4, we can indeed see how repeat migrants have the highest mean salaries and the largest difference between median and mean salaries.

Table 10.4   Median and mean salaries by migration category

Migration category	Median salary (US$)	Mean salary (US$)
Repeat migrants	79,000	92,577
Return migrants	72,000	83,180
University stayers	58,000	69,210
Late migrants	81,204	92,426
Non-migrants	57,000	67,228

Other factors also affect mean and median salaries differently. For example, the salary penalty for female workers is less if measured in terms of median rather than mean salaries (22.5 per cent in Model 1 vs 35.5 per cent in Model 4). This should not be surprising as male workers are more likely to be in the upper tail of the salary distribution. For female workers, the values of mean and median salaries are surprisingly close (US\$67,158 and US\$60,000 respectively), while male workers have a mean salary of US\$95,596 vis-à-vis a median salary of US\$83,000. The big difference in salaries between the two genders is also not surprising, given that our sample is focused on graduates in STEM subjects, which have traditionally been male-dominated (Hill et al., 2010).

Among the other controls for individual characteristics, the ethnicity dummies are significant for domestic students, with Asian students having the highest salary premium of about 17.6 per cent. Having a father with less than high-school education also seems to matter for career prospects, but this effect is only noted for bachelor's and master's graduates. The effects of different institution and occupation types are similar for both mean and median salaries, although with some differences in the magnitude of the coefficients. For example, the salary premium for governmental jobs is higher when measured in terms of mean rather than median salaries.

10.5   CONCLUSIONS

The chapter reports the first analysis of graduate migration in the United States and its effect on mean and median salaries. Following Faggian et al. (2007), graduates are classified into five categories based on their sequential migration behaviour first from their pre-university state to college and then from college to their current job location.

Our results show that the most migratory individuals – that is, 'repeat migrants' – benefit from the highest wage premium both in terms of mean (16.3 per cent) and median salary (13.2 per cent). This is consistent with the human-capital migration framework *à la* Sjaastad and with previous empirical findings on graduate migration in other countries (for example, Jewell and Faggian, 2014 for the United Kingdom).

Other migration behaviours are also advantageous, although they vary for different types of graduates. For example, domestic graduates benefit more from return migration (11.3 per cent increase in mean salary) than repeat migration (10.1 per cent), possibly because of network and family effects in the state of domicile. The return migration result is particularly interesting as it contrasts the findings from other countries, such as the United Kingdom (Jewell and Faggian, 2014). Previous studies have identified that return migration is either associated with a wage penalty or – at best – has no statistically significant effect, showing that in most cases return migration is a corrective movement following an unsuccessful outcome of the previous movement.

Irrespective of the exact magnitude of the coefficients of the migration variables, the key finding of our study is that migration behaviour does influence labour-market outcomes and salaries in particular. As such, estimating a Mincerian earning equation without accounting for individual migration behaviour would give rise to potential biases due to omitted variables. Space – in this case represented by migration flows – matters, and should always be included in the analysis.

There are a number of ways forward for our analysis. First, although we looked at the relationship between migration and salaries, we said very little about graduate migration between the different states and the reasons behind the attractiveness (or non-attractiveness) of certain states. In the current analysis, inter-state differences were simply averaged out by state fixed effects. Some states, such as Alaska, California, Maryland, Massachusetts, New Jersey and New York had positive and significant fixed effects associated with them, so it would be interesting to explore further the reasons behind this result. Second, international students could be classified according to their origin to see if there are substantial regional differences among them. The gender issue could also be investigated further, especially in light of the ongoing debate about female graduates in STEM subjects.

This study is a first step towards gaining a more comprehensive understanding of the role that migration plays in shaping the spatial distribution and dynamics of human capital across the country. This is particularly important given that the United States is the world's largest education market that continues to experience marked growth. Our findings offer the potential to contribute to a new evidence base with the capacity to inform regional development policy targeted at attracting and retaining young talent.

NOTES

1. For a review of the contributions on the determinants of graduate migration, see Faggian et al. (2015).
2. See, for example, Mincer (1974).

REFERENCES

Becker, G. (1962), 'Investment in human capital: a theoretic analysis', *Journal of Political Economy*, 70(5), 9–49.

Corcoran, J., Faggian, A. and McCann, P. (2010), 'Human capital in remote and rural Australia: the role of graduate migration', *Growth and Change*, 41(2), 192–210.

DaVanzo, J. (1983), 'Repeat migration in the United States: who moves back and who moves on?', *Review of Economics and Statistics*, 65, 552–559.

DaVanzo, J. and Morrison, P.A. (1981), 'Return and other sequences of migration in the United States', *Demography*, 18(1), 85–101.

Department of the Treasury (2012), *The Economics of Higher Education*, Washington, DC, USA.

Dotti, N.F., Fratesi, U., Lenzi, C. and Percoco, M. (2012), 'Local labour markets and the interregional mobility of Italian university students', Working Paper, BEST, Politecnico di Milano.

Faggian, A. and Franklin, R.S. (2014), 'Human capital redistribution in the USA: the migration of the college-bound', *Spatial Economic Analysis*, 9(4), 376–395.

Faggian, A. and McCann, P. (2009), 'Universities, agglomerations and graduate human capital mobility', *Journal of Economic and Social Geography [Tijdschrift voor economische en sociale geografie]*, 100(2), 210–223.

Faggian, A., McCann, P. and Sheppard, S. (2007), 'Some evidence that women are more mobile than men: gender differences in UK graduate migration behavior', *Journal of Regional Science*, 47(3), 517–539.

Faggian, A., Corcoran, J. and McCann, P. (2013), 'Modelling graduate job search using circular statistics', *Papers in Regional Science*, 92(2), 329–343.

Faggian, A., Corcoran, J. and Partridge, M. (2015), 'Interregional migration analysis', in Karlsson, C., Andersson, M. and Norman, T. (eds), *Handbook in the Research of Methods and Applications in Economic Geography*, Cheltenham, UK and Northampton, MA: Edward Elgar, pp. 468–490.

Franklin, R. (2003), 'Migration of the young, single, and college educated: 1995 to 2000', Census 2000 Special Reports, CENSR-12, US Census, Washington, DC: US Government Printing Office.

Franklin, R.S. and Faggian, A. (2014), 'College student migration in New England: who comes, who goes, and why we might care', *Northeastern Geographer*, 6, 45–60.

Gottlieb, P.D. and Joseph, G. (2006) 'College-to-work migration of technology graduates and holders of doctorates within the United States', *Journal of Regional Science*, 46, 627–659.

Haapanen, M. and Tervo, H. (2012), 'Migration of the highly educated: evidence from residence spells of university graduates', *Journal of Regional Science*, 52(4), 587–605.

Hamilton, B.H. (2000), 'Does entrepreneurship pay? An empirical analysis of the returns to self-employment', *Journal of Political Economy*, 108, 604–631.

Hill, C., Corbett, C. and St. Rose, A. (2010), *Why So Few? Women in Science, Technology, Engineering, and Mathematics*, Washington, DC: American Association of University Women.

Iammarino, S. and Marinelli, E. (2011), 'Is the grass greener on the other side of the fence? Graduate mobility and job satisfaction in Italy', *Environment and Planning A*, 43, 2761–2777.

Jewell, S. and Faggian, A. (2014), 'Interregional migration wage premia: the case of creative and STEM graduates in the UK', in Kourtit, K., Nijkamp, P. and Stimson, R. (eds), *Applied Regional Growth and Innovation Models*, Berlin and Heidelberg: Springer, pp. 197–214.

Kodrzycki, Y. (2001), 'Migration of recent college graduates: evidence from the national longitudinal survey of youth', *New England Economic Review*, 1, 13–34.

Levy, M. and Wadycki, W. (1974), 'Education and the decision to migrate: an econometric analysis of migration in Venezuela', *Econometrica*, 42(2), 377–388.

Marinelli, E. (2012), 'Graduate migration and innovation in the Italian regions', *Regional Studies*, 47(10), 1618–1633.

Mincer, J. (1974), *Schooling, Experience and Earnings*, New York: National Bureau of Economic Research.

Murphy-Lejeune, E. (2002), *Student Mobility and Narrative in Europe: The New Strangers*, London: Routledge.

NCES (2015), *Digest of Education Statistics 2013*, US Department of Education, Washington, DC, USA.

Sabot, R.H. (1987), 'Internal migration and education', in Psacharopoulos, G. (ed.), *Economics of Education Research and Studies*, Oxford: Pergamon Press, pp. 196–197.

Sjaastad, L.A. (1962), 'Costs and returns of human migration', *Journal of Political Economy*, 70, 80–93.

Spence, M. (1973), 'Job market signaling', *The Quarterly Journal of Economics*, 87(3), 355–374.

Tornatzky, L., Gray, D., Tarant, S. and Zimmer, C. (2001), 'Who will stay and who will leave? Individual, institutional, and state-level predictors of state retention of recent science and engineering graduates', Raleigh-Durham, NC, Southern Growth Policies Board, Southern Technology Council.

Venhorst, V., Van Dijk, J., Van Wissen, L. (2010), 'Do the best graduates leave the peripheral areas of the Netherlands?', *Tijdschrift voor Economische en Sociale Geografie*, 101, 521–537.

Venhorst, V., Van Dijk, J., Van Wissen, L. (2011), 'An analysis of trends in spatial mobility of Dutch graduates', *Spatial Economic Analysis*, 6, 57–82.

Yankow, J. (2003), 'Migration, job change, and wage growth: a new perspective on the pecuniary return to geographic mobility', *Journal of Regional Science*, 43, 483–516.

11. Graduate migration in the UK: an exploration of gender dynamics and employment patterns

Roberta Comunian,* Sarah Jewell** and Alessandra Faggian***

11.1 INTRODUCTION

Research on women's employment performance and gender gaps in the workplace has received great attention from a variety of disciplines, ranging from management (Maxwell and Broadbridge, 2014) to regional science (Faggian et al., 2007) to psychology (de Araujo and Lagos, 2013). In addition to differences across sectors such as media studies (Ross and Carter, 2011) and technology graduates (Gottlieb and Joseph, 2006), research also examines the time-based dynamics of the gender gap across all levels of employment, from entry-level (Weinberger, 1998) to leadership at higher-level positions (Ryan and Haslam, 2005). In the field of graduate studies and careers, there is strong evidence that later career patterns are highly dependent on the early outcomes of job search, employment and mobility soon after graduation (Elias et al., 1999). Garcia et al. (2001), for instance, show that a salary disadvantage of female workers, so often acknowledged in the news, starts as soon as female graduates enter the labour market. Manning and Swaffield (2008), using British Household Panel Survey data, find that despite an initial gender pay gap of approximately zero when entering the labour market, this gap increases over a ten-year period to as much as 25 per cent.

The scope of this chapter is to analyse the relationship between the gender pay gap and migration behaviour of graduates. Does migration help female graduates reduce the initial gap or is migration actually more beneficial (for example, in terms of salary) to male workers as found in some studies such as Del Bono and Vuri (2011) for the case of Italy? We know from the literature (Faggian and McCann, 2006; 2009; Jewell and Faggian, 2014) that highly educated individuals are more mobile and, following the 'human capital migration theory' *à la* Sjaastad (1962), that the reason behind that is that migration allows them to get higher returns on their human capital investment (Becker, 1964; Sabot, 1987). Several empirical studies have tried to estimate the salary premium of migration (Coniglio and Prota, 2008; Faggian et al., 2014; Fratesi, 2014; Jewell and Faggian, 2014), but is there a gender discrepancy in how effective mobility is in increasing salaries?

Although the relationship between graduate migration and gender has been studied in contributions such as Faggian et al. (2007), the issue of how migration might influence graduate salaries differently according to gender – and in turn reduce or decrease the gender pay gap – has not been addressed by previous studies. In addressing this, not only do we look at the general effect of migration on salaries by gender, we also classify graduates according to their sequential migration behaviour (from original domicile to university and then from university to job location) and look specifically at the effect of each migration strategy on final salaries. Moreover, we expand the data used in the Faggian et al. (2007) study, by combining data from the Destinations of Leavers from Higher Education (DLHE) survey, which follows students six months after graduation, with new data from the Longitudinal Destinations of Leavers from Higher Education (LDLHE) survey, which follows up students three and a half years after graduation to have a better sense of the longer-term career prospects of graduates.

The chapter is organized as follows. Section 11.2 discusses the interconnections between human capital, gender and migration identified in the literature, with a specific focus on the case of university graduates. Section 11.3 describes the data and methodology used, while Section 11.4 presents the results starting from some general descriptive statistics on patterns of employment and migration by gender to then look at the impact of migration on salaries by gender. The final section (11.5) draws some preliminary conclusions, suggests some possible policy implications of our results and highlights new directions for further research.

11.2 GRADUATE MIGRATION RESEARCH: GENDER, MOBILITY AND HUMAN CAPITAL

Past decades have seen a sharp increase in women's educational attainments, especially in higher education, not only across Europe and North America, but also in other countries (UNESCO, 2012). In the United Kingdom (UK), it was announced in 2014 that women were a third more likely to enter higher education than men (Garner, 2014). While access to higher education for women is no longer a problem, there still seems to be a substantial gender pay gap when entering the labour market (Ball, 2005; Jacobs, 1996).

Past research focusing on the UK case showed that, even though the return to a university degree (compared to A-levels) is higher for women than men, male graduates still earn on average more than female graduates (O'Leary and Sloane, 2005). The lower salaries are in spite of women, on average, outperforming men in higher education (McNabb et al., 2002; Smith and Naylor, 2001). Several studies (Elias and Purcell, 2004; McKnight et al., 2007; Naylor et al., 2002; Purcell, 2002; Purcell et al., 2013) have confirmed that a gender wage gap exists for UK graduates, even after controlling for industry, occupation and degree subject (Machin and Puhani, 2003).

While there is an acknowledgement in the labour and regional economics literature that migration – particularly of highly skilled individuals – has an influence on their employment opportunities and economic returns (di Cintio and Grassi, 2013; Détang-Dessendre, 1999; Faggian et al., 2014; Fratesi, 2014; Jewell and Faggian, 2014), the gender dynamics underpinning the relationship between migration and salaries are often overlooked. Faggian et al. (2007), for instance, while integrating gender, human capital and mobility within a coherent framework, do not tackle the issue of how mobility affects gender gaps. Contradicting previous studies that found that men are more geographically mobile than women, they find some evidence of the opposite, concluding that 'although women are more likely to be non migrants than men, for those students and graduates who do exhibit mobility, the results are very different. For this latter group, after controlling for human capital acquisition, previous migration behaviour, and the different types of sequential migration behaviour possible, once we incorporate both individual characteristics and the characteristics of the regions, then U.K. female university graduates are clearly more migratory than men' (ibid., p. 537). They suggest that, in support of Ravenstein's (1885) early insights, women might use migration as a way to compensate for the gender differences experienced when entering the labour market. Alternatively, it could be that women's jobs are more scattered in space than men's, hence requiring them to move more to reduce the spatial mismatch between university and job location.

There is a wide array of studies that have focused on the relation between gender and migration within the 'family migration' framework (Boyle et al., 1999). They tend to consider how, in employment-motivated family migration, the (female) partner's employment status is affected by migration. They find that 'women's employment status suffers after family migration in both GB and the US, even when the female has more occupational power than their partner suffers as a result of such a family move' (ibid., p. 123). The conclusions of these kinds of studies seem to suggest that human-capital theory cannot fully explain migration and employability decisions when family ties are taken into consideration. While this is true, our study, by looking specifically at gendered migration patterns of young adults (aged 25 or below) soon after graduation, helps shed light on gender differences minimizing the bias due to well-established family ties (such as marriage or children).[1] Our analysis also provides a powerful framework in 'relating labour market efficiency to female dropout from the labour market and the various causes of the "glass ceiling"' (ibid., p. 124) without having to consider the role of family migration decisions.

11.3 DATA AND METHODOLOGY

Our analysis is based on data from the UK Higher Education Statistical Agency's (HESA) Longitudinal Destinations of Leavers from Higher Education (LDLHE) survey for the cohort of students who graduated in 2006/07. We match these data with the 'Students in Higher Education' and the DLHE data, also collected by HESA. The Students in Higher Education data contain individual student record data, for all students enrolled in higher education, with information on: personal characteristics (such as gender, age and ethnicity), subject of study (Joint Academic Coding System (JACS) code), mode (full-time vs part-time), degree results and institution attended. The DLHE survey provides information on graduates' employment activity six months after graduation and is predominantly aimed at British domiciled students,[2] with all students graduating eligible to take part. The DLHE survey, in particular, includes information on the graduate's employment, such as: salary level, employer sector (standard industrial classification – SIC code), occupational code (standard occupational classification – SOC code) and location of employment. Of the 453,880 leavers eligible to take part in the 2006/07 DLHE survey, 332,110 (73.2 per cent) responded to the survey. A sub-sample of the DLHE respondents was then selected for the longitudinal survey. A total of 49,065 responses were received for the LDLHE survey, with some groups deliberately over-sampled (ethnic minorities, individuals with disabilities, graduates living in Wales, Scotland and Northern Ireland and those who reported being unemployed or self-employed at the DLHE stage). Weights are provided to allow comparability between the DLHE and LDLHE surveys. As our main focus is migration, we restricted our sample to British-domiciled first degree graduates, who studied full-time and, following Chevalier (2011; 2012), who were 25 years of age or under at graduation. Given these restrictions, our final sample consisted of

23,156 valid observations. Part-time students (10 per cent of the sample) were removed from the sample because 48 per cent had been in their job before graduation – suggesting a high proportion were undertaking their degree as part of their employment so were less likely to migrate for work. Second, part-time students are typically older and hence more likely to have family ties and other responsibilities, which might affect their migration propensity. Older full-time graduates (above 25) were excluded for similar reasons.

The LDLHE survey contains information on employment activity 3.5 years after graduation, similar to that of the DLHE survey, although the LDLHE is more detailed than the DLHE survey. In particular, the LDLHE survey includes information on employment activity, employment since graduation, job characteristics, occupation, industry, location of employment and salary 3.5 years after graduation.

11.4   RESULTS

11.4.1   Gender and Employment Dynamics

As HESA data suggest, an increasing number of graduates are female.[3] In our sample 57 per cent of graduates are female. Table 11.1 reports the main activity of graduates as recorded by both the DLHE and LDLHE surveys. For those in combined work and study, we classified those in full-time employment with study as being in full-time employment (70 per cent of whom obtained a professional or other diploma qualification) and those in part-time work with study as further study (with the majority, 71 per cent, obtaining an academic qualification). Since we are interested in migration, it is important to distinguish between those who are likely to have moved for work at either 6 months or 3.5 years from those who are more likely to have moved for further study.

As expected, the number of individuals in full-time employment and self-employment (as compared to those in part-time employment, further study and unemployment) has increased in the three-year period between the DLHE and LDLHE surveys. Six months is often too short a period to judge an individual's assimilation into the labour market, while 3.5 years is likely to give a more accurate picture of the graduate labour market. Men are more likely to be in full-time and self-employment than women, but also more likely to be unemployed. In contrast, part-time employment and further study is more frequent for female graduates. Overall, in the three-year period between surveys, unemployment and part-time work decreased more significantly for men than women, implying that, even if there are

Table 11.1 Destinations in the DLHE and LDLHE Surveys

	DLHE		LDLHE	
	Base obs.	Weighted %	Base obs.	Weighted %
All				
Full-time employment[a]	13,435	59.62	17,167	74.98
Self-employed/freelance	589	1.80	917	3.80
Part-time/unpaid employment	1,724	7.81	1,342	5.89
Further study[b]	4,560	19.22	2,463	9.84
Unemployed	1,789	6.22	840	3.62
Other	1,059	5.32	427	1.87
Total	23,156	100	23,156	100
Women				
Full-time employment[a]	7,594	59.52	9,626	74.31
Self-employed/freelance	253	1.33	426	3.19
Part-time/unpaid employment	1,078	8.5	907	7.02
Further study[b]	2,708	20.16	1,440	10.15
Unemployed	847	5.09	396	3.04
Other	611	5.4	296	2.29
Total	13,091	100	13,091	100
Men				
Full-time employment[a]	5,841	59.77	7,541	75.86
Self-employed/freelance	336	2.4	491	4.6
Part-time/unpaid employment	646	6.93	435	4.43
Further study[b]	1,852	18.01	1,023	9.43
Unemployed	942	7.69	444	4.36
Other	448	5.21	131	1.31
Total	10,065	100	10,065	100

Notes:
a. Includes those who work FT with study
b. Includes those who combine study with non FT work

common challenges across genders in entering or getting established in the labour market, men are more successful in facing these challenges.

11.4.2 Gender and Migration Behaviour

Following the contribution by Faggian (2005) and Faggian et al. (2007), we classify graduates into five different migration categories based on their migration behaviour from original domicile to university, and later from university to first job location (Figure 11.1).

As we require information on the locations of domicile, study and work

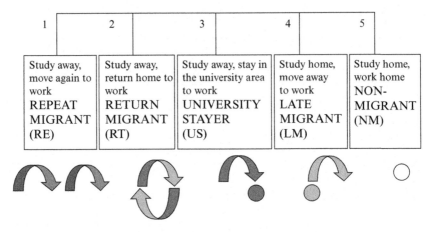

Figure 11.1   Student migration decision categories

to create our migration categories, the number of valid observations in our sample decreases. While only 47 per cent of the records in the DLHE survey have all the required information, this information is available for 88 per cent of the LDLHE respondents. For this reason, we focus more on the LDLHE survey with data collected 3.5 years after graduation. However, when appropriate we supplement and compare the longitudinal data with the DLHE data collected six months after graduation to get a more dynamic picture of migration patterns by gender over time.

At both points in time the distribution by gender is significantly differ-ent. At six months from graduation, women are significantly more likely to be return migrants and less likely to be repeat migrants than men. By 3.5 years, women are significantly less likely to be repeat migrants and more likely to be late migrants than men. It seems that the proportion of non-migrants, return migrants and university stayers have fallen between the DLHE and LDLHE, whilst the proportion of late migrants and repeat migrants has increased. This could reflect that six months, as mentioned earlier, is not enough time to really reflect assimilation into the labour market.

Table 11.2 examines the five categories of migration behaviour by gender.

It is interesting to compare the migration categories by type of employ-ment (excluding those again who are in study and not full-time (FT) employment) as provided in Table 11.3.

Part-time (PT) and self-employed graduates are more likely to belong to the non-migrants and return-migrants categories than the others, espe-cially repeat migrants (the lowest). Although we are focusing on younger

Table 11.2   Migration categories by gender

	DLHE		LDLHE	
	Men	Women	Men	Women
Non-migrant	13.22	13.99	10.17	11.94
Late migrant	5.34	5.48	6.27	5.78
University stayer	18.45	19.64	13.48	13.69
Return migrant	26.26	27.18	22.46	24.48
Repeat migrant	36.73	33.7	47.63	44.11
Base observations	3,271	4,133	7,424	9,715
Chi-squared gender difference test		*13.6403*		*33.1767*
Chi-squared p *value*		*0.009*		*0.000*

Table 11.3   Migration category and employment type, column percentages

	DLHE			LDLHE		
	Full-time	Self-employed	Part-time	Full-time	Self-employed	Part-time
Non-migrant	12.43	16.02	21.43	10.36	13.92	20.22
Late migrant	5.81	3.26	3.2	6.2	4.02	4.54
University stayer	19.48	16.35	17.2	13.51	15.75	13.33
Return migrant	24.68	33.46	39.49	22.46	28.78	35.46
Repeat migrant	37.6	30.91	18.69	47.48	37.51	26.45
Total	100	100	100	100	100	100

students, this result might be linked to family responsibilities (unfortunately, we have no information on whether the individuals are married or have children). 67 per cent of PT workers after 3.5 years (when graduates should be better integrated into the labour market) are women. At 3.5 years, almost half of FT employed individuals are repeat migrants, 35 per cent of PT students are return migrants, and 20 per cent are non-migrants.

Table 11.4 helps highlight some of the geography of the migration patterns between region of study and region of employment. It is interesting that, even if London is equally attractive to male and female students as a region of study, a slightly higher proportion of male graduates work there. The opposite is true for the northeast, Yorkshire and the Humber, and the West Midlands, where, although women are less numerous than men as students, they outnumber men in the labour market. Given that London provides better wages for recent graduates (Faggian et al., 2013),

Table 11.4   Region of institution and employment by gender

	Region of institute			Region of employment		
	All	Men	Women	All	Men	Women
Northeast	5.25	5.34	5.19	2.62	2.39	2.8
Northwest	10.28	9.7	10.73	8.25	8.03	8.42
Yorkshire and the Humber	11.17	11.44	10.96	6.8	6.57	6.97
East Midlands	9.64	10.53	8.95	5.64	5.68	5.61
West Midlands	8.19	8.49	7.96	6.42	6.35	6.47
East of England	5.27	5.4	5.17	6.1	6.24	5.99
London	10.85	10.81	10.88	27.76	28.84	26.94
Southeast	11.55	11.49	11.6	12.07	12.85	11.48
Southwest	8.95	9.77	8.32	6.72	7.18	6.37
Wales	5.8	5.08	6.36	5.38	4.71	5.88
Scotland	9.97	9.18	10.59	8.34	7.63	8.87
Northern Ireland	3.08	2.76	3.32	3.91	3.53	4.21
Chi-squared gender difference test			96.33			43.49
Chi-squared p *value*			0.000			0.000

Table 11.5   Mean salary levels by gender – 3.5 years

	All	Men	Women
All	24,964	26,679	23,650
Migration category			
Non-migrant	22,681	23,434	22,192
Late migrant	25,554	26,959	24,354
University stayer	24,708	26,283	23,508
Return migrant	22,495	23,638	21,723
Repeat migrant	26,522	28,524	24,867

this geographical composition could further exacerbate the gender salary gap problem.

11.4.3 Salary and Migration Patterns

Table 11.5 reports average salaries for FT employed individuals by gender.[4] Following HESA's approach, only FT employed individuals were included, as PT and self-employed individuals' salaries are less reliable (PT students do not always report pro-rata salaries and the response rate is lower for part-timers).[5] Men, on average, earn more than women and this is true across all migration categories. As expected, repeat migrants earn the most, followed by late migrants and university stayers. Return migrants earn less than non-migrants, which is also consistent with Faggian (2005).

To better understand the relationship between migration behaviour and salaries, we ran Mincer-type wage equations (split by gender) including migration categories as additional explanatory variables beyond the ones traditionally used in the literature, such as age, ethnicity, subject studied, institution type, pre-university qualifications (A-level tariff points) as a proxy for ability, degree class and any additional qualifications they have gained since graduation. We also included regional fixed effects for the region of employment (although we do not report them in the table of results). The models were run with and without job characteristics. Job characteristics include: firm size, industry and occupation, and contract type (temporary, fixed term, permanent), and time in current job (job tenure: before graduation, since graduation, 2–3 years, 1–2 years, less than a year). Including job characteristics in the model does reduce the magnitude of the coefficients, but leaves their significance and sign unaltered.

Table 11.6 reports the results of our wage equations. The results on the main control variables were in line with what has been found previously in the literature: better degree classification holders earn more on average, as do students with higher ability measured by A-level points. There is a salary premium associated with having earned a degree from more prestigious universities, and older graduates earn more (age being a proxy for experience). However, there are differences between genders in the magnitudes of the coefficients on these control variables, for example men's premium for having a first-class degree is higher (in fact more than double when controlling also for job characteristics), attending a more prestigious university (Russell group or other old university) is also more beneficial for male graduates with a salary premium of 8.1 per cent vis-à-vis 5.6 per cent for female graduates after controlling for job characteristics. In the pooled model with a control for gender, women earn on average about 7.6 per cent less than men, with this reducing to 5.7 per cent when we include job characteristics. One point of interest is the effect of migration behaviour on salaries, which has some variation between genders. For instance, staying in the university's area to work after graduation (university stayers) gives a significant salary premium (around 2.5 per cent) only to female graduates once the characteristics of the job are included. Late migration and repeat migration both carry a significant wage premium, but while the former is more beneficial to women (6.3 per cent vs 5.9 per cent), the latter is a better migration strategy for men (7.8 per cent vs 4.4 per cent). However, when we run a regression interacting gender and migration (Table 11.7), the only

Table 11.6 Mincer equations at 3.5 years (dependent variable: log of salaries)

	All		Men		Women	
	Without job characteristics	With job characteristics	Without job characteristics	With job characteristics	Without job characteristics	With job characteristics
Female	-0.076***	-0.057***				
	(0.008)	(0.005)				
Subject (reference: business)						
Medicine related	0.151***	0.124***	0.155***	0.142***	0.153***	0.120***
	(0.034)	(0.025)	(0.046)	(0.040)	(0.035)	(0.025)
Science	-0.065***	-0.064***	-0.067***	-0.062***	-0.061***	-0.066***
	(0.011)	(0.009)	(0.013)	(0.010)	(0.012)	(0.010)
Mathematics and computer sciences	0.071***	0.034	0.061**	0.033	0.077***	0.033**
	(0.017)	(0.021)	(0.023)	(0.022)	(0.016)	(0.014)
Engineering, technology and architecture	0.035	-0.014*	0.027	-0.022	0.012	-0.021
	(0.021)	(0.008)	(0.021)	(0.016)	(0.022)	(0.020)
Social studies	-0.009	-0.002	-0.016	-0.003	-0.004	-0.004
	(0.014)	(0.014)	(0.024)	(0.017)	(0.010)	(0.015)
Law	-0.108***	-0.090**	-0.093	-0.068	-0.113***	-0.098***
	(0.031)	(0.029)	(0.052)	(0.054)	(0.023)	(0.021)
Humanities	-0.111***	-0.079***	-0.152***	-0.103***	-0.087***	-0.065***
	(0.011)	(0.011)	(0.016)	(0.011)	(0.012)	(0.015)
Creative arts	-0.135***	-0.090***	-0.144***	-0.089***	-0.129***	-0.094***
	(0.010)	(0.009)	(0.019)	(0.018)	(0.008)	(0.011)
Education	0.040*	0.029	0.019	0.015	0.042	0.022
	(0.022)	(0.025)	(0.051)	(0.040)	(0.027)	(0.026)

Degree classification (ref: upper second)

First class	0.061***	0.047***	0.079***	0.073***	0.047***	0.030***
	(0.008)	(0.008)	(0.015)	(0.016)	(0.008)	(0.007)
Lower second	−0.057***	−0.043***	−0.068***	−0.051***	−0.051***	−0.039***
	(0.003)	(0.004)	(0.009)	(0.010)	(0.008)	(0.005)
Third/pass	−0.135***	−0.090***	−0.147***	−0.089***	−0.124***	−0.092***
	(0.013)	(0.017)	(0.021)	(0.024)	(0.015)	(0.015)
Unclassified	0.084*	0.083**	0.056	0.059	0.106**	0.102**
	(0.041)	(0.038)	(0.041)	(0.044)	(0.044)	(0.036)
Age	0.037***	0.030***	0.038***	0.031***	0.036***	0.030***
	(0.004)	(0.003)	(0.004)	(0.004)	(0.005)	(0.004)

Ethnicity (ref: white)

Asian	−0.045***	−0.027***	−0.053***	−0.03	−0.038**	−0.026*
	(0.007)	(0.009)	(0.013)	(0.019)	(0.016)	(0.014)
Black	−0.041***	−0.036***	−0.037*	−0.018	−0.043**	−0.046**
	(0.008)	(0.009)	(0.018)	(0.015)	(0.017)	(0.019)
Other	−0.02	−0.01	−0.012	0.008	−0.029	−0.026
	(0.012)	(0.010)	(0.009)	(0.012)	(0.017)	(0.016)
Unknown	−0.048**	−0.062**	−0.097**	−0.111***	0.016	−0.003
	(0.022)	(0.021)	(0.032)	(0.025)	(0.035)	(0.034)
Disabled	−0.042***	−0.030**	−0.054***	−0.043***	−0.029**	−0.019
	(0.009)	(0.010)	(0.008)	(0.011)	(0.013)	(0.013)

Institution Type (ref: post−1992)

Russell group	0.085***	0.067***	0.098***	0.081***	0.074***	0.056***
	(0.014)	(0.011)	(0.022)	(0.018)	(0.013)	(0.008)

(continues overleaf)

Table 11.6 (continued)

	All		Men		Women	
	Without job characteristics	With job characteristics	Without job characteristics	With job characteristics	Without job characteristics	With job characteristics
Other old	0.053***	0.036***	0.059***	0.036**	0.048***	0.036***
	(0.011)	(0.008)	(0.018)	(0.014)	(0.011)	(0.007)
FE/HE college	0.014	0.019	0.004	0.017	0.021	0.018
	(0.016)	(0.012)	(0.031)	(0.015)	(0.019)	(0.018)
Further qualifications (none)						
Higher/first degree	-0.046***	-0.030***	-0.048***	-0.026*	-0.042***	-0.033***
	(0.008)	(0.009)	(0.012)	(0.013)	(0.008)	(0.008)
Post-graduate diploma	0.080***	0.052***	0.036*	0.035	0.098***	0.053***
	(0.009)	(0.010)	(0.019)	(0.020)	(0.008)	(0.012)
Professional	0.100***	0.079***	0.094***	0.080***	0.107***	0.076***
	(0.016)	(0.008)	(0.018)	(0.011)	(0.016)	(0.011)
Other	-0.026***	-0.015**	0.006	0.004	-0.049***	-0.032***
	(0.006)	(0.005)	(0.012)	(0.011)	(0.007)	(0.003)
A-level points (241–340)						
<241	-0.032***	-0.025***	-0.02	-0.02	-0.036***	-0.025**
	(0.010)	(0.007)	(0.015)	(0.011)	(0.010)	(0.011)
341–420	0.016**	0.011	0.020*	0.01	0.014*	0.013*
	(0.007)	(0.007)	(0.010)	(0.013)	(0.007)	(0.006)
>420	0.053***	0.044***	0.061***	0.044***	0.048***	0.045***
	(0.005)	(0.005)	(0.012)	(0.013)	(0.006)	(0.008)
Non-A-level qualification	-0.044***	-0.030**	-0.054***	-0.048***	-0.03	-0.011
	(0.008)	(0.012)	(0.016)	(0.015)	(0.019)	(0.023)

Migration category

	(1)	(2)	(3)	(4)	(5)	(6)
Late migrant	0.088***	0.061***	0.092***	0.059**	0.088***	0.063***
	(0.016)	(0.013)	(0.023)	(0.021)	(0.017)	(0.012)
University stay	0.036***	0.024**	0.043**	0.022	0.030**	0.025**
	(0.011)	(0.010)	(0.019)	(0.014)	(0.012)	(0.009)
Return migrant	0.001	0.004	0.007	0.014	−0.004	−0.004
	(0.010)	(0.007)	(0.015)	(0.015)	(0.015)	(0.008)
Repeat migrant	0.077***	0.060***	0.107***	0.078***	0.054***	0.044***
	(0.008)	(0.006)	(0.013)	(0.011)	(0.010)	(0.006)
Observations	12,583	11,927	5,469	5,238	7,114	6,689
R-squared	0.337	0.456	0.337	0.45	0.323	0.455

Notes: All regressions include region of employment fixed effects.
Job characteristics include: current job tenure, firm size, contract type, occupation and industry.
Robust standard errors in brackets.
*** $p < 0.01$, ** $p < 0.05$, * $p < 0.1$.

Table 11.7   Gender interactions

	All	
	Without job characteristics	With job characteristics
Female	−0.040*	−0.032*
	(0.020)	(0.017)
Migration category		
Late migrant	0.091***	0.060**
	(0.022)	(0.019)
University stay	0.050**	0.030*
	(0.020)	(0.016)
Return migrant	0.005	0.012
	(0.016)	(0.016)
Repeat migrant	0.114***	0.084***
	(0.013)	(0.013)
*Migration category * female*		
Late migrant	−0.002	0.005
	(0.028)	(0.021)
University stay	−0.022	−0.009
	(0.025)	(0.020)
Return migrant	−0.008	−0.013
	(0.026)	(0.021)
Repeat migrant	−0.064**	−0.043**
	(0.021)	(0.017)
Observations	12,583	11,927
R-squared	0.339	0.456

Notes: Includes same control as Table 11.6. *** $p < 0.01$, ** $p < 0.05$, * $p < 0.1$.

significant difference between genders is related to repeat migration with a significantly lower premium for women.

11.5   CONCLUSIONS

Our findings confirm that migration is a powerful tool used by highly educated individuals to seek better economic rewards for their human capital (Becker, 1964; Sabot, 1987; Sjaastad, 1962). Confirming the findings of Faggian et al. (2007), mentioned earlier, we find that repeat migrants earn the most, followed by late migrants and university stayers. However, differences exist in the returns to migration by gender. Late migration has the greatest premium, and higher for women than men. The importance of late migration for women could be linked to the importance of establishing a stronger career profile – due for instance to the weaker salary negotiation position usually experienced by women (Babcock et al., 2006) – before making a migration decision. As reported, when we include job characteristics the salary premium associated with the different migration categories is lower. However, when we run a regression interacting gender and migration, the only significant difference between genders is related to repeat migration with a significantly lower premium for women. This again seems to confirm the argument that continuously renegotiating jobs and salaries seems to be more difficult for women. Being a university stayer is also significant only for women, which might also support the idea that women need local networks and university connections to strengthen their initial access to the labour market and build their career. The higher wage premium of repeat migration for men might be linked to the lower negotiating power of women when entering the labour market (Babcock and Laschever, 2003; Kulik and Olekalns, 2012), but this requires further and more detailed research to be confirmed. Alternatively, women might be more sensitive to the costs (including psychological costs) associated with repeat migration.

The findings have implications for women and the migration strategy they might want to adopt to maximize their wages and career advancements. However, they might also have implications for policy, especially for organizations interested in supporting gender equality and women's career progressions. For women thinking strategically about their career, migrating only when there is a real career progression offer might be a more selective strategy than moving for smaller incremental opportunities. However, for organizations interested in attracting women to specific, higher career positions, a better understanding of what would facilitate migration in the later stages of their career might be necessary. It is especially important to have the awareness that later migration might have a stronger impact on women's overall future career advancements than earlier movements.

Therefore, this initial analysis highlights the role that migration patterns can play in providing a gender-based response to the pay gap and finding better rewards for recent female graduates. However, it also suggests that migration strategies are not entirely gender-neutral and that repeat migration – although appealing economically in principle – might create barriers as it poses an advantage for individuals who are able to negotiate continuous increases in wages for their repeat migration and the literature in management and psychology seems to suggest that these individuals tend to be men. The role of job characteristics is a crucial issue that we would like to explore in more depth in the future; it would be interesting, for instance, to look at the role of different sectors and their geographical distribution (and concentration). Although Comunian and Faggian (2014) address the importance of London and the southeast labour markets, their analysis is restricted only to creative and cultural industries.

NOTES

*   Email: roberta.comunian@kcl.ac.uk.
**   Email: s.l.jewell@reading.ac.uk.
***   Email: alessandra.faggian@gssi.it.
1.   Although tied moving cannot be completely ruled out even for this young cohort of graduates, we believe that, by restricting to graduates 25 and below, the bias is relatively small.
2.   HESA has a target response rate of 80 per cent for full-time home-domiciled graduates, 70 per cent for part-time home-domiciled graduates and 50 per cent for EU graduates.
3.   HESA data show that there has been an increase in the proportion of graduates (qualifiers) who are female, from 51 per cent for the 1994/95 graduating cohort to 57 per cent for the 2013/14 cohort – this refers to British-domiciled first degree graduates. For the 2006/07 cohort it was 57 per cent as per our sample. (Statistics obtained from the HESA's free online statistics – see https://www.hesa.ac.uk/content/view/1973/239/.)
4.   Salaries were only included if they were greater than or equal to the amount that would be earned at the minimum wage rate and less than £100,000 (with high values potentially being the result of an error or being outliers).
5.   81 per cent of FT individuals at 3.5 years provided a sensible salary level; in comparison only 43 per cent of self-employed individuals and 48 per cent of PT employed individuals provided a sensible salary (reflecting that the latter may have not been reporting a pro-rata salary rate).

REFERENCES

Araujo, P. de and Lagos, S. (2013), Self-esteem, education, and wages revisited, *Journal of Economic Psychology*, 34, 120–132.

Babcock, L. and Laschever, S. (2003), *Women Don't Ask: Negotiation and the Gender Divide*, Princeton, NJ: Princeton University Press.

Babcock, L., Gelfand, M., Small, D. and Stayn, H. (2006), Gender differences in the propensity to initiate negotiations, in de Cremer, D., Zeelenberg, M. and Murnighan, J.K. (eds), *Social Psychology and Economics*, Mahwah, NJ: Lawrence Erlbaum, pp. 239–262.

Ball, S.J. (2005), *Degrees of Choice: Class, Race, Gender and Higher Education*, Stoke on Trent, UK: Trentham Books.

Becker, G.S. (1964), *Human Capital: A Theoretical and Empirical Analysis*, with Special Reference to Education Chicago, Chicago: University of Chicago Press.

Boyle, P., Cooke, T.J., Halfacree, K. and Smith, D. (1999), Gender inequality in employment status following family migration in GB and the US: the effect of relative occupational status, *International Journal of Sociology and Social Policy*, 19, 115–133.

Chevalier, A. (2011), Subject choice and earnings of UK graduates, *Economics of Education Review*, 30, 1187–1201.

Chevalier, A. (2012), To be or not to be . . . a scientist? IZA DP No 6353.

Cintio, M. di and Grassi, E. (2013), Internal migration and wages of Italian university graduates, *Papers in Regional Science*, 92, 119–140.

Comunian, R. and Faggian, A. (2014), Creative graduates and creative cities: exploring the geography of creative education in the UK, *International Journal of Cultural and Creative Industries*, 1(2), 19–34.

Coniglio, N.D. and Prota, F. (2008), Human capital accumulation and migration in a peripheral EU region: the case of Basilicata, *Papers in Regional Science*, 87, 77–95.

Del Bono, E. and Vuri, D. (2011), Job mobility and the gender wage gap in Italy, *Labour Economics*, 18(1), 130–142.

Détang-Dessendre, C. (1999), Reciprocal link between exit from unemployment and geographical mobility, *Environment and Planning A*, 31, 1417–1431.

Elias, P. and Purcell, K. (2004), Is mass higher education working? Evidence from the labour market experiences of recent graduates, *National Institute Economic Review*, 190, 60–74.

Elias, P., McKnight, A., Purcell, K. and Pitcher, J. (eds) (1999), Moving on: graduate careers three years after graduation, Manchester: CSU/DfEE.

Faggian, A. (2005), *Human Capital, Migration and Local Labour Markets: The Role of the Higher Education System in Great Britain*, Unpublished thesis, University of Reading, UK.

Faggian, A. and McCann, P. (2006), Human capital flows and regional knowledge assets: a simultaneous equation approach, *Oxford Economic Papers*, 58, 475–500.

Faggian, A. and McCann, P. (2009), Human capital, graduate migration and innovation in British regions, *Cambridge Journal of Economics*, 33, 317–333.

Faggian, A., McCann, P. and Sheppard, S. (2007), Some evidence that women are more mobile than men: gender differences in U.K. graduate migration behavior, *Journal of Regional Science*, 47, 517–539.

Faggian, A., Comunian, R., Jewell, S. and Kelly, U. (2013), Bohemian graduates in the UK: disciplines and location determinants of creative careers, *Regional Studies*, 47(2), 183–200.

Faggian, A., Comunian, R. and Li, Q.C. (2014), Interregional migration of human creative capital: the case of 'bohemian graduates', *Geoforum*, 55, 33–42.

Fratesi, U. (2014), Editorial: the mobility of high-skilled workers – causes and consequences, *Regional Studies*, 48, 1587–1591.

Garcia, J., Hernández, P.J. and Lopez-Nicolas, A. (2001), How wide is the gap? An investigation of gender wage differences using quantile regression, *Empirical Economics*, 26, 149–167.

Garner, R. (2014), Women are now a third more likely than men to opt to go to university, according to UCAS application figures, *The Guardian*, 31 January.

Gottlieb, P.D. and Joseph, G. (2006), College-to-work migration of technology graduates and holders of doctorates within the United States, *Journal of Regional Science*, 46, 627–659.

Jacobs, J.A. (1996), Gender inequality and higher education, *Annual Review of Sociology*, 22, 153–185.

Jewell, S. and Faggian, A. (2014), Interregional migration wage premia: the case of creative and STEM graduates in the UK, in Kourtit, K., Nijkamp, P. and Stimson, R. (eds), *Applied Modeling of Regional Growth and Innovation Systems*, New York: Springer, pp. 197–216.

Kulik, C.T. and Olekalns, M. (2012), Negotiating the gender divide: lessons from the negotiation and organizational behavior literatures, *Journal of Management*, 38(4), 1387–1415.

Machin, S. and Puhani, P.A. (2003), Subject of degree and the gender wage differential: evidence from the UK and Germany, *Economics Letters*, 79, 393–400.

Manning, A. and Swaffield, J. (2008), The gender gap in early-career wage growth, *The Economic Journal*, 118, 983–1024.

Maxwell, G. and Broadbridge, A. (2014), Generation Y graduates and career transition: perspectives by gender, *European Management Journal*, 32, 547–553.

McKnight, A., Naylor, R.A. and Smith, J. (2007), Sheer class? Returns to educational performance: evidence from UK graduates first destination labour market outcomes, Warwick economic research papers (No 786), Coventry, UK: Department of Economics, University of Warwick.

McNabb, R., Pal, S. and Sloane, P. (2002), Gender differences in educational attainment: the case of university students in England and Wales, *Economica*, 69, 481–503.

Naylor, R., Smith, J. and McKnight, A. (2002), Why is there a graduate earnings premium for students from independent schools? *Bulletin of Economic Research*, 54, 315–339.

O'Leary, N. and Sloane, P. (2005), The return to a university education in Great Britain, *National Institute Economic Review*, 193, 75–89.

Purcell, K. (2002), Qualifications and careers: equal opportunities and earnings among graduates, Report, Equal Opportunities Commission London.

Purcell, K., Elias, P., Atfield, G., Behle, H., Ellison, R. and Luchinskaya, D. (2013), Transitions into employment, further study and other outcomes: the Futuretrack Stage 4 Report, Manchester/Coventry: HECSU/Warwick Institute for Employment Research.

Ravenstein, E. (1885), The laws of migration, *Journal of the Statistical Society*, 46, 167–235.

Ross, K. and Carter, C. (2011), Women and news: a long and winding road, *Media, Culture and Society*, 33, 1148–1165.

Ryan, M.K. and Haslam, S.A. (2005), The glass cliff: evidence that women are over-represented in precarious leadership positions, *British Journal of Management*, 16, 81–90.

Sabot, R.H. (1987), Internal migration and education, in Psacharopoulos, G. (ed.), *Economics of Education Research and Studies*, Oxford: Pergamon Press, pp. 196–197.

Sjaastad, L.A. (1962), The costs and returns of human migration, *The Journal of Political Economy*, 70, 80–93.

Smith, J. and Naylor, R. (2001), Determinants of degree performance in UK universities: a statistical analysis of the 1993 student cohort, *Oxford Bulletin of Economics and Statistics*, 63, 29–60.

UNESCO (2012), *World Atlas of Gender Equality in Education*, Montreal and Paris: UNESCO Institute for Statistics' Education Indicators and Data Analysis Team, available at: http://www.uis.unesco.org/Education/Documents/unesco-world-atlas-gender-education-2012.pdf (accessed 8 April 2015).

Weinberger, C.J. (1998), Race and gender wage gaps in the market for recent college graduates, *Industrial Relations: A Journal of Economy and Society*, 37, 67–84.

Index